Bloom's Modern Critical Views

Bloom's Modern Critical Views

RICHARD WRIGHT
New Edition

Edited and with an introduction by
Harold Bloom
Sterling Professor of the Humanities
Yale University

BLOOM'S
LITERARY CRITICISM
An imprint of Infobase Publishing

Editorial Consultant, Brian Johnson

Bloom's Modern Critical Views: Richard Wright—New Edition
Copyright ©2009 by Infobase Publishing

Introduction ©2009 by Harold Bloom

Bloom's Literary Criticism
An imprint of Infobase Publishing
132 West 31st Street
New York NY 10001

Library of Congress Cataloging-in-Publication Data

Richard Wright / edited and with an introduction by Harold Bloom.—New ed.
p. cm.— (Bloom's Modern Critical Views)
Includes bibliographical references and index.
ISBN 978-0-7910-9622-2 (alk. paper)
1. Wright, Richard, 1908–1960—Criticism and interpretation. 2. African Americans in literature. I. Bloom, Harold. II. Series.
PS3545.R815Z814 2008
813'.52—dc22
                            2008031807

Cover design by Ben Peterson

Printed in the United States of America
Bang BCL 10 9 8 7 6 5 4 3 2 1

This book is printed on acid-free paper.

All links and Web addresses were checked and verified to be correct at the time of publication. Because of the dynamic nature of the Web, some addresses and links may have changed since publication and may no longer be valid.

Contents

Editor's Note

My Introduction, rather sadly, reflects upon Richard Wright's inadequate mastery of language.

The ten essays reprinted here all rely upon criteria that are not aesthetic. Jack B. Moore personally appreciates what he regards as Wright's "great, general human importance," while Jeff Karem admires *American Hunger,* the original version of *Black Boy.*

The symbolism of the Virgin Mary, Eve, and Mary Magdalene in Wright is expounded by Tara T. Green, after which Brannon Costello concentrates upon Wright's politicized Modernism.

Cheryl Higashida offers a feminist critique of Wright's male radicalism, while Petar Ramadanovic applies Freud to *Native Son.*

Gendered politics returns via Qiana J. Whitted, after which Cedric Gael Bryant compares Wright to Toni Morrison.

Wright's critique of Marxism and Existentialism is set forth by Jeffrey Atteberry, and this volume is then concluded by Robert Butler's adding the Loeb and Leopold case to *Native Son*'s sources.

HAROLD BLOOM

Introduction

RICHARD WRIGHT (1908–1959)

I

What remains of Richard Wright's work if we apply to it only aesthetic standards of judgment? This is to assume that strictly aesthetic standards exist, and that we know what they are. Wright, in *Native Son,* essentially the son of Theodore Dreiser, could not rise always even to Dreiser's customarily bad level of writing. Here is Bigger Thomas, condemned to execution, at the start of his death vigil:

> In self-defense he shut out the night and day from his mind, for if he had thought of the sun's rising and setting, of the moon or the stars, of clouds or rain, he would have died a thousand deaths before they took him to the chair. To accustom his mind to death as much as possible, he made all the world beyond his cell a vast gray land where neither night nor day was, peopled by strange men and women whom he could not understand, but with those lives he longed to mingle once before he went.
>
> He did not eat now; he simply forced food down his throat without tasting it, to keep the gnawing pain of hunger away, to keep from feeling dizzy. And he did not sleep; at intervals he closed his eyes for a while, no matter what the hour, then opened them at some later time to resume his brooding. He wanted to be free of everything that stood between him and his end, him and the full and terrible realization that life was over without meaning, without anything being settled, without conflicting impulses being resolved.

1

If we isolate these paragraphs, then we do not know the color or background of the man awaiting execution. The intense sociological pathos of Wright's narrative vanishes, and we are left in the first paragraph with an inadequate rhetoric: "shut out the night and day," "died a thousand deaths," "a vast gray land," "strange men and women," "with those lives he longed to mingle." Yet the second paragraph is even more unsatisfactory, as the exact word is nowhere: "gnawing pain of hunger," "resume his brooding," "full and terrible realization," "conflicting impulses being resolved." Wright's narrative requires from him at this point some mode of language that would individuate Bigger's dread, that would catch and fix the ordeal of a particular black man condemned by a white society. Unfortunately, Wright's diction does not allow us even to distinguish Bigger's horror from any other person's apprehension of judicial murder. Nor does Bigger's own perspective enter into Wright's rhetorical stance. The problem is not so much Wright's heritage from Dreiser's reductive naturalism as it is, plainly stated, a bad authorial ear.

It is rather too late to make so apparently irrelevant an observation, since Wright has become a canonical author, for wholesome societal purposes, with which I am happy to concur. Rereading *Native Son* or *Black Boy* cannot be other than an overdetermined activity, since Wright is a universally acknowledged starting point for black literature in contemporary America. Canonical critics of Wright speak of him as a pioneer, a man of rare courage, as a teacher and forerunner. None of this can or should be denied. I myself would praise him for will, force, and drive, human attributes that he carried just over the border of aesthetic achievement, without alas getting very far once he had crossed over. His importance transcends the concerns of a strictly literary criticism, and reminds the critic of the claims of history, society, political economy, and the longer records of oppression and injustice that history continues to scant.

II

I remember reading *Black Boy: A Record of Childhood and Youth* when Wright's autobiographical book first appeared, in 1945. A boy of fifteen, I was frightened and impressed by the book. Reading it again after more than forty years, the old reactions do not return. Instead, I am compelled to ask the Nietzschean question: who is the interpreter, and what power does he seek to gain over the text, whether it be his own text or the text of his life? Wright, an anguished and angry interpreter, wrote a far more political work in *Black Boy* than in *Native Son*. What passes for a Marxist analysis of the relation between society and Bigger Thomas seems to me always a kind of authorial afterthought in *Native Son*. In *Black Boy*, this pseudo-Marxism usurps the narrator's function, and the will-to-power over interpretation becomes the incessant undersong of the entire book. Contrast the opening and closing paragraphs of *Black Boy:*

One winter morning in the long-ago, four-year-old days of my life I found myself standing before a fireplace, warming my hands over a mound of glowing coals, listening to the wind whistle past the house outside. All morning my mother had been scolding me, telling me to keep still, warning me that I must make no noise. And I was angry, fretful, and impatient. In the next room Granny lay ill and under the day and night care of a doctor and I knew that I would be punished if I did not obey. I crossed restlessly to the window and pushed back the long fluffy white curtains—which I had been forbidden to touch—and looked yearningly out into the empty street. I was dreaming of running and playing and shouting, but the vivid image of Granny's old, white, wrinkled, grim face, framed by a halo of tumbling black hair, lying upon a huge feather pillow, made me afraid.

With ever watchful eyes and bearing scars, visible and invisible, I headed North, full of a hazy notion that life could be lived with dignity, that the personalities of others should not be violated, that men should be able to confront other men without fear or shame, and that if men were lucky in their living on earth they might win some redeeming meaning for their having struggled and suffered here beneath the stars.

The young man going North, scarred and watchful, in search of redemption by meaning, has remarkably little connection with the four-year-old boy, impatient for the dream of running, playing, and shouting. Wright's purpose is to explain his fall from impulse into care, and his inevitable explanation will be social and historical. Yet much that he loses is to his version of the family romance, as he himself describes it, and some of what vanishes from him can be ascribed, retrospectively, to a purely personal failure; in him the child was not the father of the man.

What survives best in *Black Boy*, for me, is Wright's gentle account of his human rebirth, as a writer. At eighteen, reading Mencken, he learns audacity, the agonistic use of language, and an aggressive passion for study comes upon him. After reading the *Main Street* of Sinclair Lewis, he is found by the inevitable precursor in Theodore Dreiser:

"That's deep stuff you're reading, boy."
"I'm just killing time, sir."
"You'll addle your brains if you don't watch out."

I read Dreiser's *Jennie Gerhardt* and *Sister Carrie* and they revived in me a vivid sense of my mother's suffering; I was overwhelmed. I grew silent, wondering about the life around me.

It would have been impossible for me to have told anyone what I derived from these novels, for it was nothing less than a sense of life itself. All my life had shaped me for the realism, the naturalism of the modern novel, and I could not read enough of them.

Steeped in new moods and ideas, I bought a ream of paper and tried to write; but nothing would come, or what did come was flat beyond telling. I discovered that more than desire and feeling were necessary to write and I dropped the idea. Yet I still wondered how it was possible to know people sufficiently to write about them? Could I ever learn about life and people? To me, with my vast ignorance, my Jim Crow station in life, it seemed a task impossible of achievement. I now knew what being a Negro meant. I could endure the hunger. I had learned to live with hate. But to feel that there were feelings denied me, that the very breath of life itself was beyond my reach, that more than anything else hurt, wounded me. I had a new hunger.

Dreiser's taut visions of suffering women renew in Wright his own memories of his mother's travails, and make him one of those authors for whom the purpose of the poem (to cite Wallace Stevens) is the mother's face. There is an Oedipal violence in Wright that sorts strangely with his attempt to persuade us, and himself, that all violence is socially overdetermined. *Black Boy*, even now, performs an ethical function for us by serving as a social testament, as Wright intended it to do. We can hope that, some day, the book will be available to us as a purely individual testament, and then, may read very differently.

JACK B. MOORE

A Personal Appreciation
of Richard Wright's Universality

Universality, once an admired achievement in an artist, has been in disrepute lately, or to be more accurate the *claim* of universality has often been severely questioned or even attacked, primarily because it is alleged that what has been presented as universal actually masks the privileged and parochial. What the observer puts forth as a theme or perception or behavior true, its depiction valued all over the world, is merely a reification of personal or class or gender specific or regional interests. That charge is often so. But the narcissistic vision of people who mistake the hole of a tunnel for a slice of the horizon, who favor presentation of concerns and conditions that are merely immediate or trendy and announce them as images of world-wide significance, should not lead viewers away from appreciating artists who strike beyond what appeals to (or profoundly troubles, for that matter) the cherished interests of bounded, exclusive groups of people.

Richard Wright's works and the critical literature his works have elicited demonstrate his universality, the fact that he is not only a powerful writer in the liberal-radical, black, male, American tradition, but that his artistic territory ranges far more extensively, that he is a writer of great, general, human importance. He may not be a writer who speaks to everyone, everywhere, at every time. He is certainly a writer who illustrates his liberal-radicalness, his blackness, his maleness, his Americanness in nearly all that he has written.

Mississippi Quarterly: The Journal of Southern Cultures, Volume 50, Number 2 (Spring 1997): pp. 365–374. Copyright © 1997 Mississippi Quarterly.

My claim for him is not the old claim of universality that would have ignored how rooted he was (and, paradoxically, how rooted humanity is, universally) in the highly personal and to an unknown extent inescapable biologic, environmental, and cultural conditions of individual identity. My claim is simpler, that he was a writer—a human being—who in his life and works traveled beyond the worlds of his roots, and showed many fellow humans that the strands of existence he dramatized in his person and literature were tangled with their own strands in fascinating patterns. In many ways his life and the lives he depicted were their lives and the lives we see around us: our lives, and finally, I suppose, my life, your life, though of course, not everybody's life.

That is rhetoric, so I will provide a story to illustrate what I mean. During the Second World War my stepfather, who was a German national but who had lived and worked loyally in America since just before the First World War, was interned with some other German nationals and perhaps a few German-American citizens, out west in a camp they could not leave without permission, or apparently, without guardianship. Many Americans think only people of Japanese origins and their families were interned, but this is not so. My stepfather was taken from the bakery he owned in New York City and moved with his family at that time (I only knew him later) to the Southwest. His bakery from that point did not exist. He said he and his family were fairly well treated—the government provided him with the special shoes he needed to compensate for a foot problem, for instance—but they lived always behind a large fence of some kind, possibly a wire fence or something like a wooden cyclone fence. One day the family was strolling the grounds of their incarceration, and his young son saw a few workers behind the fence, and asked him, "Who are those people with guns inside the fence?" And my stepfather had to tell his son that the people were soldiers outside the fence, and that he and his sister and their mother lived inside.

To a small boy, the world inside the fence was big enough to seem outside, and for a small boy with short legs the world inside gave him ample scope for movement and varied observation of others. But someone like Wright would have known who was inside and who was outside the fence, and that the first step getting outside was knowing you were inside, and could get out. His vision transcended what appeared immediately to be. He could accurately describe what appeared to be and in fact to the personal vision was—only he could also see beyond that. I would expand the dimensions of my parable just a little farther, and suggest Wright would also know that even outside that one fence around the concentrated German and American community, there were other fences, and fences beyond those, to journey beyond and describe.

The critical literature about Wright and the body of literature that was his legacy to us documents while it explores his universality. Over the past decades a number of critical collections have gathered reviews and essays that offer valuable insights into what are arguably (sometimes heatedly so) his strengths and weaknesses as a writer, that investigate the picture of life that he created in his poetry, non-fiction, and fiction. One of the first of these and still one of the most helpful was *Richard Wright: The Critical Reception* (1978), which John M. Reilly so ably edited, a thick book recording the "early critical reception of Richard Wright's works upon their publication in the United States"—contemporary newspaper and magazine reviews including nearly all the most influential reports together with a balanced sample of many other appraisals revealing a book-by-book account of Wright's general reception. Arnold Rampersad's more slender 1995 *Richard Wright: A Collection of Critical Essays* is a very good gathering of lengthier essays by academic critics who focus on one work or a limited aspect of Wright's art. *The Critical Response to Richard Wright*, edited by Robert Butler (Westport, Connecticut, London: Greenwood Press, 1995), from which I will be quoting in my remarks, stands midway between these, offering both contemporary book reviews (some of them by essentially newspaper critics) and essays or portions of essays by academics on a selected number of Wright's books, plus a "Biographical Overview" and a unit rifled "Richard Wright Today."

In an analysis of *The Outsider* that Buffer reprints, Michel Fabre quotes from a letter to Wright in 1945 in which Ralph Ellison remarks, "man is absolute in his own time, in his own environment," a statement which Fabre glosses as meaning "that the black writer will achieve universality by concentrating on the specific, by dealing with his own experience." And Wright came to know that the alembic that universal art demanded required the chemistry of unique creativity the individual writer had to possess and explore. Fabre also quotes from a letter Wright wrote "to the South American artist Antonio Frasconi: 'I hold that, on the last analysis, the artist must bow to the monitor of his own imagination, must be led by the sovereignty of his own impressions and perceptions'" (p.113). Wright must have experienced a writer's shock of recognition at what Albert Camus deplored in a 1946 lecture Fabre says Wright read, that an element of the post-war "Human Crisis" was the deadening condition that "No longer are individual passions possible, but only collective, that is to say abstract, passions" (p.115). Wright seemed to know, and proved in work after work that he knew, that one of his functions as an artist—as a human being—was to dramatize individual passions and through these to reach the passions of human communities not in the abstract, but in the particular.

One of the recurring motifs in Wright's work is the great influence environment has upon the individual, surely a fact of existence irrespective of the individual peculiarities that separate people and peoples from each other. His own life demonstrates this influence, as related in biographies of him or his reworking of his life in *Black Boy (American Hunger)*, as do *Native Son*, for example, or *Black Power*, or any number of his other works. But at the same time, at his most effective he also shows—as his life reveals—the possibility (though, sadly, not the inevitability) of traveling beyond one's environment, of getting outside it, when that would expand opportunities of enriched individual consciousness. Sometimes after observing your life, you find it possible to redirect it, change it. The journey outside the self to get back into it may be physical, or more importantly it can be intellectual. The trick is to maintain connection with what is strong in your roots while you are making the trip. Wright certainly recognized this necessity when in his "Blueprint for Negro Writing" he charged that "Negro writers must accept the nationalist implications of their lives, not in order to encourage them, but in order to change and transcend them. They must accept the concept of nationalism because, in order to transcend it, they must *possess and understand* it" (Wright's emphasis).

Look at Wright's life. Although it is possible for the gifted and even the not so gifted individual to create something significant and valuable—including a fully justified self—from the barest environmental materials, historically this ability is not easily performed anywhere by anybody. Wright did not live in the same South that William Faulkner or Thomas Wolfe or Robert Penn Warren or Eudora Welty did, because Wright was black (and Welty was female). Of course the South of whites and blacks, men and women, economically affluent or poor was culturally rich in many ways, but the South for black people was also drained of many possibilities, was diminished in terms of chances, restricted, contained, brutalizing, leached, in ways it was not ordinarily for most white people (though surely it was diminished for poor whites also, it was not impoverished precisely in the same way). Van Wyck Brooks once wrote of Sam Clemens/Mark Twain in a passage of *The Ordeal of Mark Twain* that has become infamous because of its arguability, that the land producing him was "A desert of human sand! The barrenest spot in all Christendom, surely, for the seed of genius to fall in." Still, how much more hostile that land was to Twain's (and the South's) creation Jim than to Huck. The Mississippi and South of Wright's time had, potentially, much to offer a writer but withheld much also from and greatly bruised the black people contained within its dangerous boundaries. Though viewed one way the South had great potential for the imaginations of burgeoning black artists, from another angle—the angle of actually living there—it could be a soul deadening or literally murderous place. Wright once wrote that "the environment the South creates is too small to nourish human beings, especially Negro human beings" (p.72). Certainly if you had the choice of placing the seed of a black person you hoped would become a great writer into the most nurturing soil possible, you would not place that seed in the soil and family situation Wright was born into and grew up in, if you knew anything about the environment's effect upon the body and spirit, unless you believed that the worst conditions were truly the best conditions for raising children and encouraging artistry: risky propositions few parents anywhere would wish to test for their own blood kindred.

But Wright escaped, though not fully (does anyone, anywhere?), and carried with him local relationships and materials that his imagination ultimately turned into lessons for humanity about the possibilities of emancipation—and some of the costs, and the perils that were part of the price, for him anyway. Grandson of slaves, son of an illiterate, wandering father and a very emotionally fragile mother, born black in the boondocks—the black boondocks—of possibly then the most racist state of his racist nation, during the time Rayford Logan characterized as "the nadir of civil rights," he traveled to Chicago, New York, Paris, Accra, Bandung, and at different times (not constantly) his voice was listened to (not always with welcome or positive regard) as an important voice. On these travels he listened to many voices he never would have heard in Mississippi—Camus's voice, Sartre's, Nkrumah's, Zhou Enlai's, together with echoes of great writers' voices—Dreiser's, Zola's, Dostoevski's. Amid this polylingual chorus, however, he never forgot the black rural and urban blues he heard during his black American years. Still, he came a long way from the boy who said he killed a cat and told his grandmother to kiss his ass, on a journey whose precise stops not all would have to or want to travel in life, but whose general route heading towards social betterment of condition and deepening of inner resources many around the world might find appealing or even worth attempting. His writing, from centering on a simple, poor, black Mississippi boy who was "Almos' a Man" to uncovering "The Man Who Lived Underground" who was like people underground all over the world, travels along imaginatively at least as much territory as he did in his life, and discovers about as many twists. He suggests for example that the Outsider's environment is as much the philosophy of existence within him as the world outside, which may be as true in Beijing as in New York City.

To be human is to be not exactly like anyone else, but also to be similar in a great variety of ways to many other people. Are some people more like many other people than some other people? The thought is as tortuous as the language. Wright's life—its start anyway, so seemingly starved of chance for healthy development—was like the life of many others who live in misery that is physical or of the spirit. The Monty Python routine of people competing in claimed misery—one proudly says he lives in a paper bag in a septic tank, I believe—might have near universal appeal. Wright's quest, however, was to comprehend and challenge misery, not flop and wallow in it. Wright's life, his strenuous attempt to escape his private Mississippi of pain and deprivation, is now, like a legend, a mixture of the facts of his life as they have been and are being ascertained and of his treatment of those facts as he interpreted and built upon or modified them for his audience. The emerging story is at once personal, and at the same time possesses universality, because the world possesses many such places as that Mississippi of old was for him and others like him. Ordinary people and not just gifted artists who live within them attest to that.

Amazingly, so does the story of his greatest creation, Bigger Thomas, possess universality.

Butler's collection reprints an early (1969) piece by one of the most productive and informative Wright scholars, Keneth Kinnamon, on "*Native Son: The Personal, Social, and Political Background.*" Kinnamon says Charles I. Glicksberg "is speaking hyperbolically" when he claims that "Richard Wright is Bigger Thomas—one part of him anyway," but adds "Nevertheless, there is some truth in the assertion, and not merely in the general sense, according to the formulation of James Baldwin, that 'no American Negro exists who does not have his private Bigger Thomas living in the skull.'" Kinnamon notes that both Richard and Bigger "are Mississippi-born Negroes who migrated to Chicago; both live with their mother in the worst slums of the Black Belt of that city; both are motivated by fear and hatred; both are rebellious by temperament; both could explode into violence" (p.15). Bigger and Richard Wright might share these precise, combined facts of existence and emotional responses to them with relatively few people. Far more would be drawn into commonality with the two if "opportunity-poor and oppressed" were substituted for Mississippi Negroes, "a place where they expected a better life" for Chicago, and so on. Fear, hatred, rebelliousness, and violence are not responses limited to alienated and subjugated black Americans. But Wright shows that even murderous Bigger possesses—develops—human capacities enabling him to grow beyond the roles the dominating forces represented viciously by state's attorney Buckley, and with the best intentions by Bigger's defender, Max, would impose upon him: black monster or black victim.

Like Richard Wright, Bigger grew beyond his environment and in a complicated fashion, gets outside it, escapes it by escaping the confines of the self to which his oppressive (and in Bigger's instance, white) society would limit him. He does this at first dangerously and destructively and from my own particular angle, unhealthily, through murder. Even more than *Black Boy (American Hunger), Native Son* presents a worst-case scenario for fulfilling personal development. As a station on some existentially absurd game board, murder would represent the worst starting position. In life, murder removes the human being murdered from the chance to play the game: Mary and Bessie will never win. The moral math that would balance out the women's destruction of selves with Bigger's growth is tragically flawed. And Bigger in the heightened awareness he achieves does not suggest such a formulation. But neither does he allow his crimes to accomplish the fate white society seems to have wished for him, the destruction of his humanity. Instead, through accepting what he did as self-impelled, and agonizingly pursuing the question why he acted in such deadly fashion, he strives to come to terms with who he had been, why he had been the person he was. By this terribly risky and harmful route he becomes someone different and better. Bigger may represent what Wright could have become but did not, but he also becomes by the end of *Native Son* what few would have expected him to grow into, a sign of the human spirit's potential that he was not at the book's opening. And he does so in a dramatically, which is to say convincingly, true-to-life way.

Bigger, always imperfect just as Richard Wright was, perhaps travels farther than his creator considering his psychological and intellectual starting point, so that it is possible for a reasonable observer of his life narrative to feel a sort of hard (not sentimental) pity—the pity of classic tragedy—at his destruction, and not simply because he was black and therefore badly shaped by unfair white society. His execution by the state destroys the human potential of the pained and at least partially understanding human being he has become. Here, the state seems more like the early Bigger, killing from a fear and anger it does not understand. With his death, his life is wasted to humanity except as an illustration of possibilities for an individual to redeem a self that seemed wasted practically from birth.

What Bigger illustrates, just like what Wright's life adds up to, is very complicated. Wright said he did not want Bigger to elicit easy sorrow, and at the novel's end there is that now famous "ring of steel against steel as a far door clanged shut" like a trap around the newly self-aware Bigger, whose social consciousness will not be given much more time to develop. In Butler's book, Carla Capetti says about Wright's autobiographical persona in *Black Boy (American Hunger)* that "rather than traveling from bondage to freedom," he "is condemned to travel from bondage to bondage forever, never to reach freedom" (p.90). But just as my stepfather found other boundaries he had to pass beyond once he was released from the wartime camp he and his family were confined to, so must we all proceed from boundary to boundary, or enough of us to qualify our experience as universal. Chicago was liberating for Richard Wright, but it was also confining. So was New York. So were Paris and Accra. He was buoyed by the experience of observing African liberation from political colonialism in *Black Power*, but depressed at seeing that the Africans were maybe stepping deterministically from one jail to another, where some Great White Hope above the black masses was replaced by a Great Black Hope. So he wrote a nervy open letter to Nkrumah respectfully telling him how to run his new nation. Then on to Bandung, to observe more nations with more hopes of getting out from under the heel of domination.

Frederick Douglass also showed that escape to emancipation demands a struggle that never ends until you give up or die. The Richard Wright that emerges from his life story is never fully, finally free, but he also never gives up until—fate of us all—he dies. Never giving up is one burden Wright lugged around with him on what Michel Fabre has so grandly documented as Wright's never-ending quest. In his quests Wright used the places of confinement and oppression he had experienced as he exploited the prison that Mississippi could have been for him—as so many opportunities to explore human chances for the growth as well as the destruction of spirit and soul.

Donald Gibson refers to Bigger, in an essay Butler reprints, as "Wright's Invisible Native Son," because some readers fail to see beneath his surface. "Most critics of Wright's novel see only the outer covering of Bigger Thomas, the blackness of his skin and his resulting social role. Few have seen him as a discrete entity, a particular person who struggles with the burden of his humanity" (p.35). Like Richard Wright, Bigger *is* a distinct person with a distinct black, male, American history. But his quest to understand himself and what made him is both his black and human burden, and his struggle is another. If you reject both burdens, as Wright's work and his life show Wright did not, you reject part of your humanity. What Wright dramatizes in both life and art is that the burden is the humanity, and something Bigger dramatizes when he is about to be killed is that he will die as a Negro but also as a reasoning, suffering human being, what Gibson terms a "private, isolated human" who "must face the consequences" of his actions (p.37) but also, I would add, of his humanity. He is neither a statistic nor the moral or sociological equivalent of some rat squashed by a skillet.

In his Introduction Robert Butler recalls Ralph Ellison's commentary on *Black Boy* in the *Antioch Review,* claiming that "Wright was able to triumph over his personal disasters by forming those raw experiences into art" (p.xxx). Jerry Ward wisely reminds us that "Wright himself never capitulated to the dehumanizing norms of early twentieth-century Southern culture" (p.95) nor did success ever satisfy his hunger (p.96), and Irving Howe remembers that his friend Wright died "full of hopes and projects . . . struggling toward a comprehension of the strange and unexpected world coming into birth" (p.139). This world is the same world that seems always strangely coming into birth, whether one is born black and male near Roxie, Mississippi, or some other color or gender anywhere. Readers anywhere, even if they did not share Wright's feelings of alienation and cosmic despair, might participate in what Michel Fabre, quoted in Amriyit Singh's essay "Richard Wright's *The Outsider:* Existentialist Exemplar or Critique," informs us was Wright's increasing attempts in the 1950s to acquire a "more global view of . . . the situation of contemporary man" (p.128). An element of that view, as his life and works demonstrate, was, simply, the common idea that while life was bleak, we should try strenuously to make it better.

Wright showed throughout his life and in his works that to make life better, a person could not remain what Melville called an isolatto, rejecting support and offering none. In "Blueprint for Negro Writing" he praised the early black American church for serving "as an antidote for suffering and denial," and although he eventually broke with the Communist Party he never forgot the brotherhood and sisterhood it offered him at a critical period in his maturation and never denied the visionary gleam for racial solidarity that shines so brightly in his early novella "Fire and Cloud" (though he cleverly notes at the story's end when black and white dissidents stand together, that "tears" were "blurring" the "vision" of heroic black Reverend Taylor, who is leading the mixed-races masses). But in focusing on both bleakness and betterment, Wright—finally—entered on the individual. In *Black Boy (American Hunger)*, for example, particularly its first half, the boy Richard escapes his cruel trap seemingly almost by his efforts, his striving, his cunning, his imagination alone. This depiction elides or distorts many of the facts of Richard Wright's life, but its truth may be that at heart—finally—nothing can help the individual but the individual. This may not be a truth universally acknowledged, but it is at least a frequently held belief in many places in the world, one that Wright brilliantly dramatizes. If escaping from inside the trap is ultimately the individual's job, for Wright the task of the oppressor is escaping from what looks like the outside of the trap. In "Creation of the Self in Richard Wright's *Black Boy*," Yoshinobu Hakutani emphasizes Wright's demonstration that "the oppressors are as much victims of the elemental design of racism as are the oppressed" (p.73). I would add that Wright broadened his focus on victimization to depict many other oppressors and oppressed, other political masters and slaves, other dominating men and violated women. He showed, I think, that when that steel door clanged shut, containing Bigger, whoever caused the door to shut was imprisoned also in a trap that was ultimately self made, universally.

In chapter XIII of *Black Boy (American Hunger)*, just before young Richard escapes the South, he ponders his alternatives. He could stay and fight Southern whites but does not think he would win. Otherwise he "could submit and live the life of a genial slave," or "drain off my restlessness by fighting" other Negroes, or he could "forget what I had read," put the whites out of his mind, and "find release from anxiety and longing in sex and alcohol." None of these are possible for him, since "All of my life had shaped me to live by my own feelings and thoughts," and more revealingly, "If I did not want others to violate my life, how could I voluntarily violate it myself?" He acknowledges for him, finally, the primacy of the self and asserts his refusal to contain within himself violator and victim. He will not oppress himself by giving up control of himself. To the contrary, like Bigger (and some would say Cross Damon in *The Outsider*) he insists upon self-retention as a way of resisting the trap that has been constructed around him. He compels himself to keep, in the words of Abdul Jan Mohamed, whom Frank McMahon quotes in our present issue of the *Mississippi Quarterly,* "an uncontaminated space in his mind . . . where his potential humanity remained intact." Surely this private space can be cleared and maintained—cultivated—in minds outside Mississippi, outside America, by men and women, universally.

JEFF KAREM

"I Could Never Really Leave the South": Regionalism and the Transformation of Richard Wright's American Hunger

A personal history by one of our most important writers, lying in some drawer for over 30 years—how was this possible? How could it have been "lost" or "forgotten"? . . . why we have had to wait so long for the second part we are not told.

Irving Howe, review of *American Hunger*

When published in 1945, *Black Boy* constituted a cannily truncated version of Richard Wright's original autobiography, *American Hunger* (1993). In the year leading up to the publication of this text, Wright was called upon to revise his narrative to satisfy not only his publisher, but also the Book-of-the-Month Club, which wanted to make his work a selection. In exchange, Wright was led to alter his conclusion and even to delete the section describing his experiences in the North after leaving the South. These changes effectively blunted Wright's broader critique of American race relations and confined *Black Boy* to a regional narrative of childhood and adolescence. This publishing experience may provide a literary corollary for his personal speculation at the end of *Black Boy* that "deep down, I knew that I could never really leave the South" (284). It was not until 1977, after Wright's death, that the missing portion of his autobiography would appear in print.

American Literary History, Volume 13, Number 4 (Winter 2001): pp. 694–715. Copyright © 2001 Oxford University Press.

15

Reexamining the publication history of *American Hunger* is in order because the scholarship on this subject is inconclusive and lacking in detail. Neither Wright's biographer, Michel Fabre, nor the editors of the Library of America edition of *Black Boy*, Jerry Ward Jr. and Arnold Rampersad, present a well-documented explanation for how the comprehensive critique that was *American Hunger* became the tale of triumph that was *Black Boy*. Moreover, no one has tried to place these editorial decisions and critical reception in the context of trends in publishing and political life during wartime America in the 1940s. From this broader perspective, the history of *Black Boy* affords an ideal opportunity to investigate the complex relationship among authorship, the marketplace, and politics, as well as to observe how regional narratives have formed a crucial way for America to construct its national self-image.

In his major writings leading up to *American Hunger*, Wright struggled to impress his total vision of American race relations upon his audience and to avoid writing protest fiction evoking easy sympathy. Reader-response mattered to Wright because a key purpose of his art, as he described it in "The Blueprint for Negro Writing" (1937), was "to lift the level of consciousness higher" (49), and to "deepen people's perceptions" and to "quicken their thoughts," as he explained in an interview ("This" 67). Consequently, Wright was disappointed to discover after the publication of *Uncle Tom's Children* (1938) that many reviewers had changed the inflammatory content of the work into sentimental, even reactionary responses. A reviewer for the *Memphis Commercial Appeal* wrote that, "Written by a negro . . . the book still does not rankle in the mind of the white reader. On the other hand, it provokes only his sympathy. And this is saving grace for a Southerner" (Tyus). The reviewer went on to say this "sympathetic" quality of the work ensures that it will not "inflame" people to action against the South, as did *Uncle Tom's Cabin*. The *Jacksonville Sunday Times-Union* provided a similar reading of Wright's characters—one that would seem at home in old plantation days: "These accounts of negro life sing with a plaintive melody, haunting our souls, in telling of the few simple things necessary for the happiness of the negro . . . they plead for sympathetic understanding and a chance to be left alone" (Hendry). No doubt because of such "sympathetic" reviews, which managed to harness Wright's regional fiction for distinctly sectionalist ends, Wright found himself quite troubled by the reception of this work, as he explained in the essay "How Bigger Was Born" (1940): "When the reviews of the book began to appear, I realized that I had made an awfully naive mistake. I found that I had written a book which even bankers' daughters could read and weep over and feel good about" (xxvii).

In later works such as *Native Son* (1940), Wright tried to prevent readers from transforming the radical energy of his vision into a catharsis, but different strategies emerged for containing his confrontational stance. In Bigger

Thomas, a transgressive African American living in the North, Wright produced a fearsome character that could not be sentimentalized as a hapless victim, as could the nearly angelic protagonists of *Uncle Tom's Children*. This regional shift expanded the scope of Wright's criticism of America, but several reviewers argued that as a Southerner-in-exile, Wright lacked the perspective to indict American race relations so broadly. Liberal Southerner David Cohn, in a famous scathing attack in the *Atlantic Monthly*, admitted that there was violence against African Americans in some parts of the South, but faulted this "Mississippi-born Negro" for inflating it into a national problem. He criticized Bigger's anger at "*all* whites," declaring, "Nowhere in America save in the most benighted sections of the South, or in times of passion arising from the committing of atrocious crime, is the Negro denied the equal protection of the laws" (659). Some sympathetic reviewers were also frustrated by this shift to Chicago. For one writer in the *Los Angeles Times*, "Richard Wright is a young Negro who has added much to our understanding of black life in the South. His Book-of-the-Month Club novel, however, is about a Chicago Negro; and it is not the solid piece of work I expected of him . . . Bigger is not really a Negro" (Needham 7). Significantly, the reviewer did not explain *why* Bigger was not really a "Negro," save for this mention that Wright had chosen to write about Chicago rather than the South, as if Bigger were less of a "Negro" because he was not "Southern enough." By the time he was writing *Native Son*, Wright had departed from the South in both life and literature, but many of his reviewers showed a desire to confine him to a narrow place in America's literary and cultural landscape, returning him, ironically, not only to the very land he fled, but also for the very reasons he had for leaving, the limitations the South had imposed on him.

Although the reception of *Native Son* demonstrated that Wright's Southern origins could be used against him, he would soon turn this regional affiliation into an ally, claiming a privileged perspective on American race relations because of his combination of Northern and Southern experiences. As he was putting the finishing touches on *Native Son*, Wright contemplated a broader investigation of African-American life in the South and the North, which would eventually take shape as the poetic ethnography *Twelve Million Black Voices* (1941). Edward Aswell, his editor at Harper and Row, expressed his dismay over the project to Wright, because he felt it would divert the author from other plans Aswell wanted him to pursue: "This project rather disturbs me because, if it goes through, it will completely kill an idea which I had been thinking about for you, and one which I believe is really a sounder and more important approach to very much the same subject" (Letter to Wright, 31 Dec. 1940). In a subsequent letter, Aswell explained that he wanted Wright to create something more "personal," to address these issues (30 Sept. 1941). In 1942, one year after the publication of *Twelve Million Black Voices*, Wright turned his attention to Aswell's request and began the autobiography that would garner for him more acclaim than even *Native Son* had brought.

Wright's earliest drafts of his autobiography, entitled "Black Confession," present detailed chapters describing his experiences of growing up in the South and his young adulthood in Chicago, all with an eye towards his *bildung* as a writer. Perhaps in response to the limiting perspectives with which critics had approached his previous works, Wright emphasized that he was not merely a documenter of African-American folkways by foregrounding his development as an intellectual with cosmopolitan literary interests. In later drafts, for example, Wright deleted the sections describing the importance of black dialect to him. In his first reflections on Gertrude Stein's "Melanctha" (1909), a novella focusing on the consciousness of an African-American domestic, Wright drafted in "Black Confession" a scene in which black speech inspired his writing: "Under the influence of Melanctha in Stein's Three Lives, I would spend long hours fashioning sentences which in my opinion approximated the speech of Negro people I heard around me. Negro speech was something alive for me; it was vivid in an objective and subjective way. Upon my typewriter I would pound out random and disconnected sentences for the sheer love of words" (425). For the final version of this scene, in *American Hunger*, Wright made a much more compact statement, one that elided the issue of black speech: "Under the influence of Stein's Three Lives, I spent hours and days pounding out disconnected sentences for the sheer love of words" (329).[1] Thus Wright eschewed Melanctha and African-American dialect, opting for a succinct statement of his pure "love of words." Wright may have done so in order to carve out a more distinctly modernist space for himself as an author, calling attention to his work as a wordsmith and distancing himself from the naturalistic expectations that dialect be at the center of African-American writing.[2]

One of the most striking aspects of Wright's early drafts is that although his self-portrait moves among and across regional lines (from Mississippi, Arkansas, and Tennessee to Chicago), it does not treat those boundaries as significant dividing points in the narrative. In the original draft, the transition from one region to another is continuous. Although the draft as a whole is divided into chapters, not even a chapter break separates the North from the South in "Black Confession." Wright follows his friend Shorty's admission, "I'll never leave this goddam South," with a new paragraph beginning, "I left the next day" (325). As Wright's drafting continued, the regional distinction became more pivotal to the work, however. The final version of *American Hunger* is divided into two sections entitled "Southern Night" and "The Horror and the Glory," with the transition from one region to another forming the turning point in the manuscript. When Wright submitted the final draft of this manuscript to his agent, Paul Reynolds, on 17 December 1943, he was confident that it formed a coherent whole that could not be changed: "I don't think that there is much that I will ever be able to do on this script. Perhaps a section or two here and there will have to be pulled out. But on the whole, the thing will have to stand as it is, for better or worse."

But the work did not "stand as it is." In the year and a half before *American Hunger* went to press, a decision was made to eliminate the second half of his autobiography, converting it from an account of his struggles in the North and South to a more narrow story of a Southern childhood. How and why did this happen? Although a wide range of publisher's documents are available, Wright's biographers and critics have not yet fully accounted for how this change in plans occurred. The evidence available fails to justify the classic speculations about the sources of this change, such as editorial desires for conciseness or pressures from the Communist Party. Wright's agent liked the manuscript as it was and sent him an enthusiastic telegram one week later: "Your autobiography is enthralling believe it has possibilities of a very large sale want publication this spring will see you Monday any suggested work on manuscript will be of a most minor nature" (Reynolds, Telegram). Conversations between Reynolds and Aswell revealed that Harper's did want the manuscript shortened. Fabre sees this desire for compactness as a reason behind the truncation of the manuscript. In his biography of Wright he reports that Aswell told Wright "that it might be better to limit the book to Wright's experiences in the South because it would then be more closely knit" (254). Wright's own papers, however, do not contain any mention of such an exchange, either in conversation or in letters. More significantly, Wright's correspondence with his agent makes clear that Aswell had no such wish for large-scale deletions in the work. On 19 January 1944, Reynolds wrote to Wright explaining the changes Aswell desired: "I saw Ed Aswell yesterday. He said he wanted compression of certain passages rather than cutting towards the latter part of the book." In fact, the changes requested were generally very minor, such as deletions of repetitive language or occasional tightening of themes and plot details. Not only did Aswell *not* want the latter part of the autobiography cut, he actually suggested that it be expanded: "I may be wrong but I personally would like to see some of this cut and the story carried on to the years of Wright's success—perhaps to the writing of *Native Son*" (Letter to Reynolds, 20 Dec. 1943). Desires for Wright's autobiography to end on a note of "success" would continue to haunt this manuscript, but Harper's did not demand such substantial changes at that point. Although Aswell did ask if the ending could be given a more hopeful cast, he respected Wright's polite rejoinder that he could not "step outside of the mood rendered there and say anything without it sounding false" (Letter to Aswell, 14 Jan. 1944). The galley proofs produced in April 1944 contained both sections of Wright's autobiography in its finally drafted form, demonstrating that Harper's was fully prepared to publish the entirety of *American Hunger* in the shape Wright wanted it to take.

Subsequent evidence has revealed that what intervened to change publication plans was the interest of the Book-of-the-Month Club. On 26 June 1944, Aswell wrote to the club to tell them that "Richard Wright has accepted the suggestion of your Judges to end his book, now entitled *American Hunger*, at the point where he leaves the South to go to Chicago" (Letter to Wood). Aswell's letter makes clear that the manuscript was abridged at the club's behest, but there is no explanation for why the club desired this change. Critics have not thoroughly explored this signal moment in American publishing and Wright's career. Janice Thaddeus points to the archival evidence revealing the club's interest in abridging the volume, but her brief study gives neither a close reading of the changes requested by the club nor a full-fledged account of the publication history.[3] Neither do the editors of the restored Library of America edition of *American Hunger*, who explain the abridgment according to theories that are not very well-supported. Rampersad suggests in his "Note on the Text" that "pressure from the Communists had led the book club to ask him to drop the second section" (487), which was quite critical of the Party. Although Rampersad claims that Wright expressed this fear of Communist anger in the journal he kept in 1944–45, I can find no such reference. In fact, in that same journal Wright seemed fearlessly prepared for any conflicts with Communists that would arise from his work: "If ever there came a revolutionary book from the pen of a Negro, BLACK BOY is it. I say fuck all ignorant communists who think otherwise" (59). In addition, the judges from the Book-of-the-Month Club who were involved with Wright in the revision process, Henry Seidel Canby and Dorothy Canfield Fisher, were distinctly *not* of the group of intellectuals who had communist loyalties or would be cowed by Party criticism.

In fact, evidence demonstrates that publishing these criticisms of the Party was actually perceived as a marketing point for the book. In the summer before *American Hunger* was set to be published, excerpts from the later part of the autobiography—both of which eviscerated the Party—were released in *Atlantic Monthly* magazine. Although Rampersad (488) and Fabre (254–255) give the impression that the decision to publish these pieces occurred after the decision to shorten the volume was made, publication correspondence reveals that the release of these excerpts had been planned all along. Wright's agent, Reynolds, thought this would drum up interest and wrote to Edward Aswell of Harper's on 2 May 1944 that "it ought to help the book if *The Atlantic* uses it in three installments and we shall want to publicize that fact." *Atlantic Monthly*, in fact, had already advertised the upcoming article "I Tried to Be a Communist" (1944) as an excerpt from *American Hunger*, and had to apologize to Harper's for unknowingly representing this article as part of the upcoming autobiography. Embarrassed, Edward Weeks wrote to Reynolds on 31 July 1944, explaining that the "decision to omit the latter chapters was arrived at long after our Atlantic Bulletin had gone to press, but we have taken pains not to make any further link between *American Hunger* and the two-parter which we now have in print." Such a foul-up in the release of this material shows the degree to which this change requested by the Book-of-the-Month took everyone by surprise.

But why would the Book-of-the-Month Club have such an interest in abridging Wright's autobiography? The overall effect of this truncation was that it changed Wright's work from the story of a writer's *bildung* in America to a tale of "growing up Southern" as Jerry Ward aptly describes it (xiii). The Book-of-the-Month Club judges, particularly those most connected to the selection of *Black Boy*, had an interest in literary regionalism that may give a clue as to why the story of "growing up Southern" would be of more interest to them. The chairman of the club at that time, Canby, former Yale literature professor and founder of the *Saturday Review of Literature,* had strong ideas about returning American literature to its regional origins. On 25 June 1927, Canby wrote a lead article for the *Saturday Review*, "Place and Literature," which asserted that the American writer needed "deeper roots in his soil." Canby expressed regret that the "heart for questing adventure" too often turned American writers away from "small familiar things" and left their writings "unenriched by that sort of allusion which imbues locality with significance, and in turn wins connotativeness from place" (923). In light of these ideas about place and origins, one can read the truncation of Wright's autobiography as a way of curtailing his "questing adventure" and confining his work to his "roots." Canby's ideas also revealed the way the regional was often intertwined with the rural in American literary discourse in Wright's time. Canby's career showed that he was quite willing to put his preferences for regional literature into his practice of publishing and editing. When asked by E. P. Dutton to select a series of works of American literature for young boys for their King's Treasuries series, Canby proposed anthologies favoring a regional, rural approach to American literary life, including such volumes as *Indian Stories, Narratives of Country Life, Plantation Tales,* and *Stories of the Backwoods* (Canby, Correspondence). By contributing to the club's decision to change the shape of *American Hunger*, Canby succeeded in subsuming Wright's work into his larger project of directing America's literary focus to its regions.

Regionalism as a literary force was no less important for Fisher, who was an acclaimed regional writer in her own right. In correspondence, Canby and Fisher often argued about who was more committed to regional literature. In a letter written in response to an item in Canby's memoirs that portrayed him as the champion of regionalists, Fisher denied that she showed any signs of "steering off from regional books," citing all of the works she had supported (14 Nov. 1946). Fisher also articulated a philosophy of regionalism relevant to the subject of *Black Boy*. She reminded Canby that "the 'regional' literature and subjects I often take for my subject is youth, childhood. . . . I'm in a state of revolt (have been all my life) against the literary convention that a human being can be a proper *major* subject for a serious piece of fiction (intended as an interpretation of a comment on human life) *only* if he/she has come to the age of mating." In shifting the focus of *American Hunger* to Wright's Southern childhood, the Book-of-the-Month Club's decision combined Fisher's dual preferences for narratives of youth and region.

Confining Wright's autobiography to his Southern childhood also served to blunt the political impact of his work. Revisions to the text's conclusion provide crucial evidence of the Book-of-the-Month Club's desire to contain the scope of Wright's cultural criticism. A set of proofs and correspondence bearing the note "Revised version to set from if Book Club takes it" documents the transformation of the fierce conclusion of *American Hunger* into the comparatively mild ending of *Black Boy*.[4] Wright's original ending to *American Hunger* shows him to be skeptical not only of the life offered to him in the North and the South, but of America as a whole. He begins his conclusion in a fiercely interrogative mood: "Well, what had I got out of living in the city? What had I got out of living in the South? What had I got out of living in America? I paced the floor, knowing that all I possessed were words and dim knowledge that my country had shown me no examples of how to live a human life. All my life I had been full of a hunger for a new way to live . . ." (Chapter XIV Drafts 452). As he finishes the work, Wright comes to the realization of the power of those "words," and concludes *American Hunger* with his pencil hanging expectantly over a sheet of paper. He writes, "I wanted to try to build a bridge of words between me and that world outside, that world that was so distant and elusive that it seemed unreal. I would hurl words into this darkness and wait for an echo, and if an echo sounded, no matter how faintly, I would send other words to tell, to march, to fight, to create a sense of the hunger for life that gnaws in us all, to keep alive in our hearts a sense of the inexpressibly human" (453). This passage closes *American Hunger* with a sense of expectation to be fulfilled by the author. America as a concept has failed him, has given "no examples of how to live a human life." In this conclusion, Wright will be the own arbiter of his future, who will "build a bridge of words" to bring the fulfillment that has been denied to him. This conclusion is as much a beginning as an end. Even as there is a sense of possibility, there is no complete triumph, no banishment or elimination of Wright's "hunger." In fact, it is not even Wright's purpose by the end to "satisfy" hunger, but to evoke a collective vision of the hunger all of us face.

Because the truncated autobiography only addressed the first 18 years of Wright's life, before he had decided to devote himself to literature, it would not make sense for that book to end with the birth of a writer. Consequently, one of the first things to disappear in the revision was this dimension of authorial power. Wright also could not present as broad a sense of all-encompassing "hunger," as his autobiography only depicted his Southern experience. Indeed, rather than "hunger," he writes of the "sense of freedom" he felt at the chance of leaving the South, which immediately puts a more hopeful cast on the story of Wright's life. Wright begins his closing paragraph of *Black Boy* with the suggestion that hope lies in the North: "With ever watchful eyes and bearing scars, visible and invisible, I headed North, full of a hazy notion that life could be lived with dignity . . ." (496). Wright's new conclusion in its early drafts, however, still stood as a powerful piece of social critique that had implications for all of America. In this draft of the concluding chapter, Wright asks himself where he received this inspiring hope: "What was it that made me always conscious of possibilities? From where in this darkness had I caught a sense of freedom?" Significantly, he credits books, rather than any aspect of the society around him: "The external world of whites and blacks surely had not evoked in me any belief in myself. . . . It had been only through books—at best, no more than vicarious cultural transfusions—that I had managed to keep myself alive."

As much as the club liked books, the idea that texts rather than people helped Wright to freedom did not sit well with the judges. Fisher, in particular, began to correspond with Wright about changes he might make to this conclusion. Fisher had been an ally of Wright's for some time—she had written the introduction to *Native Son* and been instrumental in making that a Book-of-the-Month Club selection. Consequently, Fisher had a voice that Wright would listen to—the voice of an influential, well-connected friend whose suggestions could not be discarded lightly. Fearing that Wright's ending did not sufficiently distinguish between North and South, friend and foe, Fisher asked if there were some way he could heighten this distinction: "In the South, it is frankly violent brutality which bars the way to Negro development. In the North it is hypocrisy, the failure to do what is admitted to be right to do" (Letter to Wright, 1 July 1944). Fisher went on to quote François de La Rochefoucauld's maxim that "hypocrisy is the tribute paid by vice to virtue" in order to suggest that at least good impulses were at the root of Northern sentiments toward race relations. Accordingly, with the conclusion of World War II still to come, Fisher wanted to know if Wright could give credit in his conclusion to the American traditions of freedom of liberty: "To receive, in the closing pages of your book, one word of recognition for the aspiration, if it were possible for you to give such recognition honestly, would hearten all those who believe in American ideals." In that same letter, Fisher even proposed an alternative answer to Wright's question "From where in this darkness had I caught a sense a freedom?": "From what other source than the basic tradition of our country could the soul of an American have been filled with that 'hazy notion' that life could be lived with dignity? Could it be that even from inside the prison of injustice, through the barred windows of that Bastille of racial oppression, Richard Wright had caught a glimpse of the American flag?" This desire for a symbolic "pledge" to the flag betrays an anxiety that Wright's critique challenges America's self-conception as a land of freedom—a challenge especially dangerous as America was mounting its decisive D-Day offensive in the European Theater. In this light, the regional narrative that the club desired from Wright provided an accepted genre into which Wright's inflammatory ideas could be funneled and defused. If Wright could confine his criticism exclusively to the South and pay tribute to American ideals as a whole (embodied for Fisher in the symbol of the flag), his critique would be a national affirmation, not a national indictment.

Wright answered Fisher with mixed feelings. He agreed to sharpen regional distinctions by changing "darkness" to "Southern darkness," but he balked at Fisher's larger request that he pay tribute to the North, explaining that the North was a place of refuge rather than salvation for him: "I fully understand the value of what you are driving at, but, frankly, the narrative as it now stands simply will not support a more general or hopeful conclusion. The Negro who flees the South is really a refugee; he is so pinched and straitened in his environment that his leaving is more an avoidance than an embrace" (Letter to Fisher, 6 July 1944). Wright told Fisher that he would be willing to explain in more detail how books helped him, "I added a paragraph to the body of the epilogue explaining this notion." Wright's paragraph enclosed in this letter elaborated the influence of books on his consciousness, but refused to give Fisher the grand vision for which she had hoped, explaining that "[i]t had been my accidental reading of fiction and literary criticism that had evoked in me vague glimpses of life's possibilities" and had provided "a tinge of warmth from an unseen light."

Fisher was not satisfied with this explanation, and in her customarily gentle but unyielding tone wrote back to Wright, arguing that he ought somehow to integrate praise for "America" into this explanation: "[S]ome of the characters in books through whom you had 'glimpsed life's possibilities' were fellow-Americans of yours. These 'unseen lights' which shone through them upon your faith were reflections of American efforts to live up to an idea" (Letter to Wright, 12 July 1944). Fisher's insistence that Wright fit America into his closing sense of hope reveals how important it was for this autobiography not to compromise America's self-image. Wright responded to Fisher on 20 July 1944 with a new draft and the statement, "I did manage, this time, to use the word American." Wright fit America obliquely into the final version of the conclusion of *Black Boy*, describing his favorite authors' treatment of America in their works: "What had enabled me to overcome my chronic distrust was that these books—written by men like Dreiser, Masters, Mencken, Anderson, and Lewis—seemed defensively critical of the straitened American environment. These writers seemed to feel that America could be shaped nearer to the hearts of those who lived in it" (282). Taken as a whole, these revisions changed the conclusion of *American Hunger* from a scene of Wright poised to begin his career as a writer, with a sense that America has yet to live up to its promises, to a scene of Wright poised to find his freedom in the North, with a feeling that national ideals have already triumphed.

The deletion of the "The Horror and the Glory," the section in which Wright described his Northern experiences, eliminated Wright's vision of racism as a *national* rather than regional system of oppression, a perspective that the author had not articulated with such detail in preceding works. Although Wright had indicted American race relations as a whole in *Native Son*, exemplified in Max's dramatic statement that African Americans constitute "a separate nation, stunted, stripped, and held captive within this nation" (364), it was only in *American Hunger* that Wright created a thorough comparison of discrimination on both sides of the Mason-Dixon line. Wright argues in *American Hunger* that African Americans have a secure place neither in the North nor in the South in America, but have been "shunted" into a "No Man's Land" (312). In sharp contrast to the hopeful ending of *Black Boy*, Wright follows his description of his flight North in *American Hunger* with a grim declaration of his disappointment: "My first glimpse of the flat black stretches of Chicago depressed and dismayed me, mocked all my fantasies" (307). Even as Wright finds freedom in the city, he also discovers the alienated character of modern urban life, in which people do not perceive one another as persons, but "seemed to regard each other as part of the city landscape" (308–309). Furthermore, he also encounters occasional moments of discrimination that surprise him, even in the face of what he suffered in the South. When the Communist Party tried to stifle his dissent, Wright reflected: "It was inconceivable to me, though bred in the lap of southern hate, that a man could not have his say" (405). All of these episodes reveal the deep ambivalence Wright held for the supposed "Mecca" of the North—complexities entirely elided in the truncated edition. As Ward aptly describes it, with the expanded *American Hunger*, readers "who might have felt free to cast aspersions on the South were compelled to inspect the dirty laundry of race, oppression, and class in the North" (xiii).

Although these excisions and revisions requested by the Book-of-the-Month Club altered Wright's text in disturbing ways, it would be an oversimplification to treat him as a mere victim. Wright was well aware of the club's power and of the benefits it could bring to his career. Writing to his editor on

25 June 1944 about the different titles suggested by the club, Wright showed a willingness to endure its choice, because whatever weakness their title might have, "their distribution alone can make up for its not being stronger" (Letter to Aswell).[5] Even as the Book-of-the-Month Club circumscribed some aspects of his text, it provided a means of giving his work greater circulation—and greater sales—than it otherwise would have had. Like anyone else, Wright was interested in sales. Since Wright had no other source of income, promoting his work was an important part of his livelihood. In fact, after the galleys of *American Hunger* were printed he sent letters to various newspaper editors in order to generate interest in his work. In one, to Marshall Field of the *Chicago Sun*, Wright called attention to the topicality of his upcoming book: "The book, as you know, deals with Negro life in which there is such an intense national interest just now." Of course, the selling power of the club was so substantial that it is doubtful that any deal proposed to a writer dependent on writing for a living could easily be refused. The club's power was evident in the fact that Harper's and Wright were willing to delay publication almost half a year, until the club was finally ready to make it a selection. Aswell wrote Wright, "Your guess as to the publication date of BLACK BOY is as good as mine. It is in the lap of the gods—meaning the Book-of-the-Month Club judges" (6 Dec. 1944).

When the "gods" came through, they did quite well for Wright. *Black Boy* was slated for publication on 28 February 1945, and everyone expected large sales. Reynolds predicted that Wright's income would nearly quadruple (from $3,800 to $15,000) on the basis of advance sales (28 Nov. 1944); Aswell wrote to Wright on 5 January 1955 that Harper's was "setting our aim high," with 30,000 copies printed for advance orders and $14,000 allocated for advertisements.[6] This advertising campaign took advantage of the changed shape of *Black Boy* in order to sell it as an Algeresque success story. As an entry in a Harper's catalog put it, "At seventeen he finally boarded a train bound for Chicago—the Mecca of the Southern Negro—a city where there might still be white against black, tyranny and suspicion, but where also there would be a difference in life from which he could at last learn who he was as an individual and who he might become" (25). The cover blurbs on *Black Boy* accentuated this spirit of triumphant arrival by emphasizing Wright's background of "growing up Southern." Such confident declarations about Wright's imminent fulfillment in the North belie the sophistication with which the author treats region in his autobiography. Even in the abridged version of his autobiography that was *Black Boy*, Wright explains that the North mattered to him not as an actual place but as a projective image for life in the future: "The North symbolized to me all that I had not felt and seen; it had no relation to what actually existed. Yet, by imagining a place where everything was possible, I kept hope alive within me" (186). The key detail ignored in these publication and review materials is that the North was most important to Wright not as an endpoint to his journey, but as an inspiration to him while he was in the South.

Using a different tone, Fisher's review in the *Book-of-the-Month Club News* deployed infantilizing language, characterizing this book as the story of a "a little Negro boy growing up in our own country." She described the regional authenticity of this portrait of "growing up" as one of the best aspects of the text: "The conversations are extraordinarily natural: . . . The book is full of picturesque folk-lore, folk-ways, colorful superstitions, dramatic happenings, pictures of daily life so vividly set down that they are like things seen with the physical eye" (2). Like many of the reviewers of *Uncle Tom's Children*, Fisher accentuated the pastoral possibilities of Wright's autobiography. Ralph Ellison aptly noted in his essay on *Black Boy*, "Richard Wright's Blues" (1945), that such gestures toward the pastoral often belied disturbing political agendas. For Ellison the pastoral "mechanism" "implies that since Negroes possess the richly human virtues credited to them, then their social position is advantageous and should not be bettered" (86). Although Fisher ultimately did not support such views—she did discuss Wright's struggle with inequality later in the article—her choice to treat the folk characteristics of the work as the centerpiece of her review reveals that her deepest sympathies lay with regional portraiture rather than cultural criticism.

Fisher's comment that Wright set things down so vividly that it was as if they were "seen with the physical eye" pointed to the strong realist aesthetic undergirding the reception of regionalist work. No doubt because this book was a piece of nonfiction, the accuracy of this portrait was a key issue in its reception. Fisher expressed admiration in her review that the work was "controlled by implication, in reticently self-controlled statements of fact, not by rhetoric" (2–3). A blurb on the dust jacket of *Black Boy* also emphasized the author's rhetorical self-possession: "It is the story Richard Wright knows best, for it is his own." Although these statements about autobiography articulate traditional expectations about the distinction between fiction and nonfictional prose, it is disconcerting to observe how this interest in "fact" and the "natural" qualities of Wright's portrait diminished what he had accomplished as a writer. In representations such as Fisher's, Wright emerged as less an artist and more a conduit of factual and folkloric knowledge. In so doing, Fisher infantilized Wright yet again, this time by removing him from the role of author. It was Wright the victimized child speaking from his raw experience, not Wright the articulate writer, who emerged as the received author of *Black Boy* for many readers. Even as these characterizations ascribed authority to Wright based on the truths of his Southern past, they diminished Wright's threatening potential for the American present by keeping his work in the generic region of Southern folk narrative.

At the same time that Harper's and the Book-of-the-Month Club were struggling to market Wright's Southern childhood to readers, Wright was consciously wrestling with questions of region in his journal writings. Reflecting on the tribulations of his Southern past, Wright perceived them as essential preparation for solving America's problems in the present. He wrote, "I feel that the burden of the solution of the Negro problem in America lies mainly with the southern Negro." Even as Wright thought his Southern affiliation important, he did not think of himself as a wholly "southern Negro," but as a figure that bridged regional boundaries, a man in a "contradictory circumstance, a plantation Negro living in New York, a peasant who is an artist of sorts" (33). In his folk study *Twelve Million Black Voices* Wright finds such regional contradictions characteristic of most African Americans' lives. Describing the urban industrial workers of the North, Wright explains that "after working all day in one civilization, we go home to our black belts and live, within the orbit of the surviving remnants of the culture of the South, our naive, casual, verbal, fluid folk life" (127). As a writer who had experienced these "contradictory circumstances" firsthand, Wright could offer multiple perspectives on America's regional and racial divides, but it was just such insight into those polarities that was crippled by abbreviating his autobiography and confining his comments to the South.

After publication, a host of positive reviews of *Black Boy* emerged. Most reviews liked the book, but differed in their reading of what message it held for America. Many reviewers showed a conventional fixation on folk life that was comparable to Fisher's. Lewis Gannett, critic for the *New York Herald-Tribune*, drew a folkways portrait in miniature in his review: "It is of the Southern soil from which he sprang; of the mush-and-lard-gravy poverty, the hunger and fear and loneliness that were his home, of the swinging doors of saloons, the cindered railroad tracks, the ribald street gangs that were his escape." Gannett accentuated local color imagery and evoked a sense of Wright as an organic folk artist in this summary of the author's background. Waxing poetic, Gannett embraced the sordidness of Wright's portrait—"This, too, is America: both the mud and scum in which Richard Wright grew up, and the something that sang within him, that ever since has been singing with an ever clearer, painfully sweeter, voice." Gannett's vision of *Black Boy* recognized the pain of Wright's work, but turned it toward the triumphant conclusion that out of this pain beauty was born. This judgment showed admirable praise for Wright's art, but was startlingly silent about Wright's desire to "clean up" that "mud."

Leftists were much more interested in the book's treatment of race relations, and refused to read it as a text with solely regional implications. Benjamin Davis, of the *Sunday Worker*, for example, wrote that "[i]n *Black Boy*, Richard Wright has written a furious and terrifying story of the impact of the Jimcrow [sic] system upon human beings in the Deep South," but warned against treating this as a purely Southern problem: "For it concerns America. Any attempt to bypass this over-all picture will lessen its force and thereby lead to an underestimation of its starkness and blunt the sharp need for correctives." The lengths to which Davis went to emphasize the "over-all picture" implied by this work suggests that he was worried that readers would "underestimate" the scope of the work because of its exclusively Southern setting. There was just cause for this concern, as many reviewers, especially moderates from the North, perceived the book as an indictment of the South rather than of the nation as whole. The *Pittsburgh Press* proclaimed that "the book is a serious indictment of our South" (Paulus); the *Minneapolis Tribune* lamented that "the South probably hasn't changed too much since the period covered in this book" (J. K. S.). Significantly, these reviewers did not attribute these problems to "America" anywhere in their reviews, nor did they consider this Southern problem deserving of attention from the entire nation.

African-American reviewers generally agreed with Wright's criticisms of the South, but were uncomfortable with the idea that this regional portrait could be read as representative of the race. Mrs. Paul Robeson, for example, praised *Black Boy*'s realism in her 8 April 1945 review in the *Hartford Courant*, but rejected the idea that Wright had captured some essence: "To my mind, *Black Boy* presents a truthful portrayal of the Negro's struggle in the South. I am, however, not so convinced that the book presents a true picture of the Negro himself." W. E. B. Du Bois presented a harsher version of that opinion in his review in the *New York Herald-Tribune* with the sarcastic quip, "Born on a plantation, living in Elaine, Ark., and the slums of Memphis, he knows the whole Negro race!" Robeson and Du Bois chafed at the idea that this regional portrait should be taken as emblematic of all African Americans, perhaps because this autobiography cast light on characters from which the urbane Northern African-American class would like to distance itself. In addition, readings of Wright as representative could be confining for other African Americans if the white majority relied upon this text as the sole key to understanding a diverse minority.

The popularity of *Black Boy* solidified Wright's image as a representative African-American and Southern writer. Even as Wright had been a successful literary figure since *Native Son*, it was the placement of his Southern childhood in a text for public consumption that catapulted him to another level of fame. By 6 July 1945, *Black Boy* had sold over 423,000 copies and was at the top of the best-seller lists. Wright received an enormous amount of fan mail for his autobiography—326 pieces, which was more than three times what he had received for *Native Son*. No doubt because of this attention to Wright's Southern past, a reinvigorated interest in his earlier fiction about the South soon emerged. Robert Stepto's claim that *Black Boy* served as a "narrative of ascent that authenticates another" narrative (128), *Native Son*, is persuasive when one considers the total picture of Wright's career, but the more immediate effect of the success of *Black Boy* was a renewed interest in his other Southern text, *Uncle Tom's Children*. The World Press published another edition of *Black Boy* that year, and reprinted *Uncle Tom's Children* as well. Significantly, in this new release of Wright's work, *Native Son* was nowhere to be found. The pairing of the complementary Southern texts of *Uncle Tom's Children* and *Black Boy* by World Press suggests that returning Wright to his Southern roots, in the minds of publishers, formed a newly lucrative package for marketing his work.

In interviews and journal writings Wright revealed his own ambivalence about this role of regional and cultural representative. At times he seemed quite comfortable with the prospect that his words were speaking for other African Americans. On the radio interview program "The Author Meets the Critics," Wright described himself as writing for a black Everyman in composing *Black Boy*: "I wanted to lend, give my tongue, to voiceless Negro boys." Wright had reasons, however, for questioning his being labeled as a representative voice. When publicity activities grew more heated as *Black Boy* was ready for print, Wright wrote of his discomfort in his journal: "I write books, but like to run away when they are published. Wish I could get out of town now. I lose my self-possession when this kind of noise starts" (46). Although Wright enjoyed the role of cultural authority, he became frustrated when the public did not pay attention to the aspects of his work he considered most significant. When the first reviews for *Black Boy* came out, Wright worried that his readers were overlooking something: "There is no doubt that the majority opinion seems to reflect the feeling that BLACK BOY is the best thing that I have done.... But one thing is missing; the American mind finds it hard to ally itself with my vision.... In no review does anyone link me with what is being done in writing in the world. They look upon it in a moral light; how bad this life was; how did he learn to write; we must do something, they all say. But no one says, yes, this is life how it is lived, and here we have a sort of meaning in it; here the Negro states the theme of modern living" (Journal 102). Wright's paraphrasing of reviewers' comments as "how bad this life was; how did he learn to write" revealed his discomfort with being an object of mere pity and wonder. Significantly, Wright was also disconcerted by the idea that he would be read simply as a moral spokesman, someone who provokes his readers to say "we must do something." As committed to social change as Wright was, comments such as this suggest that he was equally concerned with being read as a writer of broader significance than social protest, one who had language and ideas that spoke to "the theme of modern living." Unfortunately, reviewers' interest in the regional focus of Wright's work and Wright's role as ethnic representative almost guaranteed that his work would be read with less of a literary or philosophical "eye" than the works of other writers.

Wright wrote also of his concern that ulterior motives might be conditioning his celebration: "They seem so positive. . . . Are these people trying to kiss me to death, trying to make me a bought idealist or something?" (Journal 53). The disputes surrounding the publication of this volume suggest some justification for such anxieties. The publication correspondence I have examined shows that Book-of-the-Month Club judges like Canby and Fisher had regional and national interests that made it worth their while to purchase and transform Wright's vision of America. The conclusions that some reviewers drew from *Black Boy* showed that that investment had "paid off." A reviewer from the *Boston Morning Globe* perceived the very existence of this book as evidence of America's greatness: "It's to America's credit that this book has been written and will be given wide circulation. Nowhere except in America could such a rebel thrive. But what made him a rebel should be on America's conscience" (Laycock). This statement pays tribute to Wright's ordeals but also argues that the very dissent permitted to the author is evidence of our national integrity. As James Baldwin has noted, "Americans, unhappily, have the most remarkable ability to alchemize all bitter truths into an innocuous but piquant confection and to transform their moral contradictions, or public discussion of such contradictions, into a proud decoration, such as are given for heroism on the field of battle" (31). On the eve of America's victory in Europe, the *Boston Morning Globe* wrested a tribute to American exceptionalism from a book with considerable criticism for the nation's failures. Significantly, it was this review—which endorsed America more than it did *Black Boy*— that Harper's chose for national advertisements for the book. That this co-opting reading of *Black Boy* would be selected by the publisher for an advertising campaign reveals that aggrandizing America's self-image had become not only a lens for reading Wright's work but also a strategy for marketing it. And in ironic contrast to that reviewer's idea that only in America "could such a rebel thrive," Wright's dissatisfactions with America would soon lead him to become a writer-in-exile.

NOTES

1. For the convenience of readers who do not have ready access to Wright's archives, all citations of the final version of *American Hunger* refer to the HarperPerennial printing of the Library of America restored text (published as *Black Boy [American Hunger]*), which faithfully reproduces the text Wright approved in final galleys of *American Hunger*, now held in the Richard Wright Papers in the Yale Collection of American Literature at the Beinecke Rare Book and Manuscript Library.

2. Across his career, Wright showed a consistent desire, in fact, to distance himself from the representation of dialect, which had formed a crucial component of *Uncle Tom's Children*. *Native Son* is comparatively free of dialect, and even when Wright returns to the South with *Black Boy* and *The Long Dream*, dialect is largely

absent. Wright even wanted to go back to *Uncle Tom's Children* to change the dialect, "to make it appear less strange and phonetic" on the page for the expanded edition. Aswell denied this request, no doubt because resetting plates would be expensive, but also perhaps because dialect had proven such an object of praise in the reception of the first edition.

3. Besides mentioning that these changes occurred and giving a brief sketch of some of the changes, Thaddeus's article took the valuable step of calling for the publication of a restored text of *American Hunger*. Rampersad and Ward admirably answered this call in their editing of the Library of America edition of *Black Boy (American Hunger)*. Oddly, however, they appear to have overlooked Thaddeus's work, as they do not mention any of her findings or look at any of her evidence in their account of the publication history of Wright's autobiography.

4. See Chapter XIV Drafts. Rampersad, in his "Note on the Text" on *Black Boy (American Hunger)*, writes that at the Beinecke Library "a sheaf of page proofs . . . bears written instructions, under the heading 'If the Book Club Takes It,' with the proviso 'Hold till Book of the Month decides'" (488). Although Rampersad's first citation ("If the Book Club Takes It") is correct, I can find no evidence at the Beinecke for his second reference, "Hold till the Book of the Month decides."

5. Wright and the club eventually selected *Black Boy* as a suitable title from a list of choices drawn up by both parties. In light of the club's interests, one can see why *Black Boy* would be a more acceptable title than *American Hunger*. The idea of *boy* and *boyhood* is a far less contentious subject than *hunger*, and the new title suggests merely a record of youth, rather than a record of starvation. Changing *American* to *Black* shifts the impact away from the nation as whole and toward the life of this one representative *black boy*. Although it was crucial for Fisher that the tag *American* be attached to the idea of *freedom* in the conclusion, it was quite undesirable to call attention to the problems Wright faced as essentially *American* as well.

6. The publication success of this autobiography was tremendous and unprecedented for Wright. In three months after its first printing, *Black Boy* had sold over 423,000 copies; *Native Son* had sold 326,000 copies in the five years since its initial printing.

WORKS CITED

Aswell, Edward. Letter to Neredith Wood. 26 June 1944. Selected Records of Harper and Brothers. Box 33, Folder 18. Firestone Library, Princeton, NJ.

———. Letter to Paul Reynolds. 20 Dec. 1943. Selected Records of Harper and Brothers. Box 33, Folder 16. Firestone Library, Princeton, NJ.

———. Letter to Richard Wright. 31 Dec. 1940. Richard Wright Papers. Box 98, Folder 1379.

———. Letter to Richard Wright. 30 Sept. 1941. Richard Wright Papers. Box 98, Folder 1380.

———. Letter to Richard Wright. 6 Dec. 1944. Richard Wright Papers. Box 99, Folder 1381.

———. Letter to Richard Wright. 5 Jan. 1945. Richard Wright Papers. Box 99, Folder 1382.

Baldwin, James. "Many Thousands Gone." *Notes of a Native Son*. Boston: Beacon, 1984: pp. 24–45.

Canby, Henry Seidel. "Place and Literature." *Saturday Review of Literature*. 25 June 1927: p. 923.

———. Correspondence with E. P. Dutton. 1921–1943. Henry Seidel Canby Papers. Yale Collection of American Literature. Beinecke Rare Book and Manuscript Library, New Haven, CT.

Cohn, David. "*Black Boy*." *Atlantic Monthly* 165 (May 1940): pp. 659–661.

Davis, Benjamin. "*Black Boy*." *Sunday Worker* 8 Apr. 1945.

Du Bois, W. E. B. "Richard Wright Looks Back." *New York-Herald Tribune* 4 Mar. 1945: p. 2.

Ellison, Ralph. "Richard Wright's Blues." *Shadow and Act*. New York: Random, 1994: pp. 77–94.

Fabre, Michel. *The Unfinished Quest of Richard Wright*. Urbana: University of Illinois Press, 1993.

Fisher, Dorothy Canfield. "*Black Boy*." *Book-of-the-Month Club News*. Feb. 1945.

———. Letter to Henry Seidel Canby. 14 Nov. 1946. Henry Seidel Canby Papers. Yale Collection of American Literature. Beinecke Rare Book and Manuscript Library, New Haven. Box 2, Folder 70.

———. Letter to Richard Wright. 1 July 1944. Richard Wright Papers. Box 97, Folder 1333.

———. Letter to Richard Wright. 12 July 1944. Richard Wright Papers. Box 97, Folder 1333.

Gannett, Lewis. "*Black Boy*." *New York Herald-Tribune* 28 Feb. 1945: p. 17.

Hendry, Marion. "Prize Stories." *Jacksonville Sunday Times-Union* 3 July 1938.

Howe, Irving. "*American Hunger*." *New York Times Book Review* 26 June 1977: p. 1.

J. K. S. "A Searing Picture of Childhood in the South." *Minneapolis Tribune* 4 Mar. 1945.

Laycock, Edward A. "Richard Wright Records Rebellion, Horror and Despair of His Youth." *Boston Morning Globe* 1 Mar. 1945: p. 15.

Needham, Wilbur. "*Native Son*." *Los Angeles Times* 10 Mar. 1940: sec. 3: p. 7.

Paulus, John D. "*Black Boy*." *Pittsburgh Press* 18 Feb. 1945.

Rampersad, Arnold. "Note on the Text." *Black Boy (American Hunger)*. New York: HarperPerennial, 1993: pp. 487–489.

Reynolds, Paul. Letter to Edward Aswell. 2 May 1944. Selected Records of Harper and Brothers. Box 33, Folder 18. Firestone Library, Princeton, NJ.

———. Letter to Richard Wright. 19 Jan. 1944. Richard Wright Papers. Box 103, Folder 1535.

———. Letter to Richard Wright. 28 Nov. 1944. Richard Wright Papers. Box 103, Folder 1535.

———. Telegram to Richard Wright. 24 Dec. 1943. Richard Wright Papers. Box 103, Folder1534.

Robeson, Mrs. Paul. "*Black Boy*." *Hartford Courant* 8 Apr. 1945.

Stepto, Robert. *From Behind the Veil: A Study of Afro-American Narrative*. Urbana: University of Illinois Press, 1991.

Thaddeus, Janice. "The Metamorphosis of Richard Wright's *Black Boy*." *American Literature* 57.2 (1985): pp. 199–214.

Tyus, William H. L. "*Uncle Tom's Children*." Rpt. in *Richard Wright: The Critical Reception*. Ed. John M. Reilly. New York: Burt Franklin, 1978.

Ward, Jerry W., Jr. "Introduction." *Black Boy (American Hunger)*. New York: Harper Perennial, 1993: pp. xi–xxi.

Weeks, Edward. Letter to Paul Reynolds. 31 July 1944. Richard Wright Papers. Box 93, Folder 1190.

Wright, Richard. *Black Boy*. New York: Harper, 1945.

———. *Black Boy (American Hunger)*. New York: HarperPerennial, 1993.

———. "Black Confession." Ts. Richard Wright Papers. Box 9, Folder 329.

———. "Blueprint for Negro Writing." *Richard Wright Reader*. Ed. Ellen Wright and Michel Fabre. New York: Harper, 1978: pp. 36–49.

———. Chapter XIV Drafts. Richard Wright Papers. Box 12, Folder 223.

———. "How Bigger Was Born." *Native Son*. New York: Harper, 1987.

———. Journal. 1945. Ts. Richard Wright Papers. Box 117, Folder 1860.

———. Letter to Dorothy Canfield Fisher. 6 July 1944. Richard Wright Papers. Box 97, Folder 1333.

———. Letter to Dorothy Canfield Fisher. 20 July 1944. Richard Wright Papers. Box 97, Folder 1333.

———. Letter to Edward Aswell. 14 Jan. 1944. Selected Records of Harper and Brothers. Box 33, Folder 17. Firestone Library, Princeton, NJ.

———. Letter to Edward Aswell. 25 June 1944. Selected Records of Harper and Brothers. Box 33, Folder 18. Firestone Library, Princeton, NJ.

———. Letter to Marshall Field. 23 May 1944. Richard Wright Papers. Box 97, Folder 1332.

———. Letter to Paul Reynolds. 17 Dec. 1943. Rpt. in Fabre 253.

———. *Native Son*. New York: Harper, 1987.

_____. Richard Wright Papers. Yale Collection of American Literature. Beinecke Rare Book and Manuscript Library, New Haven, CT.

———. "This, Too, Is America." Interview with Charles J. Rolo. Rpt. in *Conversations with Richard Wright*. Ed. Keneth Kinnamon and Michel Fabre. Jackson: University of Mississippi Press, 1993: pp. 67–71.

———. *Twelve Million Black Voices*. New York: Viking, 1944.

TARA T. GREEN

The Virgin Mary, Eve, and Mary Magdalene in Richard Wright's Novels

The Queen thought, "'How I would love to have a child with skin as white as snow, lips as red as blood and hair as black as ebony.' Not long afterwards she had a daughter with hair as black as ebony, lips as red as blood and skin as white as snow." After the death of the Queen her successor asked her mirror: "Who is the fairest of them all? And the mirror answered . . . Snow White."[1]

Since engaging literary audiences over sixty years ago Richard Wright's works have sparked debates among men and women across the globe. A significant amount of scholarship has focused on Wright's attempts to make the "White Man listen!" as he presented arguably disturbing depictions of angry, irrational black men who commit violent acts in an effort to lash out at a racist, white male-dominated society. There have been other focuses as well particularly that of black female scholars who analyze the roles of Wright's black female characters, including his religious mothers and promiscuous lovers. While much has been said about Richard Wright's treatment of black women,[2] comparatively little work has been done in his characterization of white women. In order to fully probe Wright's treatment of women, we must now consider the next logical question: "How does Wright treat his white female characters?"

CLA Journal: A Quarterly Publication of The College Language Association. Volume 46, Number 2 (December 2002): pp. 168–193. Copyright © 2002 by the College Language Association.

In her assessment of the treatment of white women in African American literature, Anna Maria Chupa presents the theory of the "Terrible Goddess," which is based on myths evolving from Europe and Africa. According to Chupa, this goddess is the combination of all that is desired and despised; she is the Mother of Life and the Goddess of Death. Wright's white women show this goddess's many faces: the Destructive/Seductive Bitch, the Benevolent (yet inevitably destructive) Witch, the Mad Woman in the Attic, the Slob-Bitch and the Whores, Mothers, and Virgins.[3] Though Chupa's categories contribute to our understanding of the role white women play in the fiction of Wright and other African American writers, we must not overlook the two significant factors that informed Wright's life and work: racism and religion. These two factors directly influenced his characterization of white women.

In his essay "Traditional and Industrialization," Richard Wright explains his feelings regarding religion:

> I was born a black Protestant in that most racist of all American states: Mississippi. I lived my childhood under a racial code, brutal bloody, that white men proclaimed was ordained of God, said was mandatory by nature of their religion. Naturally, I rejected that religion and would reject any religion which prescribes for me an inferior position in life; I reject that tradition and any tradition which proscribes my humanity.[4]

Wright saw "that religion" as an extension of racism. Essentially, in Wright's view, religion was used to control blacks, thus making them subservient to whites. An offspring of this union between racism and religion is the ideal, pure white woman as we learned of her in *Snow White*. She is a conglomeration of ideas—a strikingly beautiful maiden and unfortunate damsel-in-distress who is the envy of others. Most of all, she is the desire of her suitor, Mr. Prince Charming, her young, white faithful protector and future husband. The ideal pure white woman—as she is deemed by white men—was at the center of white supremacy and racism: "According to the myth of white supremacy, . . . the white woman . . . is the 'Immaculate Conception' of our civilization. Her body is a holy sacrament. [She] is the great symbol of sexual purity, . . . [the embodiment] of grace."[5] If a black man defiled this "symbol of sexual purity" by talking to her socially, thinking about her, looking at her, or having sex with her, he would be guilty of committing a sin, punishable by death.

Influenced by Southern Jim Crow codes and his religious upbringing, Wright plays on Mary, the biblical virgin mother, who represents the standard for sexual behavior. To emphasize the importance of her purity are two other biblical women—Eve, the fallen temptress and mother of life (both Se-ductive/Destructive); and Mary Magdalene, a repentant sexual sinner (both whore and virgin, both good and bad). Each of these biblical women is related by the significance of Mary to the history of human kind and of sexual his-tory. Mary and Mary Magdalene, as with all humans, are the descendants of Eve, the mother of life; Mary, who gives birth to the Savior, redeems Eve; finally, Mary Magdalene incorporates characteristics of both Eve (temptress) and Mary (virgin). Specifically, each member of this female biblical trinity is a model for the white woman in four of Wright's novels: Mary Magdalene as Mary Dalton in *Native Son;* Mary as Eva Blount in *The Outsider;* and Eve as "Mrs. Carlson" in *The Long Dream* and as Mabel in *Savage Holiday.* Wright's women's role is comparable to that of their biblical sisters: to lead their male associates along a journey towards self-actualization and spiritual growth. As a result, the men emerge empowered and free of inhibitions.

At the heart of the female trinity is the Virgin Mary. Accordingly, she is the Bride of God—the heart of the Holy Trinity, which also includes Jesus and the Holy Spirit. In her assessment of Mary as a literary image, Sally Cun-neen notes, ". . . the broadly Protestant culture of England and the United States in the nineteenth century tended to idealize women while still denying them equality or a public voice."[6] The "Immaculate White Woman" literary image stems from the historical perception of Mary, a young Jewish woman who bore a son in 7–4 B.C.E. (27). What is known about the Virgin Mary is derived from the four gospels, which were written by four males "thirty to sixty years after the events they recorded" and are based largely on oral tradition (29). Thus, men formed Mary's image. These male perceptions have influenced many Christians' acceptance of the story of Jesus' birth. John Gatta notes that Mary "took on a distinctive and integral significance within the development of Christian doctrine" found in Luke's account of the Nativity and the An-nunciation, and in Matthew's account of the Nativity. In 431 the Ecumenical Council of Ephesus named her the "new mother of the church and the human race." However, she also became a "cultus figure through the course of patristic and medieval history in both Byzantine and Western Christianity."[7] Her im-age has had an enormous impact on religious cultures.

In his travel narrative, *Pagan Spain,* Wright observes the cult of Mary. In this nonfiction text, he shows how the male-dominated society of Spain places pressures on women to be Mary-like and how these pressures have not been restricted to the "protestant culture of England and the United States." Like most men in *Pagan Spain,* Andre adores virgins or "good women," but cannot resist the sexual lure of "bad women":

[H]e had to worship [his fiancee] from afar and wait until he
had money enough to marry her with the ceremonial blessings of

the church. And that is why he had to go so often to seek "bad" women in the dark and fetid alleyways, and it was why, in his confused and embattled heart, he hated those women and yet had to be with them.[8]

Because of Spain's Catholic society, Andre perceives women as belonging to two categories: good and bad (Madonna/Whore). Good ones are virgins; they are the respectable women men marry and worship. Bad ones are "whores," who are not worth marrying. Yet, the bad ones can become good and respectable like Mary Magdalene. According to Wright, "a prostitute can at any time enter a church and gain absolution" (152). Wright was clearly fascinated by the Spanish culture—namely, its categorization or "cultural idealization" (Cunneen 256) of women and the effect Catholicism had on female/male relations. Notably, in much of the fiction—novels, short stories, poetry—Wright published before his 1954 travels through Spain, white women fall into these categories: good (Mary), bad (Eve), and bad/good (Mary Magdalene).

In his first published novel, *Native Son* (1940), Wright presents a Mary Magdalene type. Mary Dalton represents the kind of spiritually pure and sexually enticing woman that Wright is intrigued by in *Pagan Spain*. St. Mary Magdalene is probably the most infamous of all biblical women. Although there is no definitive evidence that she was a prostitute, she has been labeled one, and, notably men have been the ones to place this label. Gospel writers Luke and Mark describe Mary Magdalene as being healed of "evil spirits and infirmities." These spirits could have been "psychological, that is, seen as madness, rather than moral or sexual."[9] Mary Magdalene's sexually scandalous identity is the result of two factors. One is her birthplace. Her second name indicates that she was born in "el Medjel, a prosperous fishing village on the north-west bank of the lake of Galilee." This town was later destroyed in "AD 75 because of its infamy and the licentious behavior of its inhabitants" (15). Second, in the sixth century, Pope Gregory the Great declared that Mary Magdalene, Mary of Bethany, and the woman thought to be a prostitute who washed Jesus' feet with her tears and dried them with her hair in a plea for forgiveness were one and the same (16). Consequently, Mary Magdalene, the woman who loyally followed Christ even when his own disciples fled in fear of persecution at the time of their leader's crucifixion, has been labeled a "penitent whore." Mary Magdalene is henceforth thought to be a woman who defied social order through sexual promiscuity, but who later redeemed herself by seeking forgiveness by serving Christ.

Whether or not Wright was aware of the lack of evidence to support Mary Magdalene's identity is not known, but given his strong religious and cultural upbringing, it is more than mere coincidence that Mary Dalton bears the namesake of the biblical figure. The name "Mary" is the Greek form of Miriam, meaning rebellion.[10] As the name given to the mother of Christ, it is also associated with purity. Mary Magdalene is both rebellious and pure. Through the use of this name, Wright implies that his character Mary Dalton embodies both a rebellious nature by defying expectations, but by nature of her being, her body is a symbol of purity. The narrator describes Mary as being like "a doll in a show window: [with] black eyes, white face, and red lips."[11] Though a member of the upper class, she is the girlfriend of a Communist, an enemy of the 1930s government. Mary will ultimately place Bigger in the situation that will change his life; yet, since she is society's symbol of purity, Bigger will be sentenced to die for raping and killing her (and other white women).

From the voices of two patriarchal narrators, we are introduced to the dualistic nature of Mary Dalton. Bigger views a newsreel which features a rich debutante basking on the sands of sunny Florida. John Lowe in his analysis of "Big Boy Leaves Home" finds that Wright uses a reference to the prelapsarian Garden of Eden in his description of the Hawkins's lake before the white woman arrives.[12] Wright uses this reference again in *Native Son*. While Bigger watches the newsreel, he is struck by the image of Mary. The novel's narrator describes Bigger's reaction: "As the scene unfolded his interest was caught. . . . He saw images of smiling, dark-haired white girls lolling on the gleaming sands of a beach. The background was a stretch of sparkling water. Palm trees stood near and far."[13] As we would expect, the innocence of this space is subverted by the act of the white female inhabitant. Acting as the voice of "Big Brother," the narrator of the film remarks that Mary Dalton "shocks society by spurning the boys of LaSalle Street . . . and accepting the attentions of a well-known radical" (35). Society's disapproval of Mary's unrestrained sexuality is implied when the camera—society's eyes—focuses on the couple's legs and their intimate touches. At one point, Mary teases her lover, and Wright's narrator echoes the critical scrutiny of the film's commentator as the footage is described: ". . . the next scene showed only the girl's legs running over the sparkling sands; they were followed by the legs of a man running in pursuit." Suggestive in the description of her actions is that she is not only rebellious but also a temptress. Mary's behavior is watched and judged by an invisible, omniscient being who is perhaps the one who intrudes into the narrative through the eyes of the Dalton's cat as it watches Bigger sever Mary's head (105). Further, as Bigger watches, he too is sexually attracted to her and believes "them rich white women'll go to bed with anybody, from a poodle on up" (36). As critical eyes judge Mary, they watch Bigger as well, for his attraction to her—or at least the expectation of a black man's attraction to a white woman—will be the ultimate reason for the state's conviction of him.

When Bigger meets her, he recognizes her defiant nature and appears to be immediately intimidated by her: "On the screen she was not dangerous and his mind could do with her what he liked. But here in her home she walked over everything, put herself in the way" (62). At the first opportunity, Mary orchestrates a series of rebellious acts. First, she insists that Bigger not take her to school as her father expects but instead take her to pick up Jan. Her rebellious side emerges further when she insists that Bigger be her guide into his community, where she can see how his people live. Finally, after drinking too much liquor, her sexually enticing side surfaces. While Bigger reluctantly chauffeurs around Mary and Jan, he notes that they engage in sexual activity in the back seat of the car. Like her biblical archetype, Mary, particularly from the protagonist Bigger's point of view, is dangerously intriguing and alluring.

Though the interaction between Bigger and Mary actually occurred within a few hours, the young white woman's treatment of this young black man proves to be the most significant part of the novel. Certainly, Mary is aware of the "danger" of not keeping Bigger at a respectable distance from her, yet she insists that Bigger sit next to her in her father's car and that he call her by her first name. This white woman's defiance of social order is as sacrificial an act as her public interactions with the Communists. Suggestive of her rebellious behavior is a desire to treat Bigger as her equal. She takes her defiance a step further when she allows herself to become inebriated, trusting that Bigger will get her home without sexually assaulting her. Mary does not appear to view her body as a symbol of purity. This perception is one that is male-defined, a label that she vehemently rejects. She, like the redeemed Mary Magdalene, rejects the focus that men place on her body as sexual property. What's more, her attempt to get to know Bigger is a redemptive act. Perhaps, subconsciously, Mary is attempting to repent for the sins of her father and other racists.

Her ultimate sacrifice, however, is her death. Before meeting Mary Dalton, Bigger says, "Half the time I feel like I'm on the outside of the world peeping in through a knothole in the fence" (23). After killing Mary, the symbol of oppression, Bigger erupts with a sense of spiritual freedom that he feels will allow him to coexist with ease in a world in which he has previously felt excluded. As a result of Mary's death, Bigger feels like an unstoppable superhero—he aims his gun at Jan, and then he confidently boards a bus and sits among the white passengers. He feels so confident in his newfound "power" that he tries to extort money from the Daltons while still working for them. He finds a road to freedom by accidentally murdering Mary Dalton, and he is able to confidently live in the society that he previously had viewed as oppressive. He thinks he now can "see":

> The whole thing came to him in the form of a powerful and simple feeling; there was in everyone a great hunger to believe that made him blind, and if he could see while others were blind, then he could get what he wanted and never be caught at it. (120)

This is perhaps the most revealing passage in the novel. As a result of Mary's death, Bigger's self-consciousness emerges and he develops a plan of survival the logic of which can be discerned in W. E. B. Du Bois's remarks about double-consciousness.[14] Bigger, although he does not possess the articulateness of Du Bois, can "see," whereas whites—not being gifted with the veil—cannot. As such, Mary's death is a gift to Bigger, making it a "justified" act. In essence, Mary had to die in order for Bigger to live, if not physically, then spiritually.

Not until his conversation with Max does Bigger begin to fully realize the impact that Mary has had on his life. Bigger explains:

> "She acted and talked in a way that made me hate her. She made me feel like a dog. I was so mad I wanted to cry. . . . Aw, Mr. Max, she wanted me to tell her how Negroes live."
>
> "But, Bigger, you don't hate people for that. She was being kind to you. . . ."
>
> ". . . All I knew was that they kill us for women like her."
> (405)

What Max takes for Mary's kindness, Bigger perceives as an intrusion. Bigger's reaction is informed by his experiences as a black man. Despite his anger he confesses his attraction to Mary:

> "I don't understand, Bigger. You say you hated her and you say you felt like having her when you were in the room. . . ."
>
> "Yeah; that's funny, ain't it? Yeah; I reckon it was because I knew I oughtn've wanted to. I reckon it was because they say black men do that anyhow. . . . Mr. Max, when folks say things like that about you, you whipped before you born." (406)

Max and Bigger clash because of historical and cultural conditioning. Bigger perceives Mary as being the sexual temptress that society would not allow him to touch. Max, a white man, can never fully understand how Bigger feels and neither could Mary. Acting as the minister to whom Bigger confesses, Max tells Bigger "[I]f you die, die free. You're trying to believe in yourself. And everytime you try to find a way to live, your mind stands in the way" (499). His journey to spiritual freedom allows him to accept responsibility for Mary's death. During this last meeting, Bigger explains to Max how he feels: "When a man kills, it's for something. . . . I didn't know I was really alive in this world until I felt things hard enough to kill for 'em . . ." (501). Accepting the reality of his circumstances and his fate, Bigger feels empowered by the act that led to his physical demise.

While Mary Dalton is a Mary Magdalene figure, Eva Blount of *The Outsider* is a Mary figure that closely resembles the highly revered biblical figure. According to some believers, Mary is a second Eve. By accepting the responsibility of giving birth to the Savior, she provided the world with a chance at eternal life, which was lost when Eve fell from grace and convinced Adam to follow. According to Matthew's gospel, Jesus is born to a virgin, for he was conceived before Mary and Joseph "came together," and this is confirmed when the angel tells a skeptical Joseph, "That which is conceived in her is of the Holy Ghost" (Matthew 7:20).[15] As Mary is a servant to God, who will redeem the world with their son, Eva Blount serves as a symbol of "freedom" for Cross. A relationship with Eva allows Cross to enjoy freedom from the depressing and oppressing black women in his life—a religious, psychologically overbearing mother and two women: his young mistress, Dot, and his estranged, angry wife, Gladys—whom he does not love. Eva's purpose is "Cross's cure from his aimless life and self-hatred."[16]

Eva Blount is the sexually and spiritually pure woman that captures Cross's attention. In a letter to his editor, Paul Reynolds, Wright stated, "I must confess that she [Eva Blount] is still the weakest character in the book, but I cannot think of anything else to do with her."[17] Wright depicts Eva as a "childlike," innocent, pure, and "lovely girl."[18] Eva is the artistic wife of a Communist, and she finds out after she has wed that her husband, Gil, has married her as part of a political move by order of the Communist Party. She is too distraught to paint certain colors and feels trapped by Gil and the rest of the Communist Party. She is incapable of demanding liberation from people whom she apparently never wished to know. Her dislike of the Party makes her a perfect match for the protagonist.

Religion and sex are as relative in *The Outsider* as they are in *Pagan Spain*. Cross worships women in much the same way that the Spanish *must*, in Wright's view, worship the Black Virgin. Each time Cross sees a woman, he thinks she is "body of woman," an image of a body—a sexual being. Cross's pious mother named him after the cross of Jesus and taught him that sex is a sin unless shared with one's spouse. Consequently, this forbiddance causes him to want the very thing he has been taught to avoid. Likewise, in Spain, sex, unless it is performed with one's own spouse, is a sin. In Cross's life and in the lives of the Spanish, religion and sex are inseparable.

As two characters that are associated with biblical figures, notably Mary and Jesus, both Eva and Cross are outsiders of the world or the society in which they find themselves. The Party, whose ideology Eva does not accept, traps her. Cross is a black man who is an intellectual outside the realm of his family and friends. As a result of these kindred differences, Cross finds his soul mate only in Eva Blount. Once Cross becomes aware that Eva is an outsider, he bonds with her as with no other woman, for no other woman could understand Cross's life as an "outsider": "He knew that Eva, too, had been forced to live as an outsider; she, too, in a different sort of way was on his side" (350).

There is a significant difference between Wright's characterization of black women and white women. Certainly, the feelings of contempt that Cross has for his pregnant, teenaged mistress and for the estranged mother of his two sons are feelings he could never have for Eva. On one level, Eva is no different from the black women who depend on the black protagonist for emotional support. During an emotional episode, Eva opens herself up to Cross:

> Her soul was reaching gropingly toward him for protection, advice, solace. Cross smiled, feeling that he was listening to her words as perhaps God listened to prayers. . . . A wave of hot pride flooded him. She was laying her life at his feet. With but a gesture of his hand he could own her, shield her from the Party, from fear, from her own sense of guilt. . . . (348)

The connection between Cross and Eva sets Eva apart from the black females of the novel. Feeling himself akin to God, his "spiritual" connection to Eva/Mary, Mother of God, is no mystery. His attraction to her is maternal, yet sexual. This ambiguous attraction is typical of Wright's work. Wright may have been a Freud scholar, for his Freudian studies become evident in *Pagan Spain* as he discusses his observations of the Black Virgin, a statue commemorating Mary—the virgin mother. In response to his visit of the Black Virgin, he concludes, "Man senses that if there is anything at all really divine or superhuman in us, it is linked to, allied with and comes through sex, and is inescapably bound up with sex" (64). After aligning sex with belief in supernatural entities, he gives a brief history of the concept of virgin worship: "The concept of the Virgin Mary antedates Christianity by some two thousand years. Maya, the mother of Buddha, was supposed to have been a virgin" (65). Wright suggests that humans' desire for sex is as natural as their need to be acknowledged by a maternal being. The Black Virgin is not only a manifestation of that need, but the statue also represents humans' desire to detach maternity from sexuality, resulting in a sexually pure entity—an existence that can only be achieved by a divine being. This attraction to an idealized, sexually pure woman is what Cross feels for Eva.

Further, Cross's relationship with Eva is motivated by the author's experiences. Interrelatedness between mothers—both Eve and Mary are mothers—and religious worship is prominent in Wright's fiction. Claudia Tate suggests that Wright's interest in Freud's theories was an attempt by him to understand his own life and to inform his work: "Wright accords himself greater freedom for symbolizing the 'plowing up' of his own consciousness as the mode of creation."[19] Further, in her extensive psychoanalysis of Wright's *Savage Holiday,* Tate argues that the feelings of "fear," "guilt," and "hostility" found in his romantic relationships stem from his relationship with his mother. His own feelings extend to his work, where there is an inseparable connection between the sons' relationship with their mothers and, subsequently, with their lovers. Tate comments further, "With sheer force of will power, Wright deliberately detached himself from his mother and those who reminded him of her" (115). His black male characters find the "nurturing" they need in white women. Cross Damon is no exception.

Though he is a man who initially seems to be incapable of emotion, he lays *his* life at *her* feet. When initially he confesses to her, she understandably thinks he is delirious:

> He had told her his horror and had expected to hear her scream and run from him; and now she was surrendering herself, giving her gift to the man she loved, hoping to cure his distraction of his mind by placing a benediction upon his sense. (432)

Instead, she shows her love for him by having sex with him, an act that has a remarkable effect on Cross's character. As a result of her giving herself to him body and soul, Cross shows feelings of unselfishness for the first time and moves towards spiritual reconciliation: "Something close to a prayer rose up from his heart. . . . [S]how me a way not to hurt her. . . . Not to let her know . . . I don't want to kill this sweet girl clinging to me . . . I should not have let it happen . . ." (433). Although he does not believe in God, Cross's state of mind is reminiscent of the "conversion experience," where a person undergoes a literal "turning" resulting in a change in behavior and a "change of heart."[20] As he experiences this process, he feels compelled to defend his newfound freedom by killing Hilton, a Communist. The process ends when, seconds before he dies, he says to Houston, "Tell them not to come down this road. . . . Men hate themselves and it makes them hate others. . . . We must find some way of being good to ourselves" (585). He has come to a point of self-realization only because of his relationship with Eva, a white woman.

Cross may have benefited from Eva's presence in his life, but Eva suffers for having known Cross. When Eva becomes aware of his heinous activities, Cross commits the religious act of begging Eva to "save" him from the guilt he feels and to absolve him of his sins: "I'm praying to you to understand me . . . I'll die if you don't understand me" (532). His actions are similar to those of the Spanish who journey to see the Black Virgin in an act of worship and to seek absolution for their sins. Cross seeks absolution from Eva, but she is unable to offer him the saving grace that he desperately needs. Instead, repulsed by Cross's sadistic acts, she throws herself out of a window. Nagueyalti

Warren notes, "Morally she is superior even to Cross. When faced with his demonic acts of murder, she commits suicide to escape the reality of her situation."[21] Since Eva is pure, she is incapable of accepting the gravity of Cross's malicious actions—the acts of murdering his friend and acquaintances and of abandoning his family. Eva is unable to look upon the face of sin.

Wright moves from well-meaning white women to contemptuous ones as he revisits the story of Eve in his later fiction. Nehama Aschkenasy, in her analysis of *Paradise Lost* argues that John Milton further develops the first three chapters of Genesis, making Eve appear to be sexually destructive. Aschkenasy's argument is applicable to Wright. The biblical story associates Eve with evil "since she is the one who first surrendered to temptation and violated God's law." Second, she is primarily a "sexual being," which she puts to use "by going master over man." Third, only Eve has "dealings with the serpent," showing that she has an "affinity with the devil."[22] Thus, Eve is a seductress/temptress whom men should avoid. The significant difference between Mary Magdalene and Eve is that Eve does not seek absolution for her promiscuous behavior. In *The Long Dream* and *Savage Holiday*, Wright's male protagonists meet Eve.

Unlike Cross, who embraces a white woman in the North, Fishbelly of *The Long Dream* must avoid Eve, the Southern white woman. *The Long Dream* acts as a continuation of the lynching theme introduced in "Big Boy Leaves Home." Of course, Big Boy is forced to flee his home because of his nakedness in close proximity to Eve, a white woman, as he trespasses in Eden. Eve, a sexual temptress whose mere presence is dangerous to black men, is the proverbial forbidden fruit. As Fish will learn, his dealings with Eve, whose name means "giver of life," will further his maturation, allowing him to identify himself (as opposed to being identified by others) from a true sense of consciousness.

Fish is initiated into the environment that breeds the mythical taboo through the lynching of Chris. The socially conscious narrator voices the importance of this act for Fish: "This was a ceremony. He did not think it; he felt it, knew it. He was being initiated; he was moving along the steep, dangerous precipice leading from childhood to manhood."[23] Tyree teaches his black son the first commandment of Jim Crow: "NEVER LOOK AT A WHITE WOMAN! YOU HEAR? . . . When you in the presence of a white woman, remember she means death!" (64) Later, Tyree says that Chris had to die: "Chris died for us" (71). Thus Chris becomes a Chris(t) figure, not unlike BoBo in "Big Boy Leaves Home." Trudier Harris notes, "There is nothing Christian about the act . . . unless it is viewed as a crucifixion."[24] There is a lesson found in Chris's death as in Christ's—to avoid temptation. While Christ rejected temptation, Chris, like Adam, does not.

Through the symbolic act of lynching Chris—indeed, his death has social as well as literary significance—Fish becomes consumed with interest in the forbidden. While seeking time alone in the bathroom during the heat of Chris's lynching, he finds a picture of a white woman in a magazine and wonders, "Why had black men to die because of white women?" Then he "fastened his imagination upon the seductive white face in a way that it had never been concentrated upon any face in all his life" (69). Fish's interest in Eve, "the forbidden fruit," becomes a part of him mentally and physically. While being held in the back of a police car for trespassing, and after being threatened with castration for looking at a white woman while still in custody, he remembers that he still has the picture of the white woman in his wallet. In a desperate attempt to prevent the police from finding the picture, he *eats* it. This act of devouring the "forbidden fruit" shows his internalization of the danger that black men face. The narrator says, "It was inside of him now, a part of him, invisible. He could feel it moving vaguely in his stomach, . . . burning with a terrible luminosity in the black depths of him" (118). The image of the white woman becomes a part of his "solar plexus," as Bigger says is true of white people in general. Earle Bryant notes that "Fish's ingestion of the newspaper photograph is one of the most telling incidents in the novel, for it indicates that Fish has enthroned within himself the image of the white woman, has incorporated it into his being forever."[25] Indeed, by nature of his dark skin color, the powerful image of the white woman will never escape him.

He explores his curiosity of the forbidden fruit through Gladys, a biracial prostitute with Caucasian features. According to the narrator, Gladys represents for Fish a "shadowy compromise that was white and not white" (219). Wright leaves no doubt that Fish is attracted to her because of her Caucasian features: "He loved her tawny skin, . . . her tumbling brown hair. . . . He loved her because she was whitish" (215). Although Fish will not admit his obsession with "white meat," either consciously or verbally, Maybelle, a dark-skinned prostitute, does:

> They want white meat! But you sluts ain't white! You niggers like me! But you the nearest thing they can get to white! If you all just dying for white meat, why don't you go 'cross town where there ain't nothing but white meat? You scared of being killed like a dog! (177–178)

She acts as the voice of the social consciousness. All are aware of the danger that black men face. Fish's curiosity about white women is revealed after he loses his virginity:

[H]e knew deep in his heart that there would be no peace in his blood until he had defiantly violated the line that the white world had dared him to cross under the threat of death. . . . *You are nothing because you are black, and proof of your being nothing is that if you touch a white woman, you'll be killed!* (165)

His desire is not about love or even about sex. Fish feels that white women are an extension of Jim Crow. To have one would be an act of social defiance no different from sitting in the "reserved for whites" section of a segregated bus.

Fishbelly is perhaps a spokesperson for Wright himself, who married two white women. Michel Fabre concludes that Wright's own attraction to white women was

revenge for the years of sexual and emotional frustration during adolescence; he certainly felt additional pleasure in flaunting the taboos that for a black man in Mississippi, were the equivalent of a castration. . . . To possess a white woman was a way of eradicating painful memories. . . . [A] black man suffered many humiliations in public places. (197)

I argue further that Wright ultimately avenges those who tried to *master* him with the white-woman code by controlling the image of this woman in his fiction. In this way, Wright's "revenge for the years of sexual and emotional frustration" is not limited to his personal relationships with white women, but is manifested in his publications.[26] Perhaps Lazarus of Eldridge Cleaver's *Soul on Ice* says it best: "Every time I embrace a black woman I'm embracing slavery, and when I put my arms around a white woman, well, I'm hugging freedom. . . . I will not be free until the day I can have a white woman in my bed and a white man minds his own business" (161). For black men who have sexual relations with white women, they are exercising a freedom—a right—that white men guard.

Having grown up with the threat of a rape accusation and lynching, Fish finds himself in jail under such a charge. The police, in an effort to find Tyree's incriminating checks, know that the only way to jail Fish without question is to have a white woman "cry rape." Harris asserts, "The role she plays in the drama is just as historically determined as is the role Chris plays" (*Exorcising* 123). Fish knows that history allows the police to arrest him on such a charge and that there is literally nothing that he can do to defend himself. "Mrs. Carlson" and the police play their historical roles effectively. Fish's eventual imprisonment suggests the attempt to confine his desire for power through social equality. Since Fish is reared in the South,

Wright implies that dark shadows loom over his head. One such shadow is the specter of death that will descend if Fish acts upon his forbidden desire to have sex with a white woman.

While in jail, Fish reaches a level of understanding about his attraction to white women:

> Other than a self-justifying yen for imitating the outward standards of the white world above him, there had not come within the range of his experience any ideal that could have captured his imagination. (356–357)

Fishbelly realizes that his behavior had been motivated by his desire to attain all that had been kept from him because of his race. His dangerous dealings with the underworld had given him a certain kind of power, especially since he had a working relationship with the white officials of the town. His attraction to white women is likely a subconscious desire to be part of the white world.

This subconscious longing for unattainable power expresses itself in his dreams.[27] One such dream includes Fish drowning in the blood of his slain friend, Chris: "It was engulfing his head and when he opened his mouth to scream he was drowning" (83). Yoshinobu Hakutani argues, "In a free democratic society he has the right to associate with women of his choice."[28] Fishbelly may be in the United States of America, but he is an African American who lives in the South. Thus, his access to American freedoms is limited. Through Fish's dreams, Wright suggests that American black males have dreams for freedom and nightmares resulting from a lack thereof. In "How 'Bigger' Was Born" Wright says,

> Any Negro who has lived in the North or the South knows that times without number he has heard of some Negro boy being carted off to jail and charged with "rape." This thing happens so often that to mind it had become a representative symbol of the Negro's uncertain position in America. (532)

Fish's (and Wright's) "flight" from Mississippi is an attempt to free himself from the restraints of the codes—jail of the South—that oppress him racially and sexually. As a result of their "uncertain position in America," both Wright and Fish become expatriates, moving to a place where their freedom is not jeopardized.

Eve appears in her most powerful form in Wright's *Savage Holiday*. When the novel opens, Erskine Fowler's employers and colleagues are honoring him at a retirement dinner. At the age of forty-three and after thirty years of service to the company, he has been forced to retire so the boss's son can replace him and add a "younger generation" spin to the insurance company. The next day he inadvertently locks himself out of his apartment when he steps outside to collect his newspaper; unfortunately, he is naked. Literally fearing the idea of being found nude and after failing to contact the superintendent of the building for help, he attempts to climb to the open window of his bathroom above his balcony. Fowler charges outside to the balcony where his neighbor's son is playing, trips over the boy's tricycle, and scares the child, who falls over the balcony to his death. Once Fowler climbs through his window and the child's body is found, he, a Christian, decides not to confess his involvement to the police. While at church (all of this happens on a Sunday morning), Fowler, who has never missed a Sunday service, reaches an epiphany: he thinks that God has allowed him to take part in the child's accidental murder so that he can save the child's promiscuous, alcoholic mother. Fowler befriends the mother, Mrs. Mabel Blake, and convinces himself that he will marry her to keep her from suspecting his part in the child's murder. Yet, although he is repulsed by her promiscuous behavior, he is also attracted to her. We later find out, after he stabs her numerous times in the stomach, that his attraction to her is influenced by the relationship he has had with his own promiscuous mother and his desire for her to die: she was, as Tate describes, a "bad mother."

Eve's identity is strikingly similar to the one Wright constructs for Mabel Blake. Warner describes Eve as "cursed to bear children rather than blessed with motherhood" (58). In contrast to Immaculate Mary, a "good woman/mother," Wright's Mabel Blake is representative of the "bad woman/mother." Mabel is a "bad mother" who later confesses to Fowler that she met Tony's father, married him almost immediately, and conceived the day before her husband went off to the war, where he was killed. Furthermore, she maintains that it was his idea that she become pregnant, not hers. Mabel's thinking reflects that of theologians. For Mabel, her son's presence was a nuisance and not a blessing.

Wright develops the idea of the cursed mother in *Savage Holiday*. Just a few hours after the accident, Fowler reads and interprets a scripture to his church congregation that is vital to this assessment of the Eve character. The scripture is St. Matthew 12:46–50 and is prefaced by the narrator's description of a picture in the Sunday School text which "depicted Jesus speaking to a vast crowd at the edge of which stood Mary, Jesus' mother, and her sons."[29] The biblical passage involves a visit from Jesus' "mother and brethren," who desire to speak with Him. Jesus replies,

Who is my mother? And who are my brethren? And he stretched his hand toward his disciples, and said, Behold my mothers and my brethren. For whosoever shall do the will of my Father which is in heaven, the same is my brother and sister, and mother.

This scene also appears in a slightly different version in Mark. According to Marina Warner, Jesus' friends decided he had "lost his mind, and wanted to prevent him from teaching (Mark 3:21). . . . The sequence of events implies strongly that Jesus' "friends" have marshaled his mother and relatives to help stop his ministry. . . . Thus Jesus rebuffs His earthly family to embrace the larger family of His spiritual fellowship."[30] Although it is certainly possible that Jesus has a conversation with His mother after this public incident, He certainly does seem to separate Himself from His earthly family, particularly His own mother, to embrace a spiritual family. This biblical reference to the son's rejection of the mother is a reminder of the experience Fowler endured when he was forcibly separated from his own mother when he was a child. According to Evelyn Bassoff, "For mothers and sons, separating is a normal part of their relationship; severing the bond between them is not."[31] As an adult, Fowler suffers from being the son of a mother who did not love and nurture him.

It is in this biblical text, however, that Fowler discerns an answer to the dilemma regarding his part in the child's untimely demise: "Wasn't this a clear call for him to regard Mrs. Blake as his sister in Christ?" (86). In his need to reconcile Mrs. Blake with his own moral convictions, he must disassociate her with his life. Readers later learn that Fowler does not see Mrs. Blake as a "sister," but as his mother. At one point he thinks she is "alone sensual, impulsive . . . [and] he remembered his own mother" (38). Fowler's memories of his own mother are not good ones; they include "[i]mages of the many men who always surrounded her laughing face—men who came and went, some indulgent toward him, some indifferent. Gradually, as he'd come to understand what was happening, he'd grown afraid, ashamed" (38). Feelings of fear, dread, shame, and guilt are typical of Wright's male protagonists. Consequently, they often react violently to alleviate themselves of these feelings.

Fowler reconciles his actions while he is in church. It is also here that he seems to think of Mrs. Blake as Eve. He thinks, "That accident was God's own way of bringing a lost woman to her senses. . . . God had punished her by snatching little Tony up to Paradise—had garnered Tony home from the evil of this world" (87). Fowler, who aligns Mrs. Blake with his own mother (an absent Eve figure), becomes like Cain, who asserts a right to take the life of his brother, Abel. According to Fowler, it is Mrs. Blake's fault that her son dies. His thinking does not differ from those who credit Eve with introducing sin into the world, thus making her indirectly responsible for her son's death. It is Mrs. Blake's fault that her son dies, just as it is Eve's fault that her son Cain killed her other son, Abel (which sounds like Mabel). As a result of "logically" categorizing Mrs. Blake, Fowler can justify his actions and place the blame on her: "How right he'd been in refusing to accept blame for Tony's death; it hadn't been his fault at all. Only an ignorantly lustful woman could spin such spider webs of evil to snare men and innocent children!" (105).

Fowler's act of murdering Mabel has an additional significance for the novel. As with Bigger's murder of Mary, Mrs. Blake's death frees Fowler from his past. He is now able to remember suppressed parts of his life, and he is additionally able to "confess his sins" to the police officers. Prior to the murder, Erskine Fowler is timid and shy. Unlike the other white men in Wright's fiction, Fowler seems powerless. He is a man who cannot express his feelings of outrage to his employers for forcing him to retire, nor can he even admit to himself that he is outraged. Fowler's mental state of freedom and ability to talk or to confess is reminiscent of Wright's most famous murderers, Bigger and Cross. Further, like the black male protagonists, Fowler gains a certain level of freedom resulting from the murder of a white woman. In Genesis the serpent convinces Eve to eat the fruit, saying, "Your eyes shall be opened, and ye shall be as Gods, knowing good and evil" (Genesis 2:5). After Adam and Eve eat the fruit, "the eyes of both were opened" (Genesis 2:7). Just as Eve helps to open the eyes of Adam by convincing him to eat the forbidden fruit, Wright's Eves help to open the eyes of his male protagonists.

Richard Wright's white female characters play significant roles in the lives of his male protagonists. Specifically, the Virgin Mary, Eve, and Mary Magdalene figures give the male protagonists a chance for a new life either through death or in another venue. These women have dual roles, acting as a threat to the men and as a link to the spiritual freedom the men desire. Bigger's act of accidentally murdering Mary and his acceptance of his act results in his reaching a point of self-realization. Cross forms an emotional and spiritual connection with Eva and eventually confesses to his malicious acts, warning others not to follow his lead. Fishbelly, through his association with sexual taboos, realizes that the only way he can be physically free is to leave the oppressive South. Though he is a white man, Fowler also benefits from his dealings with Eve, as he is now ready to examine the disturbing experiences of his past. Wright's men may have ambiguous feelings about women, but they seek, crave, and, in ironic ways, benefit from the white women's presence in their lives.

NOTES

1. *Snow White*, adapted from the Brothers Grimm (Winchester, MA: Faber, 1983).

2. See Maria Mootry, "Bitches, Whores, and Woman Haters: Archetypes and Typologies in the Art of Richard Wright," *Richard Wright: A Collection of Critical Essays*, ed. Richard Maskey (Englewood Cliffs, NJ: Prentice-Hall, 1984);

Sherley Anne Williams, "Papa Dick and Sister Woman: Reflections on Women in the Fiction of Richard Wright," *American Novelists Revisited: Essays in Feminine Criticism,* ed. Fritz Fleischman (Boston: G.K. Hall, 1982); Sylvia Keady, "Richard Wright's Woman Characters and Inequality," *Black American Literature Forum* 10 (1976): pp. 124–128; Trudier Harris, "Native Sons and Foreign Daughters," *New Essays on Richard Wright,* ed. Keneth Kinnamon (New York: Cambridge University Press, 1990).

3. Anna Maria Chupa, *Anne, the White Woman in Contemporary African American Fiction: Archetypes, Stereotypes, Characterizations* (New York: Greenwood Press, 1990): p. 10.

4. Richard Wright, *White Man, Listen!* (New York: HarperPerennial, 1995): p. 55.

5. Calvin C. Hernton, *The Sexual Mountain and Black Women Writers: Adventures in Sex, Literature, and Real Life* (New York: Doubleday, 1987): pp. 84–85.

6. Sally Cunneen, *In Search of Mary: The Woman and the Symbol* (New York: Ballantine, 1996): p. 256. Hereafter cited parenthetically in the text.

7. John Gatta, *American Madonna: Images of the Divine Woman in Literary Culture* (New York: Oxford University Press, 1997): p. 7.

8. Richard Wright, *Pagan Spain* (New York: Harper, 1957): p. 87.

9. Susan Haskins, *Mary Magdalen: Myth and Metaphor* (New York: Harcourt, 1993): p. 14. Hereafter cited parenthetically in the text.

10. James Boyd, *Bible Dictionary* (New York: Crown, 1958): p. 62.

11. Mary Dalton bears a remarkable resemblance to the character description of Snow White.

12. John Lowe, "Wright Writing Reading: Narrative Strategies in *Uncle Tom's Children,*" *Modern American Short Story Sequences: Composite Fictions and Fictive Communities,* ed. Gerald Kennedy (Cambridge: Cambridge University Press, 1995): p. 38.

13. Richard Wright, *Native Son* (New York: HarperPerennial, 1993): p. 34. Hereafter cited parenthetically in the text.

14. W. E. B. Du Bois, *The Souls of Black Folk* (New York: Penguin, 1989): p. 5. Italics mine.

15. Bible, King James Version and New Living Translation, People's Parallel Edition (Wheaton, IL: Tyndale House, 1997).

16. Sylvia H. Keady "Richard Wright's Women Characters and Inequality," *Black American Literature Forum* 10 (1976): p. 127.

17. Michel Fabre, *The Unfinished Quest of Richard Wright,* trans. Isabel Barzan (New York: William Morrow, 1973): p. 368. Hereafter cited parenthetically in the text.

18. Richard Wright, *The Outsider* (New York: HarperPerennial, 1993): pp. 319, 347. Hereafter cited parenthetically in the text.

19. Claudia Tate, *Psychoanalysis and Black Novels: Desire and the Protocol of the Race* (New York: Oxford Press, 1998): p. 94. Hereafter cited parenthetically in the text.

20. Albert Raboteau, *A Fire in the Bones: Reflections on African-American Religious History* (Boston: Beacon, 1995): p. 152.

21. Nagueyalti Warren, "Black Girls and Native Sons: Female Images in Selected Works by Richard Wright," *Richard Wright: Myths and Realities,* ed. James Trotman (New York: Garland, 1988): p. 69.

22. Nehama Aschkenasy, *Eve's Journey: Feminine Images in Hebraic Literary Tradition* (Philadelphia: University of Pennsylvania Press, 1986): pp. 39–40. Hereafter cited parenthetically in the text.

23. Richard Wright, *The Long Dream* (New York: Harper, 1958): p. 64. Hereafter cited parenthetically in the text.

24. Trudier Harris, *Exorcising Blackness: Historical and Literary Lynching and Burning Rituals* (Bloomington: Indiana University Press, 1984): p. 103.

25. Earle V. Bryant, "Sexual Initiation and Survival in *The Long Dream*," *Richard Wright: Critical Perspectives Past and Present*, ed. Henry Louis Gates, Jr., and K. A. Appiah (New York: Amistad, 1993): p. 430.

26. Black Boy was forbidden to talk about white women. This prohibition of speech is indicative of the social climate of Wright's time. Ironically, his speech as an artist was depressed even further when the original bedroom scene that described Bigger kissing Mary was deleted: "to retain such highly charged sexual scenes would risk censorship" (Keneth Kinnamon, "How Native Son was Born," *Richard Wright: Critical Perspectives Past and Present*, ed., Henry Louis Gates Jr. and K. A. Appiah (New York: Amistad, 1993): p. 110.

27. For a discussion about the dreams, see Katherine Fishburn, *Richard Wright's Hero: The Faces of a Rebel Victim* (Metuchen, NJ: Scarecrow, 1977): p. 19.

28. Yoshinobu Hakutani, "Richard Wright's *The Long Dream* as Racial and Sexual Discourse," *African American Review* 30 (1996): p. 254.

29. Richard Wright, *Savage Holiday* (Jackson, MS: Banner, 1954): p. 86.

30. Marina Warner, *Alone of All Her Sex: The Myth and the Cult of the Virgin Mary* (New York: Knopf, 1976): p. 14.

31. Evelyn Bassoff, *Between Mothers and Sons: The Making of Vital and Loving Men* (New York: Penguin, 1994): p. 65.

BRANNON COSTELLO

Richard Wright's Lawd Today! *and the Political Uses of Modernism*

Readers have long considered *Lawd Today!*, Richard Wright's first written and last published novel, an anomaly—when they have considered it at all. The novel, which Wright began perhaps as early as 1933 and which he continued to compose and revise until 1937, [1] simply seems inconsistent with our image of what a Wright text of the 1930s, a decade which saw the publication of Wright's radical poetry and the short-story collection *Uncle Tom's Children*, should do or be. Set in Chicago during the Great Depression, *Lawd Today!* features petit bourgeois postal worker Jake Jackson as its protagonist. Jake, a drunken, abusive lout who spends his days lusting after prostitutes and beating his wife, never achieves any real revolutionary awakening, and indeed continues to endorse capitalism and the American success myth and to condemn "'Commoonists'" despite his own debtridden and fundamentally unsuccessful life. When the small publishing house Walker and Company released the novel posthumously in 1963, critics greeted it with a mixture of confusion, qualified praise, and disgust. Indeed, Nick Aaron Ford, the novel's most vociferous early critic, found this "dull, unimaginative novel" so impossible to reconcile with his vision of Wright that he wrote, "It is difficult to believe that *Lawd Today* was written by Richard Wright. . . . It is doubtful that the mature Wright ever would have agreed to its publication" (368). Although Ford may have articulated the most extreme critique of the novel, he was by

African American Review, Volume 37, Number 1 (Spring 2003): pp. 39–52. © 2003 Brannon Costello.

no means completely out of step with his fellow reviewers. Granville Hicks' unenthusiastic comment that "it is less powerful than either *Native Son* or *Black Boy*, but it has its own kind of interest" (363) typifies the lukewarm response that continues to guide critical discussion—or the lack thereof—of the novel today, with a few notable exceptions.[2] Yoshinobu Hakutani, a more recent Wright critic, claims that few readers can "deny that *Lawd Today* lacks the tension of *Native Son*." Although he admires certain satiric elements of the novel, he takes it to task primarily for its failings as a work of naturalistic protest fiction, à la *Native Son*: "On the one hand, [Wright] has accumulated documentary detail characteristic of a naturalistic style. But his manner is flawed because his selected scenes are imparted with gratuitous metaphors and images" (222).

The stylistic "flaw" that Hakutani identifies here—the preponderance of "metaphors and images"—speaks to another difficulty critics have had in reconciling *Lawd Today!* to the traditional view of Wright, and indeed of literature in general, in the 1930s. The novel seems influenced less by the naturalism or social realism that we typically associate with Wright and more by modernist aesthetic and thematic concerns. Wright, however, was an active member of the Communist Party throughout the 1930s,[3] and he served as head of the Chicago branch of the literary John Reed Club, published pieces in Party-sponsored and Party-friendly magazines like *New Masses* and *Partisan Review*, and rose to prominence as a poet, short story writer, literary critic, and journalist. Since official Communist Party doctrine treated modernism as irredeemably bourgeois and counterrevolutionary, goes the conventional argument, its stable of critics would doubtlessly have roundly condemned Wright's novel. Indeed, Granville Hicks asserts that the novel "would have been disturbing to most orthodox Communists in the Thirties" (364), and Edward Margolies claims that "even a cursory glance at its contents will reveal what the party would have found objectionable" (91).

True, *Lawd Today!* has little to do, on the surface, with socialist realism, the literary mode ostensibly endorsed by the Communist Party. Mike Gold, one of the Party's most famous aesthetic theorists, lobbied for a "proletarian literature [that] will reflect the struggle of the workers in their fight for the world. It portrays the life of the workers . . . with a clear revolutionary point" (205–206). Gold draws a sharp distinction between proletarian writers and the "bourgeois writers" who "tell us about their spiritual drunkards and super-refined Parisian emigres; or about their spiritual marriages and divorces" (206). While modernist art deals with "precious silly little agonies," proletarian novels offer a vision of "not pessimism, but revolutionary elan" (206–207). Gold, certainly, would have disliked *Lawd Today!*'s similarities to James Joyce's *Ulysses*: The novel takes place in the course of one day, and, as Eugene Miller argues, Jake's "quotidian routine is parasyntactically laminated over Lincoln's birthday radio speeches and other media pronouncements"; his "activities . . . are patently and ironically rendered more meaningless by playing the myth over them," much as Leopold Bloom's life is rendered more meaningless in *Ulysses* through ironic contrast with patterns from classical mythology (59). Craig Werner also argues that the novel "is a conscious rewriting of *Ulysses*. Filled with direct allusions to Joyce and Eliot, the novel emphasizes a mythic parallel and multiple styles" (190). Moreover, the incorporation of newspaper headlines, popular songs, and radio broadcasts also recalls Joyce. Gold would surely have turned up his nose at the epigraph from T. S. Eliot's *The Waste Land* that begins the novel's third section, "Rats' Alley," and Don Graham has gone so far as to argue that Eliot's archetypal modernist poem and *Lawd Today!* share the theme of "spiritual death and the possibility of rebirth" (329), although he finds this theme unrelated to the novel's socio-political concerns.[4] Jake and his fellow postal workers even have a conversation about Gertrude Stein. As Margolies observes, Jake suffers from "spiritual poverty"— a fundamentally modernist dilemma — in addition to the usual economic poverty. Wright's text, then, has little in common with Daniel Aaron's description of the Party ideal: "Black proletarian and white proletarian, two massive figures . . . standing arm in arm" (44). The Communist Party, Margolies claims, "would have disapproved" (93).

But would it have? Drawing on recent leftist revisions of the literary history of the 1930s, I would like to argue that stereotypically modernist subject matter and aesthetic strategies were actually available and indeed very attractive to Wright at this time. Further, far from being an apolitical or anti-leftist anomaly in Wright's 1930s' output, *Lawd Today!* is actually very much in keeping with Wright's original conception of the relationship between his art and his political ideology. In *Black Boy*, Wright writes,

> The Communists, I felt, had oversimplified the experience of those whom they sought to lead. In their efforts to recruit masses, they had missed the meaning of the lives of the masses, had conceived of people in too abstract a manner. I would make voyages, discoveries, explorations with words and try to put some of that meaning back. I would address my words to two groups: I would tell Communists how common people felt, and I would tell common people of the self-sacrifice of Communists who strove for unity among them. (377)

This passage is frequently cited in critical surveys of Wright's work, often as a way of introducing his overtly Communist-influenced 1930s' writings, especially the short-story collection *Uncle Tom's Children*. Such studies tend to focus on how Wright addresses the second of the two groups that he discusses, how he makes Communism a palatable and viable strategy of resistance to the "common people."[5] However, I would argue that a fuller consideration of the first part of Wright's plan—to "tell Communists how common people felt"—is appropriate to help us better understand *Lawd Today!*

In *Lawd Today!*, Wright focuses on the modernist dilemmas of "fragmentation, alienation, sense-making; the shoring up of fragments against our ruins; what to make of a diminished thing" (Werner 11) to describe not just the social, political, and economic dis-enfranchisement of African Americans fleeing from the South to Chicago in the Great Migration, but also the personal, spiritual disenfranchisement that comes from being separated (or, sometimes, from separating themselves) from the forms of community and means of connection with each other—church and folklore, for example—that sustained them in the South. Though not a proletarian novel in Mike Gold's formulation, the novel does serve a political purpose: It shows how the popular myths of consumerist, capitalist American culture have disrupted these forms of community and stresses the need for new forms or for the revival of the old. Ultimately, to paraphrase Wright, *Lawd Today!* tells Communists how common people feel so that they might not oversimplify the experience of the masses and that they might better know how to appeal to them.

***

In recent years, leftist historians and literary critics have begun to challenge the narrow definition of proletarian literature and the stereotypical view of the Communist Party that I have outlined above and that is implicit in many dismissals of *Lawd Today!*. Barbara Foley's *Radical Representations: Politics and Form in U.S. Proletarian Fiction, 1929–1941*, offers perhaps the most comprehensive treatment of this issue. Foley criticizes "the model of a philistine, coercive, and anti-modernist party [that] has routinely been invoked in treatments of the relationship between writers and the organized left" (46). This inaccurate model, says Foley, promotes the view that "through writer's foundations and critical organs where their influence dominated . . . the party critics who were based in the *New Masses* issued directives about matters ranging from politics to subject matter to style" (45). Moreover, "it is charged [that] writers were cut off from the most exciting and productive developments in contemporary literature and consigned to a sterile, banal, and—ironically—conservative realism" (54). Foley, however, argues for a radically different model of the relationship between the Communist Party and leftist literary production. She contends that, although the party did offer directives, and though prominent members such as Mike Gold argued long and loud for the inherent decadence of modernism, the notion that American literary proletarians "repudiated literary innovations simply does not stand up under the evidence" (57). Foley argues that, "although the 'commissars' of leftist criticism have been

criticized for dogmatism and arrogance, they were quite ready to acknowledge that not merely proletarian literature but American Marxist criticism
was in its infancy" (51). Indeed, even "the organs most closely identified
with the Communist party—the *New Masses* and, especially, the *Daily
Worker*—were quite hospitable to literary innovations of various kinds"
(58–59). As she puts it, "In short, much Depression-era literary radicalism
was intimately involved in the project of 'mak[ing] it new'" (62).[6]

Of course, Richard Wright, as a Party writer, book reviewer, journalist, and
head of the Chicago John Reed Club (until the clubs were disbanded in 1935),
would have been fully steeped in this decidedly heterogeneous attitude toward
proletarian fiction. Foley cites the 1935 Writers Congress, which Wright attended, as a particularly significant moment in the ongoing redefinition of proletarian literature, when the primary emphasis for acceptable proletarian fiction
moved from "authentic" proletarian authorship to a more general articulation
of a Marxist perspective (118). At this conference, Wright met Edwin Seaver,
literary critic for the *Daily Worker* (Fabre 118), and Wright would surely have
read Seaver's essay "What is a Proletarian Novel?: Notes Toward a Definition,"
which appeared in *Partisan Review* around the time of the conference. Here,
Seaver argued that proletarian literature need not be "written by a worker, about
workers or for workers . . . . it is possible for an author of middleclass origin
to write a novel about petty-bourgeois characters which will appeal primarily
to readers of the same class, and yet such a work can come within the clas-
sification, Proletarian novel" (5). He asserted that the primary concern for the
proletarian writer was not "the period of history in which he sets his story, or
the kind of characters he writes about, but his ideological approach to his story
and characters, which approach is entirely conditioned by his acceptance of the
Marxian interpretation of history" (7).

Indeed, the pages of Philip Rahv and William Phillips' prominent
leftist magazine *Partisan Review* were almost certainly already familiar and
quite influential for the young Wright, since it served as a primary organ of
the John Reed Clubs. Further, Wright served as an associate editor for *Partisan Review* in 1936. Though the post, Michael Fabre claims, was largely
honorary, Wright doubtlessly followed the magazine's ideological discussions, and he was at least engaged enough to contribute a book review (of
Arna Bontemps' *Black Thunder*) and a letter to the editor in defense of an
artist who had been accused of being too concerned with aesthetics and
insufficiently radical.[7] Wright's involvement with *Partisan Review* is important to an understanding of his use of aesthetic and thematic elements
of modernism. As Harvey M. Teres has discussed in his recent study of
Partisan Review's development, *Renewing the Left: Politics, Imagination, and
the New York Intellectuals*, William Phillips and Philip Rahv, the magazine's
two chief editors from 1934 to 1936, consciously rejected "narrow-minded

sectarian theories and practices" in favor of an "increasingly heterodox literary and critical project" (40). As early as 1934, Phillips and Rahv attacked "critical positions that demanded that literature make explicit appeals for socialist revolution, or present a dialectical-materialist world outlook, or render working-class life in a favorable light" (43); instead, they believed that, "through publishing the movement's 'best creative work,' the magazine would be a participant in political struggle" (40). Most significantly for our discussion of Wright, Phillips and Rahv worked for "the attainment of an unprecedented degree of autonomy, tolerance, and rigor for literature and criticism . . . within left discourse; and . . . the creation of a compelling, though highly unstable union between modernism and political radicalism" (41–42). The editors found it ludicrous that Marxist critics would reject modernism out of hand as "an aesthetic and decadent source of counter-revolutionary ideology" (48) and therefore make unavailable to Marxist-oriented writers a wide range of formal innovations that these writers could potentially incorporate into their works with powerful results. Instead, Phillips and Rahv tried to "respond productively to 'bourgeois' literature, especially as it impinged on the shaping of the new proletarian literature" (43).

One of Rahv's earliest pieces in this vein was his 1934 review of Ernest Hemingway's *Winner Take Nothing*. Wright particularly admired Hemingway (Fabre 141, 170, 176) and would surely have been interested in a review of his work. Rahv argued against completely discarding Hemingway's "cluster of formal creative means" because of his bourgeois subject matter. He argued that such an approach "makes the proletarian artist insensible to those few—largely external—features of contemporary art that are class determined in such a slender and remote manner as to render them available for use by the creator of the new art who is seeking an effective artistic method" (58). Three issues later, William Phillips forcefully articulated an even more liberal version of this theory. In his essay "Three Generations," he argued that current Marxist writers were the inheritors of two sets of literary ancestors: the pioneering social realists who wrote in the vein of Dreiser, and the modernist experimenters of the 1920s. He claims that, while many critics wish to ignore the innovations of the '20s, "the spirit of the 1920s is part of our heritage, and many of the younger revolutionary generations are acutely conscious of this. . . . The job of our generation is to tie these threads, to use whatever heritage there is which gives color to our pattern" (52). He criticizes the tendency to "repudiate the bourgeois heritage, and fall into primitive, oversimplified and pseudo-popular rewrites of political ideas and events" (53). Harvey Teres argues that Phillips and Rahv were particularly interested in modernist representations of "felt experience," though they believed that "felt experience must carry more than personal significance—it must bring the reader face to face with broader social contradictions" (45).

In "Three Generations," Phillips argued that T. S. Eliot could provide a useful model for such an articulation of felt experience: "In his poetry, however reactionary its ultimate implications may be, Eliot has perfected a new idiom and tighter rhythms for expressing many prevailing moods and perceptions" (53). As these passages indicate, while some doctrinaire Marxist critics found modernist forms of representation such as stream-of-consciousness or a reliance on metaphor and imagery inevitably and intrinsically bourgeois, the *Partisan Review* editors argued that these same forms could be marshaled in the service of the left.

The modernist forms of expression championed by Rahv and Phillips would serve Wright well in his attempt to tell how a common person like Jake Jackson feels alienated in his barren existence in the urban wasteland of Chicago. Mark Sanders has argued that, after the Great Migration, "African American individual and cultural identity was forced to adjust to the new demands of the city and industrialization. As a result, African American culture entertained new concepts of individuality and tried to rationalize new feelings of alienation" (11). Though Jake never reaches a level of self-awareness that would allow him to begin to rationalize his feelings of alienation, the text is riddled with descriptions of his essentially isolated and empty life. For example, Wright frequently deploys images of sleep and dreaming to underscore Jake's alienation. Though the novel opens with Jake's awakening from a dream, Wright often describes Jake as though he were still partially asleep, not fully aware of or engaged with the world around him. When he rises, he is confronted by a vision of dissolution: "He saw the bed and the dresser and the carpet and the walls melting and shifting and merging into a blur" (6). When he leaves the house, he walks down the street with "his mind lost in a warm fog" (37). Repeatedly, Wright characterizes Jake as tired or sleepy (36, 66, 115, 158, 213, and passim), as longing for a deathly peaceful oblivion. Indeed, Jake seems constantly on the verge of falling asleep in the midst of whatever he is doing, whether he is playing bridge, getting a haircut, talking with friends, or working at the post office. In one case, Jake muses that his "arms and legs felt heavy and slightly numb, as though they were watersoaked. He licked his lips, mumbling *Gawd, but I'm sleepy.* If he could only sleep right now, if he could only close his eyes and rest his head upon something soft" (68). Later, he and his post office cronies talk about how they like "slipping off into nothing" (158).

Jake never manages to articulate his feeling of alienation, which he also feels both as an unexplainable nervousness and as a lack, a hunger. During a lull in the opiatic distraction of conversation and bridge with his friends, he feels "empty, missing something," and thinks, "*I'm getting nervous as hell.* And he knew that as long as he sat this way his nervousness would increase. . . . Jake's mind fished about, trying to get hold of an idea to cover his feeling of uneasy emptiness" (89). Elsewhere, Jake thinks that "he wanted something, and that something hungered in him, deeply" (68), and he feels "a haunting and hungering sense of incompleteness" (51). When he faces his shift at the post office, he feels "a dumb yearning for something else; somewhere or other was something or other for him" (116). The vagueness of Wright's language here appropriately reflects the haziness of Jake's desires. Although, when a white supervisor criticizes Jake for improperly sorting several letters, Jake thinks that *"It ain't always going to be this way!"* he can get no further than that rudimentary expression of frustration:

> His mind went abruptly blank. He could not keep on with that thought, because he did not know where that thought led. He did not know of any other way things could be, if not *this way*. Yet he longed for them *not* to be this way. He felt that something vast and implacable was crushing him; and he felt angry with himself because he had to stand it. (142–143)

This inability to articulate or even understand his feelings, this loss of meaning, plagues Jake in other ways over the course of his day. In the dream that opens the novel, Jake endures a Sisyphean torment, running frantically up a flight of steps at his boss's urging but never making any progress. Though the dream carries (for us, anyway) an obvious symbolic meaning relating to Jake's racial and economic exploitation, he spends much of the morning just trying to remember what he dreamed in the first place: *"Now what was I dreaming?* He tried to think, but a wide gap yawned in his mind" (6). Worse, when the sight of some children playing on a flight of stairs reminds him, he does not ponder over any possible social significance the dream might have had, but instead uses it as a guide for picking numbers for a "policy" game, an elaborate numbers racket. Even more problematically, Jake cannot intuit the numbers from the dream himself; instead, he must go through two intermediaries. He tells one woman, Mabel, his dream, and she picks out the important elements; then she shouts those elements to a woman named Martha, who matches them up with the numbers found in *King Solomon's Wheel of Life and Death Dream Book*. Jake is not allowed to see this book, so he must get the information thirdhand before he bets his money. Finally, complete recovery of the dream's meaning is not possible even in the terms of this corrupt system, because "a dream sometimes had so many possible interpretations, it referred to so many different combinations of numbers, that it was impossible to 'cover' the dream" (45). Jake can only access as many different interpretations of the dream as he has money to spare.

Jake's fellow postal laborers offer little more than Mabel and Martha in helping Jake understand the meaning of their alienated and exploited existence. Jake spends much of his day with overweight national guardsman Al, clap-ridden Bob, and tubercular Slim. Most of their conversation, whether at Bob's house playing bridge or at the post office sorting letters, revolves around such topics as the treacherous nature of women and the admirable success of millionaires like Henry Ford and John D. Rockefeller. But the grinding monotony of their labor exhausts them and makes genuine communication all but impossible. Wright says that "often they were on the verge of speaking, but the sheer triviality of what they wanted to say weighted their tongues into silence" (150), and that "when they talked it was more like thinking aloud than speaking for purposes of communication. Clusters of emotion, dim accretions of instinct and tradition rose to the surface of their consciousness like dead bodies floating swollen upon a night sea" (158). The connotations of Wright's imagery are clear: Jake and his friends speak in a dead language devoid of meaningful ideas.

However, in one very specific instance, language does offer something more than a distraction from the nervous hunger of alienation, and this instance helps us begin to understand Wright's fundamental argument about African American life in the urban, Northern wasteland. After a game of poker with his friends, Jake feels "empty, missing something." While casting about for a way to ease this feeling, he notices Al resting calmly on the couch nearby and decides that he wants to "make some of the strength of that repose his own" (89). He chooses to do this by playing the dozens with his friend. This is significant, because in playing the dozens, an African American folkloric form, the two men who comically insult each other forge connections, albeit satirical ones, with their cultural heritage in the South and in Africa. For instance, Al tells Jake that "'when old Colonel James was sucking at my ma's tits I saw your little baby brother across the street watching with slobber in his mouth,'" and Jake, a few exchanges later, tells Al that, "'when my greatgreatgreat grandma was smelling them pork chops, your poor old greatgreatgreat*great* grandma was a Zulu queen in Africa. She was setting at the table and she said to the waiter: "Say waiter, be sure and fetch me some of them missionary chitterlings ..."'" (91). Though the images invoked are humorous, they also connect Al and Jake with the heritage of ancestors who occupied, in varying degrees, positions of authority (or at least importance) in relation to white people in their respective societies. However, once their game ends, they return to business as usual.

This moment of connection with his cultural heritage brings Jake an unusual feeling of joy; it also suggests Wright's overall project in *Lawd Today!* Rather than simply and pessimistically dramatizing the alienation of his protagonist, as Gold might accuse a decadent bourgeois writer of doing, Wright offers specific cultural reasons for this alienation and suggests possible solutions compatible with leftist ideology. The text strongly suggests that Wright locates the source of Jake and his fellow Chicago-dwellers' alienation and un-easiness in their separation from African American cultural traditions such as folklore and the black church, traditions that forged community and helped to explain and make bearable the oppression they suffered in the South. These traditions are, of course, the very ones that Wright would endorse in his "Blueprint for Negro Writing" (1938) as part of a black culture that "has, for good or ill, helped to clarify [the black individual's] consciousness and cre-ate emotional attitudes which are conducive to action" (39). Though Jake has renounced these traditions and indeed anything that recalls black life in the South, he has not yet found any other means of meaningfully relating to the world and has instead adopted the exploitative myths of American popular culture, with disastrous results.

Throughout the novel, Jake reiterates this disavowal of the South and any aspect of African American culture that he associates with it. When Jake asserts the superiority of America over "Commoonist" Russia, Lil reminds him that "'they burned a colored man alive the other day,'" but Jake dismisses her story by saying "'Aw, that was down South, anyhow.'" When Lil goes so far as to remind him that "'the South's a part of this country,'" Jake accuses her of being a Red (33). Later, Jake says that "'they ought to lynch 'em if they ain't got no better sense than to stay down there'" (193). Similarly, when Duke, the novel's only Communist organizer (and not a very successful one) tries to encourage a group of black men to see the ills of capitalism by pointing to "'all them sharecroppers,'" Jake, in characteristically individualist fashion, tells him to "'let 'em look out after themselves'" (60). This rejection of the South even affects Jake's work habits: When he transports letters, he prefers to "carry a Northern state rather than a Southern one. He never wanted to carry Missis-sippi, his home state. *That's one state I'm damn glad to be from.*" Wright explains Jake's feelings when he describes his tastes in current cinema: "When he went to the movies he always wanted to see Negroes, if there were any in the play, shown against the background of urban conditions, not rural ones. Anything which smacked of farms, chaingangs, lynchings, hunger, or the South in gen-eral was repugnant to him. These things had so hurt him once that he wanted to forget them forever" (138).

Only once does Jake seem on the verge of reclaiming his Southern cul-tural heritage. When he and his cohorts stop to watch a parade sponsored by a black nationalist group, they find themselves profoundly affected by the music: "They were feeling the surges of memory the music had roused in their minds. They did not agree with the parade, but they did agree with the music. There came upon them the memories of those Sunday mornings in the South when they had attended church." Wright stresses here the potential that this cultural tradition can have as a way of appealing to African Americans, for Jake says, "'Maybe them folks is right, who knows?'" He does, however, say this "out of the depths of a confused mood" (110); perhaps his confusion stems from his momentary attraction to something he has so thoroughly repudiated. Though Jake and his friends at one point ambivalently describe the South as "Heaven and Hell all rolled into one" (180), Jake attempts to renounce the South altogether, and though he has escaped the Hell that caused him such pain, he also denies the redemptive potential of Heaven.

Indeed, although Jake often pays lip service to the necessity of faith, he apparently rejects the possibility that religion can have any meaningful effect on people's lives. His wife Lil, whom Jake once tricked into having an abortion and who now suffers from a tumor because of it, draws some of the strength that allows her to survive from a magazine called *Unity,* "DEVOTED TO CHRISTIAN HEALING" (7). Though *Unity,* with its picture of a "haloed, bearded man draped in white folds," with his hand "resting upon the blond curls of a blue-eyed girl," certainly seems a far cry from the traditions of the African American church, for Lil, whose husband dislikes her talking even to her neighbors or the milkman, it is perhaps the only access to religion or to any sort of broader community. Jake nearly flies into a rage every time he sees this magazine, calling it "trash" and ripping it from her hands. When Lil asks him for money to have an operation for her tumor, he thinks, cruelly, "*Yeah, she ought to ask Gawd to get rid of that tumor for her.... The very next time she tells me about that damned tumor I'll tell her to let Unity take care of it. Let them bastards send up a silent prayer!*" (20). He criticizes Lil for not being as up-to-date with current events as he is, and he tells her that "'you could learn something if you didn't keep that empty head of yours stuck into the Gawddamn *Unity* books all the time.'" When Lil protests, telling him that "'this is Gawd's word.... Don't you know Gawd can slap you dead right where you is?'" Jake responds, "'It's a gyp game, that's all! ... don't be dumb!'" (31).

However adamant and complete his renunciation of Christianity seems, Jake has difficulty sticking to it. Because of his condition of oppression and alienation, he deeply needs to believe in something that can interpret the world for him and explain why things are the way they are. He sometimes lapses into an almost rote repetition of Christian ideals; indeed, only a few pages after he condemns religion as a "gyp game," he tells Lil that "'the good Lawd's done got it all figgered out in his own good fashion. It's got to be that way so there can be some justice in this world, I reckon ....' His voice trailed off uncertainly" (34). Perhaps his uncertainty stems from the obviously (even to Jake) contradictory nature of his statement. At other times it seems as though Christianity is the only thing Jake does *not* believe in. When he goes to his post office box, he finds it crammed full of advertisements hawking everything from supernatural numbers-picking schemes to proto-Viagra vitality tonics. Oddly, given his apparent disdain for belief in things divine,

Jake seems to have some faith in the supernatural powers of the products advertised here. He says that "there might be something to this" ad for "THE MYSTERIOUS THREESTAR MEDIUM" (38). Of another that promises to "MAKE THE UNSEEN WORLD VISIBLE" with "Second Coming Incense," he ruminates that "maybe there's something in it if it comes straight from the spirit world" (39). He thinks that a good dose of "VIRGIN MARY'S NEVERFAIL HERB AND ROOT TONIC FOR NERVOUS AND RUNDOWN WOMEN" for Lil might save him the cost of her operation (40–41). Moreover, when it comes to picking his numbers for the policy game, he relies on dream interpretation because "he was much too shrewd to trust such a small thing as numbers to fortune tellers, spiritualists, and the like; these people were consulted only in case of a deep, life-and-death crisis" (45). Jake's inconsistency here—attempting (with limited success) to reject Christianity but replacing religious faith with a faith in charlatans and scam artists—further emphasizes his alienation and his need to believe in something that gives his life meaning.

However, if Jake does have a primary alternative belief system, another master narrative that explains the world to him, he finds it in the American success myth pervasive in the popular culture—newspaper, radio, films—that he consumes. Wright subtly drives this point home from the novel's opening sequence. As Jake climbs futilely up the neverending staircase, compelled ever upward by a booming voice, he thinks, *that old sonofabitch up there sounds just like my boss, too!*" (5). Of course, when Jake awakens, he realizes that the voice in his dream actually belongs to Lil's radio, broadcasting the life-story of Abraham Lincoln, icon of bootstraps ideology. Wright suggests, then, that popular culture, or, more specifically, the success myth of limitless opportunity that it endorses, is Jake's "boss," the force that keeps him in this squirrel's cage. Jake constantly articulates his affirmation of this belief system. He tells Lil that "'nobody but lazy folks can starve in this country'" (33). He rejects Franklin Roosevelt's attempts at economic reform because "'old Hoover was doing all right, only nobody couldn't see it, that's all.'" Moreover, he thinks that the New Deal is doomed to fail because nobody can tell his heroes "'old man Morgan and old Man Rockefeller and old man Ford what to do.... Why them men owns and runs the country!'" (29). Jake is fascinated with and envious of these men, and so his assertion that "'cold, hard cash runs this country, always did and always will'" is not intended as a social critique; instead, he simply wants to get enough money so that he can emulate these giants of capitalism that he so admires.

Jake's chief local example of the embodiment of bootstraps success is Doc, his local barber. When Doc rails against Communist organizer Duke, Jake "follow[s] the movement of Doc's lips with his own and nod[s] approval" (58). Doc, who owns his own store and has a modicum of political influence, refuses to accept that anyone might be out of work for any reason but laziness. In order to explain his success, Doc likens himself to a frog, trapped in a churn of milk, who kicked until he turned the milk to butter, then "jumped on top of that ball of butter and hopped right out of the churn" (60). Further, he tells Jake that, if Communists "'kept their damn mouths shut and tried to get hold of something, some money, or property, then they'd get somewhere'" (63).

Interestingly, religion does play a part in this success myth, but not the community-forming, potentially radical and oppositional Christianity that we see in "Fire and Cloud" and "Bright and Morning Star," or even the simply sustaining Christianity of Lil's *Unity* magazines. Instead, this religion, a fairly inactive and excessively general faith in the goodness of God's longterm plan, simply serves to endorse and authorize the status quo; it becomes an explanation for how the rich get rich and a justification for keeping them that way. For instance, when Jake and his friends discuss Thomas Edison, Benjamin Franklin, Abraham Lincoln, and John D. Rockefeller, they claim that these men "'got to be successful by following the Golden Rule. . . . they did to other men what they wanted them men to do to them . . . and Gawd rewarded 'em. . . . You'll get your reward if you do right'" (166–167). Moreover, the men particularly admire a circular that depicts two trains, one headed for Hell and the other for Heaven. The first, "THE EVERLASTING DAMNATION RAILWAY CORPORATION," advertised as "the Quickest and Shortest Route to the Hottest Depths of *H E L L*," makes stops not just at the predictable "Murderer's Gap" and "Atheistville," but also at "Radical Hill," "Thomas Paine Avenue," and "Communist Junction" (162), thus clearly aligning any attempt at radical change to the status quo with soul-imperiling evil. The second, "THE SALVATION AND REDEMPTION RAILWAY COMPANY," as one would expect, stops at "Sacrifice Harbor," "Temperanceville," and "Honesty Line," thus diametrically opposing these positive values to the negative values of Communist radicalism. Jake and his friends think that the creator of this circular has "'done figgered out every *single* thing'" and that "'Gawd sure must've been with the guy to make 'im write a thing like that'" (165), statements that clearly indicate their acceptance of these values (although one suspects that they have only adopted the political and economic values, since, despite the fact that the hell-bound train stops at "Prostitution Boulevard," their after-hours destination is a cathouse).

Jake never manages to see the problems inherent in his uncritical belief in capitalist bootstraps ideology or to form any kind of meaningful community or interpersonal relationship that would help him to overcome his overwhelming sense of alienation. Indeed, the novel's last section, "Rats' Alley," begins with an epigraph from Eliot's *The Waste Land*, and it describes a scene as bleak and empty as any in that high-modernist poem. Despite his already large debts, Jake goes another hundred dollars in the hole so that he can finance a night out with his cohorts and play the big-spending high-roller he so idealizes. Jake and his friends cavort and dance with a group of prostitutes "with an obvious exaggeration of motion" (195) in an attempt to distract themselves from their alienation and their emptiness. Wright further underscores the false promises of popular culture: "The music caroled its promise of an unattainable satisfaction and lured him to a land where boundaries receded with each step he took" (203). Wright's description here clearly recalls the Sisyphean staircase that opens the novel and points out the impossibility of Jake's ever achieving the kind of success he desires. Even the fleshly pleasures that the house should offer often seem instead like pain. As Blanche, a prostitute that Jake picks up, dances in "orgiastic agony," "a thin black woman grabbed her boy friend and bit his ear till blood came" (205). When, in mid-dance, Blanche tells Jake, "'That's murder, Papa,'" he replies, "'I want to be electrocuted'" (203). Moreover, even this ambiguous sensation turns out to be inauthentic, an empty ruse; Blanche only dances with him so that her partner can pick his pocket. When Jake stumbles drunkenly home and finds that Lil has fallen asleep kneeling in prayer, he assaults her; Lil must stab him in the head with a piece of glass in order to stop his attack. Wright leaves Jake sinking into unconsciousness, circled with "fumes of darkness," feeling like "a black whirlpool was sucking him under," as "outside an icy wind swept around the corner of the building, whining and moaning like an idiot in a deep black pit" (219).

***

Clearly, *Lawd Today!* does not end with the revolutionary élan that Mike Gold advocated for the proletarian novel. However, Wright does not leave the door of radical enlightenment completely shut for the characters in this novel. Instead, he holds out hope, however slight, for the possibility of the development of a revolutionary or proletarian or at the very least community-oriented sensibility in Jake and his cronies. In one passage in which all four men speak without dialogue tags to identify the speaker, they achieve a rare moment of potentially meaningful conversation. They remark, "'Ain't it funny how some few folks is rich and just millions is poor? . . . And them few rich folks owns the whole world . . . and runs it like they please . . . and the rest ain't got nothing?'" (173). At first, it seems that the men will dismiss this glaring injustice with the typical quasireligious bootstraps fatalism that makes social change seem so untenable; they remark that "'Gawd said the poor'll be with you always . . . and he was right, too,'" and that "'some folks just ain't got not brains, that's all. If you divided up all the money in the world right now we'd be just where we is tomorrow'" (174). However, the men soon return to the topic of economic and racial oppression, and they even see the Communist Party in a positive light when they remember that "'the Reds sure scared them white folks down South

when they put up that fight for the Scottsboro boys'" (176). Even more strikingly, the men begin to exhibit an inkling of community-minded consciousness
and a desire, however haltingly expressed, to change the current system. One
says that "'a lot of times I been wanting to do things I just wouldn't do. . . . And
I bet a lot of other folks feel the same way.'" Another responds with "'Now . . .
Wait a minute. . . . Now, you see, if *all* the folks felt like that, why in hell don't
they *do* something?'" "'Ah, hell,'" says another, "'some guy's got something *you*
want, and you got something *he* wants, and when you do something you bump
into each other . . . like you see trains crashing up in the movies.'" However,
another of the workers wonders, "'But shucks, if we all was in the same train
going in the same direction . . . .'" This line of thought, unfortunately, does
not develop far beyond this point; one of the men finally says, "'Aw, man, ain't
no sense in talking about things like this,'" and the conversation moves on to
other topics (183).

In this brief but significant conversation, Jake, Slim, Al, and Bob demonstrate that their indoctrination into the hegemonic values of acquisitive,
individualistic capitalist culture is less than complete, however slightly so.
Here, Wright argues that, even in the most apparently irredeemably bourgeois characters, there exists the possibility for an awakening of revolutionary sensibility. In *Lawd Today!*, rather than offering an oversimplified vision
of a romanticized proletariat worker, class-conscious and heroic, struggling
against his capitalist oppressors, Wright draws on modernist techniques and
themes to paint a complex, unflinching, honest, and sometimes brutal picture
of four "common people." These men who feel alienated and hollow after
their move to the urban wasteland of Chicago desperately desire something
that will lessen their alienation, that will offer some reasonable explanation
for their oppressed condition. By showing the pitfalls that Jake encounters
when he loses the cultural traditions that helped to sustain him in the South
—such as an equally wholehearted belief in the "spirit realm," in the evilness
of radicalism, and in the American success myth—Wright both offers us and,
perhaps more importantly, sought to offer his 1930s' comrades, a better, more
complicated and complete vision of how actual common people might feel
about society and their position in it, a vision that Communist organizers
could use to determine how best to nurture that seed of proletarian consciousness—perhaps, as he would later suggest, by attempting to re-establish
some of those forms of community disrupted by urban Depression life.

NOTES

1. I am citing the version of *Lawd Today!* collected in Arnold Rampersad's
Richard Wright: Early Works (1991). Rampersad's edition is based on a completed
typescript dating from 1937–1938, the latest version of the work that we know of,
and the one that apparently incorporates Wright's handwritten revisions on earlier

drafts. The original edition of the book was emended by its editors at Walker and Company, who made substantial changes to Wright's "experimental punctuation, capitalization, and usage, and . . . also introduced a number of verbal changes, particularly to eliminate words considered obscene and to regularize colloquialisms" (909). Rampersad also restored the exclamation point to the title.

2. A few very early critics championed *Lawd Today!*. William Burrison, in "Another Look at *Lawd Today:* Richard Wright's Tricky Apprenticeship," argues that Wright achieves a formal unity in the novel through his use of the "trickster motif" and the repeated use of the number three. In "*Lawd Today:* Richard Wright's First/Last Novel," Lewis Leary argues that *Lawd Today!* stands "securely on its own merits" as a portrayal of "the essential bleakness of black life" (412).

3. Wright became a member of the John Reed Club in 1933, although he did not actually join the Communist Party until 1934.

4. Like Don Graham, Linda Hamalian has also noted the modernist— specifically Eliotic—influence on *Lawd Today!*. In "Other Writers, Other Looms: Richard Wright's Use of Epigraphs in Two Novels," she focuses on how the modernist epigraphs that Wright uses to introduce his chapters help illuminate themes; however, she argues that, while "the texture of a rather thin novel is enriched by its accompanying thematic allusion . . . the reader may feel that Wright allowed himself to be overwhelmed by the pessimism of his sources. He was either ignorant of or indifferent to the other side of Black life that Langston Hughes often celebrates in his poetry" (78).

5. Timothy P. Caron's essay "'The Reds are in the Bible Room': Political Activism and the Bible in Richard Wright's *Uncle Tom's Children*," in which Caron examines how Wright links Christian and Communist ideals, is an interesting and insightful recent example of this approach.

6. A number of other recent critics have followed Foley's lead. C. Barry Chabot argues that, while "the proletarian writers of the thirties are typically thought to be an interruption of literary modernism in the United States," in fact "self-consciously proletarian writers produced a variant within American literary modernism, not an alternative to it" (215). Valentine Cunningham similarly asserts that "no hard and fast divide existed in the thirties along the lines conventional literary-historical storytelling is prone to suggest"; there is no "clear-cut opposition between realism and modernism, socialists and modernists, social realism and Joyceanism" (14). Alan Filreis's *Modernism from Right to Left* studies the relationship between Wallace Stevens and various radical poets, and Betsy Erkkila's "Elizabeth Bishop, Modernism, and the Left" examines Bishop's work in a political context in order to "challenge traditional — and gendered — readings not only of Bishop but of literary modernism itself." (284)

7. In the May 1936 issue of *Partisan Review,* Sydney Justin Harris published an article entitled "Letter from Chicago," in which he lamented that, "out of this city which promised to become the intellectual hub of the Middle West, the past many years have produced nothing but sterility and superficial sophistication" (23). Harris cites the lack of significant literary output (he takes particular and understandable glee in mocking a cookbook composed of recipes submitted by the local literati) as well as city policies that ban *New Masses* and controversial plays such as *Tobacco Road* and *The Children's Crusade.* Harris asserts that Chicago has only one literary clique, a "corset of culture," "sealed and cemented" by their reactionary ideals; *Esquire,* in particular, "ignor[es] the wealth of revolutionary literature in America today" (23).

He criticizes one prominent editor who dismisses a leftist critique of Ezra Pound as a "merely economic issue," an action that he believes characterizes the Chicago literary scene's attitude toward class struggle. He regrets that these editors, poets, and critics "influence the literary tastes and opinions of millions of readers in Chicago, the Middle West, and, as in *Esquire* and *Poetry,* the entire country. It is they who obfuscate the real issues of the day with their chatter of 'immortality' and 'intelligent patriotism' and 'beauty' and 'latter-day sophistication' " (24).

Harris's article prompted Richard Wright to respond in a letter to the editor. Wright claims that in some ways the situation in Chicago is even worse than Harris describes it: "The truth of the matter is, some of the things are much blacker than Harris paints. Most of the young writers and artists with a tinge of talent flee this city as if it were on fire." However, he does argue that Harris neglects a few "young writers and artists who stand clear of the mire he paints." Moreover, he takes exception to the inclusion of one artist in particular, playwright and sometime *Esquire* reviewer Meyer Levin, in Harris's "dismal gallery." Though Levin does not receive extensive critique from Harris, Harris does number him among those who are insufficiently concerned with proletarian struggle and too concerned with decadent aesthetics. Wright challenges Harris by asserting Levin's Communist credentials: He notes that Levin "is a member of the League of American writers, an organization which commits its members to a struggle through their craft against war, against Fascism, for the protection of national minority groups and for the preservation of culture." Moreover, he points out that Levin "has been active in the left-wing theatre movement in Chicago," and that his play *Model Tenant,* about a rent strike, was prohibited from being performed because it was too "Red." Wright's defense of Levin here seems to indicate that he felt that radical political beliefs and more aesthetic concerns could coexist quite peacefully.

Works Cited

Aaron, Daniel. "Richard Wright and the Communist Party." *Richard Wright: Impressions and Perspectives.* Ed. David Ray and Robert M. Farnsworth. Ann Arbor: University of Michigan Press, 1973: pp. 35–46.

Blair, Sara. "Modernism and the Politics of Culture." *The Cambridge Companion to Modernism.* Ed. Michael Levenson. Cambridge: Cambridge University Press, 1999: pp. 157–173.

Burrison, William. "Another Look at *Lawd Today:* Richard Wright's Tricky Apprenticeship." *CLA Journal* 29 (1986): pp. 424–441.

Chabot, C. Barry. *Writers for the Nation: American Literary Modernism.* Tuscaloosa: University of Alabama Press, 1997.

Cunningham, Valentine. "The Age of Anxiety and Influence; or, Tradition and the Thirties Talents." *Rewriting the Thirties: Modernism and After.* Ed. Keith Williams and Steve Matthews. London: Longman, 1997: pp. 5–22.

Erkkila, Betsy. "Elizabeth Bishop, Modernism, and the Left." *American Literary History* 8 (1996): pp. 284–310.

Fabre, Michael. *The Unfinished Quest of Richard Wright.* Trans. Isabel Barzun. 2d ed. Urbana: University of Illinois Press, 1993.

Filreis, Alan. *Modernism from Right to Left: Wallace Stevens, the Thirties, and Literary Radicalism.* Cambridge: Cambridge University Press, 1994.

Foley, Barbara. *Radical Representations: Politics and Form in U.S. Proletarian Fiction, 1929–1941.* Durham: Duke University Press, 1993.

Ford, Nick Aaron. "The Fire Next Time?: A Critical Survey of Belles Lettres by and About Negroes Published in 1963." Reilly pp. 367–68.

Graham, Don B. "*Lawd Today* and the Example of *The Waste Land*." *CLA Journal* 17 (1974): pp. 327–332.

Gold, Mike. "Proletarian Fiction." *Mike Gold: A Literary Anthology*. Ed. Michael Folsom. New York: International, 1972: pp. 205–209.

Hakutani, Yoshinobu. "Richard Wright and American Literary Naturalism." *Zeitschrift* 36.3 (1988): pp. 217–226.

Hamalian, Linda. "Other Voices, Other Looms: Richard Wright's Use of Epigraphs in Two Novels." *Obsidian II* 3.3 (1988): pp. 72–88.

Hicks, Granville. "Dreiser to Farrell to Wright." Reilly pp. 363–365.

Leary, Lewis. "*Lawd Today*. Richard Wright's First/Last Novel." *CLA Journal* 15 (1971): pp. 411–419.

Margolies, Edward. *The Art of Richard Wright*. Carbondale: Southern Illinois University Press, 1969.

Miller, Eugene A. *Voice of a Native Son: The Poetics of Richard Wright*. Jackson: University Press of Mississippi, 1990.

Phillips, William (Wallace Phelps). "Three Generations." *Partisan Review* 1.4 (1934): pp. 52–53.

Rahv, Phillip. Rev. of *Winner Take Nothing*, by Ernest Hemingway. *Partisan Review* 1.1 (1934): p. 58.

Reilly, John M., ed. *Richard Wright: The Critical Reception*. New York: Burt Franklin, 1978.

Sanders, Mark A. *Afro-Modernist Aesthetics and the Poetry of Sterling A. Brown*. Athens: University of Georgia Press, 1999.

Seaver, Edwin. "What is a Proletarian Novel?: Notes Toward a Definition." *Partisan Review* 2.2 (1935): pp. 5–7.

Teres, Harvey M. *Renewing the Left: Politics, Imagination, and the New York Intellectuals*. New York: Oxford University Press, 1996.

Werner, Craig. *Playing the Changes: From Afro-Modernism to the Jazz Impulse*. Urbana: University of Illinois Press, 1994.

Wright, Richard. *Black Boy (American Hunger)*. 1945. New York: New American Library, 1993.

———. "Blueprint for Negro Writing." 1938. *Richard Wright Reader*. Ed. Ellen Wright and Michael Fabre. New York: Harper, 1978: pp. 36–50.

———. *Early Works: Lawd Today!, Uncle Tom's Children, Native Son*. Ed. Arnold Rampersad. New York: Library of America, 1991.

———. "Letter to the Editor." *Partisan Review* and *Anvil 3* (June 1936): p. 30.

CHERYL HIGASHIDA

Aunt Sue's Children: Re-viewing the Gender(ed) Politics of Richard Wright's Radicalism

In *American Hunger*, Richard Wright recounts the attempt by Chicago's Federal Negro Theatre to stage agitprop drama about chain gang conditions in the South, which met resistance from the Theatre's African American actors. Wright, the Theatre's publicity agent, was enthralled by the idea of creating a "genuine Negro theatre" that would "lead [the actors] toward serious dramatics."[1] The actors, however, wanted "a play that will make the public love us"—a vaudeville, according to Wright, filled with "stereotypes of clowns, mammies, razors, dice, watermelon, and cotton fields" (*AH*, 114, 115). The actors indicted the social drama as "indecent" and untruthful. "I lived in the South," one actor claimed, "and I never saw any chain gangs" (*AH*, 114). Frustrated with their myopia, Wright "felt—but only temporarily—that perhaps the whites were right, that Negroes were children and would never grow up" (*AH*, 115). When Wright sided with the Jewish director, the "children" threatened him; a black girl publicly denounced him as an "Uncle Tom"; and "a huge, fat, black woman, a blues singer, found an excuse to pass [him] as often as possible and she hissed under her breath in a menacing sing-song: 'Lawd, Ah sho hates a white man's nigger'" (*AH*, 116).

Wright's account portrays the political conflicts that the Federal Theatre Project—one of Roosevelt's social relief programs for cultural workers—faced in creating art for the people. The tensions that wracked the Chicago Project

American Literature, Volume 75, Number 2 (June 2003): pp. 395–425. Copyright © The Duke University Press.

73

are illuminated by Mark Naison's discussion of its Harlem counterpart: theater that best appealed to an audience of Southern migrants was "bawdy, funky, and humorous entertainment" drawing on "the *existing* folk culture of the black urban masses."[2] Many Communists involved with the Project, however, objected to the stereotypes of African Americans that vaudeville perpetuated. In promoting social drama of African American life, the Communists hoped to educate and politicize while bringing serious art to the people. But class-conscious art and African American folk culture, as seen in Wright's account of the Project, were frequently polarized.

Moreover, for Wright, the opposition was gendered. In *American Hunger,* he channels his resentment toward the actors into a misogynist, paternalist gaze under which they are reduced to rebellious, ignorant "children"; meanwhile, the folk culture that he repudiates in favor of social realism is embodied in the "huge, fat" female blues singer. This moment in *American Hunger* shores up dominant narratives of Wright that frequently yoke his denigration of folk culture, his misogyny (especially toward African American women), and his Marxist perspective, which he retained long after leaving the Communist Party in 1937.

Wright's public antifolk, antiwoman dogmatism stems from his exchange with Zora Neale Hurston in their reviews of each other's books. In *New Masses,* the leftist journal of culture and politics, Wright lambasted the folk romanticism of Hurston's *Their Eyes Were Watching God.* When the first edition of Wright's collection of novellas, *Uncle Tom's Children,* appeared (1938), Hurston returned the favor in a review for the *Saturday Review.* She linked the overwhelming violence in the novellas with their hypermasculine perspective: "There is lavish killing here, perhaps enough to satisfy all male black readers." She also mocked Wright's "tone-deaf" rendition of African American Southern dialect and decried his Communist didacticism, which she paraphrased as "state responsibility for everything and individual responsibility for nothing, not even feeding oneself. And march!"[3]

Hurston's critique has been amplified by recent feminist criticism that analyzes the painful limitations of Wright's representations of African American women, which continue to be associated with his Marxism. In her analysis of *Native Son,* for example, Trudier Harris claims that Wright's adherence to Communism is partly to blame for his inability to conceive of Bessie's agency.[4] This argument resonates with Sherley Anne Williams's assertion that Wright's representations of African American women in the novellas of *Uncle Tom's Children* are "subsumed under larger political or philosophical themes."[5] Discussing Wright's "pathological" treatment of female characters, Nagueyalti Warren also examines *Uncle Tom's Children* and finds that the portrait of Sarah, one of its protagonists, is "grounded in paternalistic, male chauvinist, materialist perceptions of woman as man's sexual property."[6]

It is no coincidence that *Uncle Tom's Children* holds a prominent position in African American feminist scholarship, for among Wright's published works, it features his only two female protagonists, both of them African American.[7] Sarah, of "Long Black Song," and Sue, of "Bright and Morning Star," have been read as reiterating Jezebel and Mammy stereotypes that justify the rape and exploitation of black women. My point here is not to dismiss feminist criticism of Wright but rather to engage with its uncritical anti-Communism, which has led to grossly oversimplified views of his gender(ed) politics.[8] Marxism, nationalism, gender, and sexuality were fundamentally interlinked for Wright, but not quite in the way these critics would have it. It was precisely in some of his most pro-Communist work that Wright developed a nuanced critique of patriarchy in conjunction with racialized, capitalist exploitation. Attempting to conceptualize radical praxis, Wright grappled with the ideological contradictions between Communism and black nationalism. In doing so, he found it necessary to rearticulate both Jim Crow society's and the Left's racialized conceptions of masculinity and femininity. In my own feminist rereading of *Uncle Tom's Children*, I will argue that the novellas initially espouse but then move away from a masculine aesthetic, in tandem with Wright's evolving representations of political consciousness. *Uncle Tom's Children* ultimately critiques the limitations of individualistic race rebellion, which is associated with black masculinism; in the latter novellas, Wright re-presents the transcendental perspective outlined in his "Blueprint for Negro Writing" (1937), which advocates the synthesis of black cultural nationalism and Communist integrationism. Significantly, a primary site for engendering this transcendental perspective is rural, working-class (folk), black, female subjectivity. Understanding how and why Wright articulates these gender(ed) politics provides a more nuanced perspective on his work and a much needed corrective to narrow forms of identity politics.

Communism, Black Nationalism, and Manly Men

The connections drawn in recent scholarship between Wright's Marxism and his antifolk aesthetics reiterate larger discourses around the Communist movement and its supposed role in stifling the development of African American writers and, more broadly, African American culture. This thesis has been forcefully advanced by Wilson Record and Harold Cruse, both of whom invoke Wright as a prominent example of political naïveté and subsequent illumination.[9] The Communist Party undoubtedly constrained Wright's artistic career at times and opportunistically touted his accomplishments as an African American. Yet it also fostered his literary talents through the John Reed Club and journals like *New Masses* and *International Literature*. Furthermore, exaggerating Wright's "naïveté" obfuscates his agency in critically engaging Marxism. He could be mechanistic in his thoughts on culture and class, as passages from *Twelve Million Black Voices* show (1941), but in other texts, Wright transforms Marxism to account for African American histories and subjectivities.

Uncle Tom's Children and "Blueprint for Negro Writing" are just such texts, addressing the stultifying opposition between class-conscious art and folk culture that plagued the Federal Theatre Project. Wright most clearly expressed his thoughts on this matter in "Blueprint," published soon after he had drafted the bulk of the *Uncle Tom's Children* novellas. With its analysis of contradictions within black nationalism, "Blueprint" crystallizes the structure of feeling that was African American literary radicalism in the thirties.[10] Wright discerns nationalism's "warping" influences insofar as the movement is the product of segregation, given official voice by "cowardly and incompetent" "Negro institutions." However, he also extols nationalism's "living and powerful" manifestations in African American folk culture, asserting that everyday, informal networks and forms of knowledge are the bases for "the emergence of a new culture in the shell of the old," the beginning of a revolutionary process whereby "the civilization that engenders that suffering [of the black masses] is doomed" ("B," 1383). Wright's indictment of "specious and blatant nationalism" ("B," 1382) thus does not dismiss or denigrate African American culture but, rather, targets the black bourgeoisie, whose members accept the racialized system of capitalist exploitation and promote "a Negro way of life" within it ("B," 1383). However, African American writers cannot simply dispel this ideology, Wright asserts, for it functions in the Althusserean sense as the means through which people imagine their relationships to the social totality: "Negro writers who seek to mould or influence the consciousness of the Negro people must address their messages to them through the ideologies and attitudes fostered in this warping way of life" ("B," 1383). Potentially revolutionary and reactionary, nationalism should not be accepted uncritically but *"possess[ed]* and *under[stood]"* and thereby transformed ("B," 1383). To this end, the strength and resilience of black collective history inherent in folklore can be "mould[ed]" with historical materialism. And by effecting this synthesis, African American writers can create the values, myths, and symbols "by which [the] race is to struggle, live and die" ("B," 1384).[11]

"Blueprint" articulates the motivating spirit behind the novellas, four of which were published together as *Uncle Tom's Children* in 1938, followed by a new edition in 1940 that includes the novella "Bright and Morning Star" and the autobiographical sketch "The Ethics of Living Jim Crow." Critics have observed that Wright structured the novellas to cohere, with each successive protagonist depicting a more developed social consciousness, a progression that reflects Wright's own evolving thought on black will. More specifically, this progression instantiates the transcendence of nationalism—its transformation by, and of, Marxism—outlined in "Blueprint."[12]

Of special concern is that this political progression is predicated upon conceptions of masculinity and femininity in ways that are elided or only implied by the more abstract "Blueprint."[13] Sexual ideologies were central to narratives of working-class solidarity, as Robin D. G. Kelley observes in his discussion of African American Communist poets:

> [W]hereas racial themes might have been in conflict with the Communists' version of proletarian realism, these black artists— including most male writers outside the Party—found common ground on the terrain of gender. Proletarian realism consciously evinced masculine images and defined class *struggle* as a male preserve.[14]

Writers on the Left frequently associated the revolutionary might of the proletariat with heterosexual male virility, contrasted with a doomed capitalist class figured in terms of diseased, effete, and decadent homosexuality or femininity. Although marriage, family, and sexuality figured prominently in men's proletarian fiction, they were generally metaphors for the larger history of class struggle, rather than actual structures of oppression and sites of liberation for women.[15] Such trends in the literary Left seemingly would have strengthened the link between Wright's political philosophy and his sexism.

However, through the dialectical progression of political consciousness that *Uncle Tom's Children* presents, proletarian masculinism is significantly revised and critiqued. In "The Ethics of Living Jim Crow" and the first three novellas in the collection, masculinism is linked not with collective, class-based action but with individual, racial rebellion. The turf battles waged against the white boys by the young Wright in "Ethics" serve as a leitmotif for the first three novellas. Big Boy's coming of age in "Big Boy Leaves Home" involves killing a white soldier in self-defense after trespassing on land belonging to the soldier's father; in "Down by the Riverside," Mann shoots the white townsman Heartfield, whose boat he has taken to save his wife; and in "Long Black Song," Silas fatally confronts and stands his ground against a lynch mob storming his property. "Long Black Song" shifts the terrain of militant struggle through the subjectivity of Silas's wife, Sarah, who dreams of a utopia in which black and white men are not alienated from themselves and each other. The last two novellas, "Fire and Cloud" and "Bright and Morning Star," explore Communist struggle undertaken by cross-racial alliances as the means to achieve this utopian vision. Concomitant with this political shift in the second half of *Uncle Tom's Children*, African American female subjectivity becomes the terrain on which Wright negotiates the contradictions between Communist integrationism and black nationalism. Ties to folk culture and community, seen as the province of black women, serve not as the basis for accommodationism but for a new radicalism that infuses class struggle with the history and experiences of African Americans in the rural South. Black female sexuality and motherhood provide the primary tropes and modes of experience through which Wright critiques reductive conceptions of both nationalism and Marxism. In doing so, he does not merely subordinate the Woman Question to other political themes; rather, *Uncle Tom's Children* insists that issues of gender—especially those pertaining to African American working-class women—are integral to conceptualizing revolutionary praxis and subjectivity.

Moreover, Wright's representation of African American female radicalism in *Uncle Tom's Children* was not an isolated phenomenon within a male-dominated Left. As I will show, his conceptualization of the revolutionary potential of folk culture was critically influenced by the Scottsboro trials of 1931 through 1937, which were instrumental in reconfiguring the gendered terrain of working-class struggle. In the international antilynching campaigns that accompanied the trials, black and white women on the Left countered the masculinist rhetoric that erased their agency in fighting racialized economic exploitation. By examining the sociohistorical contexts that encouraged Wright to depict African American, rural, female subjectivity as the primary site of political development, I will demonstrate that *Uncle Tom's Children* is symptomatic of larger struggles within the Left to account for working women's histories and experiences.

Big Boy and Little Mann:
Initial Meditations on the Will of Black Folk

Uncle Tom's Children begins with an epigraph that presents both context and call for the "Newer Negro":

> The post Civil War household word among Negroes—"He's an Uncle Tom!"—which denoted reluctant toleration for the cringing type who knew his place before white folk, has been supplanted by a new word from another generation which says:— "Uncle Tom is dead!"[16]

Ostensibly generational, accommodationism is soon shown to be gendered: black women expect sons and husbands to accommodate themselves to white supremacy in order to survive. In "The Ethics of Living Jim Crow," Wright reports that after soundly thrashing him for battling the white boys who live across the tracks, his mother tries to impart "gems of Jim Crow wisdom" (*UTC*, 2). Likewise, in the novellas, after Big Boy shoots a white man, his mother, another instrument of Jim Crow socialization, can do little more than reprove him for missing school; Sarah tries to dissuade

Silas from confronting the posse that comes to avenge the death of the white man whom Silas has killed; and the Reverend Taylor's wife in "Fire and Cloud," with "lungs suspiring in one gasp of amazed helplessness," is afraid to help him confer with the Communists, lest they jeopardize her son's future (*UTC*, 170). Accommodationist black men are also feminized: Rev. Taylor's nemesis, Deacon Smith, meets his fate at the hands of a "fat sister" who slaps him. Killing the legacy of Uncle Tom appears to be the duty of native sons but not black wives, mothers, or daughters.

Exploring African American subject formation under systemic, racialized violence, Wright initially links individual rebellion to the psychosocial development of the African American male, allegorized by the movement from Big Boy in the first novella to Mann in the second. "Big Boy Leaves Home" is the coming-of-age story of African American boys whose recognition of the Law of the White Father entails killing or being killed. This entrance into manhood is precipitated when Big Boy and his friends sneak into a swimming hole on white-owned land where they are caught skinny-dipping by the wife of the property owner's son. The son, a soldier, fulfills his duty to state, property, and propriety by fatally shooting two of the children. Big Boy, however, wrests the gun away and kills the soldier, thereby saving himself and his friend Bobo.

The crux of the novella lies not in the depiction of racist terrorism, however, but in the birth of militant racial consciousness. Preparing to flee to Chicago, Big Boy hides in a kiln, where the raw material of his experiences is fired and hardened into a new subjectivity; foreshadowing Bigger in his prison cell, Big Boy reauthorizes himself. At first he longs for the ties of community, family, and home, symbolized by the womb-like kiln built by the collective labor of black kin, and by his mother's corn pone, which he saves so that he and Bobo can eat together. However, as Big Boy reflects on the day's events, he realizes that he must sever these maternal bonds in order to survive. First and foremost, this entails ridding himself of his mother's survival strategies, whereby he would be subjected to the ideological apparatuses of the Southern state, epitomized by the school:

> Yeah, he shoulda went on t school tha mawnin, like Ma told im t do. But, hell, who wouldnt git tireda awways drivin a guy t school! Tha wuz the big trouble, awways drivin a guy t school. He wouldn't be in all this trouble now ef it wuznt fer that Gawddam school! (*UTC*, 49–50)

"[D]emolishing the little red school house" in his mind, Big Boy dismisses any vestigial guilt by imagining the headlines he would create facing the lynch mob single-handedly: "NIGGER KILLS DOZEN OF MOB

BEFO LYNCHED! Er mebbe theyd say: TRAPPED NIGGER SLAYS
TWENTY BEFO KILLED! He smiled a little. Tha wouldnt be so bad,
would it?" (*UTC*, 50). Dreams of self-made martyrdom become more
compelling than communal comfort in corn pone, a realization confirmed
by witnessing Bobo's lynching; the sheer brutality of white supremacist
domination renders effete all attempts to preserve ties of kinship. In order
to make a new life for himself in Chicago, Big Boy must repress knowledge
of Jim Crow savagery and betray all memories of home: "Once he heard the
crow of a rooster. It made him think of home, of ma and pa. He thought he
remembered hearing somewhere that the house had burned, but could not
remember where. . . . It all seemed unreal now" (*UTC*, 60).

Like Big Boy, the protagonist of "Down by the Riverside" transgresses the
boundaries of white property and is driven to defend himself through the individual acts of violence that Big Boy valorizes. But as his name implies, Mann
is the head of a household who does not have Big Boy's "freedom" to fend for
himself. His militance is articulated through patriarchal family relations that
perpetuate the theme of phallocentric, racial struggle. Mann's duty as husband
and father entails confronting and killing his white counterpart, Heartfield,
whose boat Mann has taken in order to get his pregnant wife to the hospital.
Unwittingly stopping at Heartfield's residence to ask for help, Mann is forced
to shoot the white man as the latter's son looks on. In doing so, Mann defends
his family but is unable to prevent the deaths of his wife and unborn child,
who have been denied medical treatment too long. Mercilessly conscripted
into flood relief, Mann returns through fatal coincidence to the Heartfield
house. This time, he is put in the position of having to kill Heartfield's son in
order to save himself, but Mann hesitates and loses his opportunity. Emascu-
lated, he ends up rescuing the remaining members of Heartfield's family under
the orders of the boy, whom Mann obeys "[l]ike a little child" (*UTC*, 112).
Heartfield's son then exacts vengeance for his father's death, identifying Mann
to National Guardsmen who shoot him to death.

Depicting Mann's inability to live up to his name, "Down by the Riverside"
allegorizes the futility of the type of rebellion into which Big Boy is inducted.
Although Mann kills the white property holder, Heartfield's son assumes authority and unmans the guilty "nigger" by interpellating him as such. Heartfield's
wife and son manage to survive—due to Mann's conscripted labor, no less—
while Mann's own wife and unborn child are killed by racist state flood relief
policy. Mann can be said to redeem himself at the end, when "fear subside[s]
into numbness," enabling him to "die before he would let [the soldiers] kill him"
(*UTC*, 123). With this final assertion of resistance, Mann articulates the will to
die, but Wright's masculinist naturalism prevents him from capturing the will
to live.

The Sexual Politics of Transcending Nationalism

Admittedly "dissatisfied" with his portrait of black will in "Riverside," Wright "tried to say the same thing in yet another way in 'Long Black Song'" (*AH*, 88–89). Thematically similar to the first two, this third novella continues to explore the meaning and aesthetics of African American social protest through individual, racial militance. Like the protagonists of the two previous novellas, Silas resorts to killing the white men who would keep him in his place, but his stand against a lynch mob represents a greater triumph than Big Boy's or Mann's defiance of Jim Crow force. As a relatively success-ful cotton farmer and landholder, Silas articulates most fully the systemic racism that prevents him from providing for and protecting his family.

Feminist critics tend to represent Silas's heroism as the focus of the sto-ry, even as they discuss the implications of Wright's decision to make Silas's wife, Sarah, the main protagonist and narrator of "Song." Consequently, less attention has been given to how "Song" shifts the trajectory and terrain of *Uncle Tom's Children*'s gendered politics of radicalism. In fact, the point of the novella is not Silas's militance but Sarah's protest against the perpetuation of racial warfare and her utopian vision of racial harmony within a social order based on freedom rather than necessity. African American female desire and plenitude, rooted in folk culture, are the basis for this alternative to mascu-linist nationalism. In adapting the expression of folk culture to a critique of patriarchy and petit bourgeois values, "Song" offers a model for embodying Wright's "Blueprint" of radical black aesthetics.

At the outset of "Song," Sarah is alone in the house, tending her baby, because Silas has left for town to sell his cotton and purchase goods and more land. The physical ache of loneliness coupled with the baby's banging on a clock transports Sarah to an earlier time with a former lover, Tom, who left to fight in World War I. As the baby continues to bang away, she further remembers her lovemaking with Tom, which she contrasts with her marriage to Silas, who "had not quite filled that hole" left by Tom's departure (*UTC*, 129). In the midst of these reveries, a white salesman of clock-graphophones enters, and in attempting to sell one of his contrap-tions to Sarah, he seduces and rapes her in a scene that renders her volition ambiguous. When Silas returns, he discovers Sarah's infidelity and kills the white man. Sarah unsuccessfully pleads with Silas to escape retribution and leave with her, but he remains to die defending his property against a lynch mob.

Contrasting Sarah's inarticulateness and weakness with Silas's eloquence and heroism, critics have frequently assumed that Wright has created yet an-other damning portrait of African American women. Sarah herself realizes the ethical and political dimensions of betraying a man who was as good to her as any black man could be to a black woman. Most of the black women worked in the fields as croppers. But Silas had given her her own home, and that was more than many others had done for their women. . . . He had worked hard and saved his money and bought a farm so he could grow his own crops like white men. (*UTC*, 147)

Williams points to Sarah's penitence as the pinnacle of her moral and political growth, since Sarah understands that

she has betrayed a rare personage in early Afro-American experience, a black man who has succeeded in acquiring the legitimate economic means to care for his family almost as well as the average white man. And most significantly, she has betrayed the collective dream, the idea that given a decent chance at economic stability and upward mobility black people could build stable families and viable communities.[17]

However, the novella does not equate Silas's desire to be "as good as any white man" with the possibility of strengthening the bonds of family and community. Silas's emulation of the petit bourgeois husband-provider, who can keep his wife out of the fields and in the home, produces Sarah's isolation. From the beginning of "Song," we see that Sarah's "long hope of white bright days and [her] deep desire of dark black nights" (*UTC*, 129) are unfulfilled because Silas is more concerned with accumulating land and commodities than with human relations. Although Sarah primarily experiences her resulting lack of personal fulfillment as sexual hunger, her desire is symptomatic of the alienation wrought by Silas's petit bourgeois ethos and by warfare and displacement as men like Tom are drafted into the army. Sarah laments not only the literal but also the social death effected by war; her comment that "go[ing] so far away from home was a kind of death in itself" refers both to World War I and the Great Migration that it helped to fuel (*UTC*, 127).

Sarah also rejects the racial militance that Silas eloquently articulates and enacts. After killing the salesman, Silas curses the whites who "ain never give no black man a chance," and he vows to "be hard like they is" (*UTC*, 152). Yet once he resolves to go down defending what is rightfully his, rage suddenly turns to pathos: "But Laws, Ah don wanna be this way! It don mean nothin! Yuh die ef yuh fight! Yuh die ef yuh don fight! Either way yuh die n it don mean nothing . . ." (*UTC*, 153). Silas's own comprehension of the ultimate futility of his heroism is amplified by Sarah, who imagines the cycle of racial warfare as "the old river of blood" that Silas follows, "cursing and whimpering" and "knowing that it meant nothing" (*UTC*, 154). Sarah thus underscores the emptiness of the masculinist racial militance that *Uncle Tom's Children* has so far upheld as the only means of resistance.

Over against the oppressive, alienating conditions that such militance perpetuates, Sarah envisions a utopic alternative:

> Somehow, men, black men and white men, land and houses, green cornfields and grey skies, gladness and dreams, were all a part of that which made life good. Yes, somehow they were linked, like the spokes in a spinning wagon wheel. She felt they were. She knew they were. (*UTC*, 154)

Sarah's vision draws from her experiences of sexual fulfillment, as well as her consciousness of "that which made life good." The lyrical images of green cornfields and grey skies, which represent the realization of unalienated existence, echo "the long gladness of green cornfields in summer" and "the deep dream of sleeping grey skies in winter" associated with loving Tom (*UTC*, 129). In other words, Sarah generalizes from the wholeness she has felt most strongly with Tom to imagine how all aspects of human life could enable "men" to actualize their dreams. This vision begins to shift the political terrain of *Uncle Tom's Children* in two important ways. First, it hints at the possibility of interracial cooperation, as opposed to segregation; second, it inchoately perceives the social field as a unity of interconnected levels rather than isolated moments. This latter perspective gropes toward "a nationalism whose reason for being lies in . . . the consciousness of the interdependence of people in modern society" ("B," 1384). The spinning wagon wheel Sarah invokes is a folk symbol of such a holistic consciousness.

It is precisely because Wright adopts this perspective in "Long Black Song" that we cannot reduce Sarah's striving for self-realization to nostalgia for an unadulterated folk way of life.[18] Wright dispels such notions by showing that the rural South is inextricably part of the world system. International warfare and the economic structures of Southern agriculture shape Sarah's social consciousness, as African American men are drafted to fight in Europe, raise crops for exchange in the market, and leave their homes in search of better pay in industry. Sarah's personal longings for love and connection therefore constitute a political as well as emotional response to the anomie that arises out of racialized, patriarchal systems of accumulation. Protest against Silas's militance rather than penitence for wronging her man marks the zenith of Sarah's development and constitutes the narrative thrust of the novella, which concludes with her resounding cry, "Naw, Gawd!" as Silas is destroyed by the posse (*UTC*, 156).

Of course, Sarah's political consciousness is circumscribed by her disposition and the conditions in which she lives. Beyond voicing her lone note of protest against racial warfare, she can do no more than flee "blindly across the fields" (*UTC*, 156). This literal blindness echoes the figurative one in her inchoate sense that *"somehow,"* black and white men are linked: "She felt it when she breathed and knew it when she looked. *But she could not say how*" (*UTC*, 154, my emphases). The consequences of Sarah's isolation are such that she is bereft of any opportunity to understand better why she thinks as she does or what the implications of her thoughts might be. This impasse reverses the trajectory of her development as a historical subject; political consciousness, which comes out of the physical ache of desire, now returns to the body: "[W]hen she thought hard about it it became all mixed up, like milk spilling suddenly. Or else it knotted in her throat and chest in a hard aching lump, like the one she felt now. She touched her face to the baby's face and cried again" (*UTC*, 154).

Nevertheless, acknowledging Wright's paternalistic circumscription of Sarah within the boundaries of a "simple peasant woman" should not blind us to the ways that her experiences of desire and domesticity enable her to critique Silas's petit bourgeois values and the racial violence that sustains them. Like the mothers of Mann, Big Boy, and the young Wright of "Ethics," Sarah espouses a communal-familial ethos, in contrast to the individualistic militance of the male protagonists. However, the integrationist tactics formerly associated with the black mother are here unmoored from accommodationism, as Sarah imagines black men not as subordinates but as equals to white men. Drawing on rural folk values, specifically the black peasant woman's sense of "that which made life good," she challenges the naturalness and permanence of segregation. Consequently, she is able to imagine, however inchoately, an alternative to the anomie of modern life. As Wright wrote of "Long Black Song" in his unpublished preface to *Uncle Tom's Children*, "it was as if the foundation upon which future building could go on had been discovered. What was that?"[19] If Wright could not yet know the exact shape this future building would take, we can hardly expect Sarah to imagine it. Nonetheless, Sarah's narrative lays the groundwork for the last two novellas to explore the possibilities of social revolution through sustained, collective resistance.

Bringing the Revolutionists Home: From Uncle Tom to Aunt Sue

In the first half of *Uncle Tom's Children*, Wright was concerned with "tell[ing] the truth from the Negro point of view," for "the lives of fifteen million Negroes in America were practically unknown. The most significant thing about the whole question is not so much the brutality of their lives as that millions of people do not even know their lives are brutal, nor why."[20] With the second half of *Uncle Tom's Children*, Wright would continue to flesh out the conditions that brutalized both black and white Americans, but he further endeavored to create a semiology for radically transforming these conditions:

> There is a gap here, a sort of "no man's land" between the Negro I see daily and the Negro I see in the revolutionary struggle. The courage of the revolutionist, its interior mechanism, is not of Big Boy, or Mann, or Sarah, either singly or collectively. Really the revolutionists are another people, a people apart, living in terms, images, symbols all their own; terms of the future no doubt. These revolutionists have not come home to us; they do not as yet act or live within the folk consciousness of our lives.[21]

What remained to be done, in other words, was to find terms, images, and symbols that would mediate the realities of the present and the goals of the future, the ideological conflicts between Communism and black nationalism, and the political and psychological differences between revolutionaries and the masses.

"Fire and Cloud" marks an important step in Wright's development of aesthetic strategies for such mediations; it symbolically enacts his thesis that "[Negro writers] must *possess* and *understand*" nationalism in order to transcend it. As discussed earlier, Wright asserts that the "warping" aspects of black nationalism cannot be dismissed as false consciousness, as they are the means through which African Americans understand their relationships to the social order, and to each other. Wright sees the African American church as the foremost ideological apparatus, and in "Fire and Cloud" he engages the beliefs and symbols of its Christianity to show the need for interracial working-class alliances to contest Jim Crow regimes.[22] The socialist conversion of Rev. Taylor, the story's protagonist, is based on and transformative of African American Christianity.[23]

Equally important, however, to Wright's representation of interracial solidarity is a version of proletarian masculinism. Taylor is not only a spiritual and political leader but also a farmer and father who exemplifies a specifically male ideal of the worker-hero. Walking past some fields on his way home, he reminisces about the good, muscular work of plowing. Undergoing his political conversion after being whipped by the white mayor's lackeys for his intransigence, Taylor reflects on his hard-earned wisdom in a moment of male bonding with his son. Within the march of poor blacks and whites at the story's conclusion, racial boundaries dissolve, but the patriarchal structure of Taylor's family is distinctly maintained: "[Taylor] felt [his wife] clinging to his sleeve. [His son] was peering ahead" (*UTC*, 220). Rev. Taylor's wife remains a virtual nonentity, while the son to whom he has passed on his wisdom is positioned as the heir apparent of the struggle.

Nevertheless, it is an unnamed "fat sister" who represents the revolutionary black masses; when Deacon Smith refuses to acknowledge the parishioners' decision to march in demand for food, she slaps him across the face (but is dragged away before she can inflict further damage). It is also she who reveals the power of folk culture to illuminate the meaning of their suffering, as she leads the marchers in song: *"[T]he sign of the fire by night/ N the sign of the cloud by day"* translates Sarah's "hope of white bright days" and "desire of dark black nights" into symbols of class warfare (*UTC*, 218). Both Taylor and the sister represent the emergence of African American peasants as historical subjects who meld the tenets of class struggle with their worldview as the descendants of slaves. At the same time, the African American female body is once again the repository for folk culture, as well as the substitute for African American female subjectivity. Although ambivalent, this recognition of African American women's revolutionary energies sets the stage for "Bright and Morning Star," the culmination of radicalism in *Uncle Tom's Children*.

While acknowledging that Sue, the protagonist of "Star," is the most articulate of Wright's female characters, feminist critics have emphasized that she remains subject to Wright's sexism. Williams, for example, reads "An Sue" as a Mammy figure vis-á-vis the young white Communist, Reva. However, as I will argue, Sue's relationship with Reva, her struggles to define her faith and alliances, and her subsequent heroism challenge masculinist representations of black militance and proletarian solidarity. In order to account for the radicalism of this last novella's gender(ed) strategies, I now want to examine the ideologies of working-class solidarity and black womanhood that Wright incorporates and rearticulates. Rather than a Mammy, Sue is Wright's rendition of a Popular Front symbol—the radical black mother—that arose out of a historic moment, formed in part by the U.S. Communist Party's involvement in the Scottsboro trial.

At the heart of the Scottsboro case were the lives of nine African American boys who came of age in the Southern penitentiary system after two white women falsely accused them of rape. The boys had been riding a Chattanooga train bound for Memphis on 25 March 1931, when state authorities indiscriminately herded them off, in response to the claims of white hoboes that a "bunch of Negroes" had started a fight and wounded them. Victoria Price and Ruby Bates, who had also been found on the train, then asserted that they had been raped by the youths so that Price would not be charged with escorting Bates, a minor, across state lines. Two weeks later, eight of the nine boys were sentenced to death by a series of all-white juries; the juvenile status of the ninth boy, Roy Wright, provided grounds for a mistrial. As Dan T. Carter observes, such legalized lynching was nothing new in the South, but the nature of the trials—the youth and numbers of the condemned, the summariness with which they had been found guilty, and the extremity of the punishment—catapulted the Scottsboro boys to national attention.[24]

The Communist Party's defense of the nine boys through its legal arm, the International Labor Defense (ILD), was instrumental in moving African Americans leftward in the thirties. Although African Americans never became Communists in substantial numbers, the Communist Party nonetheless achieved an unprecedented level of prominence in African American communities.[25] Eager to increase its black membership and strike a blow to the white supremacist South, the Communist Party and its allies waged intense ideological warfare.[26] In particular, a Communist "Scottsboro rhetoric" became one important weapon, which William Maxwell identifies in his discussion of Langston Hughes's literary contribution to the campaign. This rhetoric arose in response to the triangulation of race and gender relations that justified lynching by constructing white men as the virile defenders of virtuous white women against black rapists. As part of its defense of the Scottsboro boys, the ILD emphasized Bates's and Price's backgrounds as prostitutes to discredit their allegations of rape, while calling on black and white workers to unite in support of the boys. The Southern "lynching triangle" was thus countered by a Communist "homosocial triangle" as African American and white male workers bonded through negatively libidinizing white women. In addition to negating the possibility of white women's radicalism, this rhetoric erased altogether the presence of African American women.[27]

From the outset, however, this rhetoric received significant pressure from black and white women inspired by the heroism of the Scottsboro boys' mothers. In making their sons' trials the Communist Party's cause célèbre of the 1930s, the work of these women cannot be underestimated. Securing their permission to defend their sons was a coup for the ILD in their battle with the NAACP over legal representation. As the Scottsboro mothers Janie Patterson, Ida Norris, Viola Montgomery, Ada Wright, and Mamie Williams marched on the Capitol, spoke to the press on behalf of their sons, and toured the United States and Europe to raise awareness and campaign funds, they drew attention to the need for interracial solidarity against American fascism. Recounting how her son Andy "was put all by himself in a solitary cell next to white women prisoners so he can be framed some more," Ada Wright called for "all the workers and the farmers and all the Negro people to get behind the International Labor Defense."[28] It would be easy to read these women as pawns of Communist Party opportunism, but it would be both unhistorical and paternalistic to assume their lack of agency. Most of the mothers became fiery orators who "enthusiastically embraced the Communist program as [they] understood it."[29] Because of their fortitude—Ada Wright was even arrested in Czechoslovakia for her activism—they came to exemplify a new heroine of the Left, the radical black mother, whose "likeness [was] made familiar by pictures published everywhere."[30]

Along with the ILD photojournal *Labor Defender*, *Working Woman*—the Communist Party's periodical for female industrial, agricultural, and domestic workers—was instrumental in publicizing the work of the Scottsboro mothers. From 1933 to 1934, *Working Woman* featured the mothers regularly in order to generate readers' support for the Scottsboro boys' defense. The magazine's presentation of the mothers coincided with a larger shift in leftist discourse about women's radicalism: as the Communist Party segued from proletarianism to populism, "revolutionary girls became partisan mothers," for "images of stable family values anchored by the working-class woman as sacrificing mother" helped the Communist Party form alliances with middle-class organizations.[31] The Scottsboro mothers were often placed within this patriarchal framework, depicted as mothers who had sacrificed for their sons and were now being sacrificed along with them to the fascist South.[32] However, *Working Woman* also exhorted black and white mothers to be militants by publishing the Scottsboro mothers' rousing words. Mrs. Montgomery, for example, was quoted as saying: "They think by sending Heywoad [sic] to the chair they will stop the mothers from fighting. But these are lies because if all the mothers felt like I do about this in place of stopping the fight it will be just begun."[33]

In April 1933 Ruby Bates further promoted interracial solidarity when she recanted her charges of rape. Previously discredited by the defense as a white female prostitute and capitalist stooge, Bates was now championed by the Communist Party as "a Southern white worker."[34] Describing the shacks, mud, and litter of the hometown where Bates and Price had worked in the cotton mills, Left journalist Mary Heaton Vorse represented both women as products of the living conditions that degraded the working class as a whole.[35] Bates herself wrote: "If we, fellow-workers, let the bosses murder our boys it will mean a great blow and a great disgrace for the working class."[36] Formerly marked and marred by hypersexuality, Bates's feminine difference from an implicitly masculine norm had to be erased to bring her into the fold of "fellow" workers.

Nonetheless, Bates's work with the Scottsboro mothers undeniably presented a specifically feminized version of interracial working-class solidarity that refuted the homosocial rhetoric of black-white bonding. Once Bates joined the Scottsboro mothers on their tour, images of their marching, riding, and standing together reiterated the challenge to masculinist conceptions of interracial labor solidarity. This challenge would not have been lost, especially on Communist women like Louise Thompson, the prominent African American organizer then serving as executive secretary of the National Scottsboro Action Committee. In her report on the 1933 March on the Capitol for the release of the Scottsboro boys, Thompson wrote: "Janie Patterson and Ruby Bates, the vanguard of the marchers, are the living symbol of that increased unity [between the black and white masses]."[37] In the accompanying photo, Thompson herself is shown arm in arm with Bates. While not speaking explicitly to the fact that black and white women, herself among them, were redefining the terms of solidarity, Thompson's text hardly requires us to read between the lines to see that this was the case. The "vanguard" and "living symbol" of the revolutionary masses, black and white women radicals refuted the racialized, patriarchal rhetoric that marginalized their work within the Left.

In the same year that Janie Patterson and Ruby Bates led the march in Washington, D.C., Wright commenced his engagement with Communism when he joined Chicago's John Reed Club, the Communist Party's organization to cultivate proletarian writers. Given Scottsboro's prominence, it is not surprising that Wright would have incorporated it into his work. However, on the advice of Whit Burnett of *Story* magazine, Wright expunged allusions to the Scottsboro boys and the ILD from "Bright and Morning Star."[38] Yet Scottsboro remains a subtext in the novella, which revises the rhetoric of proletarian masculinism to recognize the struggles of women radicals like Patterson, Bates, and Thompson. In "Star," male bonding is not the cement of worker solidarity, as the black organizer, Johnny-Boy, is betrayed by the white stool pigeon, Booker. Instead, such unity is depicted in Sue and Reva's empowering, if problematic, mother-daughter relationship. More compellingly, "Star" illuminates the development of revolutionary consciousness through experiences specific to Sue, a rural, Southern, African American mother and domestic worker initially peripheral to the Party activity of her sons. In contrast to her sons' monolithic Communism that uncritically privileges class over race and gender, Sue constantly negotiates and eventually transcends the contradictions between black nationalism and Communist integrationism. It is precisely by transforming and uniting both ideologies into a synthetic perspective that Sue saves the Party from being destroyed by the state.

At the outset of "Star," we see a version of the sacrificing mother who serves as the repository of family values, precisely the patriarchal construct that Rabinowitz identifies as the Left's dominant image of Popular Front womanhood. From her mother's lips, Sue has imbibed the spirituals that sustain her as she endures the hardships of farm work and domestic service. This matrilineal religious heritage has reinforced Sue's sense of self as bound up with sacrifice: "Long hours of scrubbing floors for a few cents a day had taught her who Jesus was, what a great boon it was to cling to Him, to be like Him and suffer without a mumbling word" (*UTC*, 224). However, Sue's sons, Johnny-Boy and Sug, reject her religion when they join the Communist Party. She is distressed by their sacrilege, "[b]ut she had loved them, even as she loved them now; bleeding, her heart had followed them" (*UTC*, 225).

And a follower Sue remains, for as an African American woman and mother she occupies a subordinate, auxiliary position vis-á-vis the male-dominated Party. Her contribution to the struggle takes place not in the field but at home, "washing and ironing to feed Johnny-Boy and Sug so they could do party work." Despite the drudgery of domestic work, Sue accepts the sexual division of labor as "natural" (*UTC*, 223, 228).

As a result of her experiences of work and motherhood, Sue tries to balance Christianity and Communism in her worldview. When her work and worry about her sons become nearly too much to bear, Sue cannot help but return to the spirituals that she has supposedly renounced for Communism. Indeed, it is through Christianity that she had embraced Communism in the first place: "The wrongs and sufferings of black men had taken the place of Him nailed to the Cross; the meager beginnings of the party had become another Resurrection" (*UTC*, 225). Similarly, Sue draws on her experiences with her community to analyze the need for both race- and class-based alliances. While seeing that "black men could not fight the rich bosses alone," she argues with Johnny-Boy that they cannot jettison distinctions between "white folks" and "*our* folks" (*UTC*, 233). Hence, Sue embraces the young white Communist Reva while believing that "Johnny-Boys too trustin. . . . Hes trying t make the party big n hes takin in folks fastern he kin git t know em. You cant trust ever white man yuh meet . . ." (*UTC*, 233).

In contrast to their mother, Johnny-Boy and Sug rigidly view Christianity and Communism, race and class, as discrete and opposed. Just as Johnny-Boy makes Sue choose between Christ and the workers, he cannot tolerate her identification with the community, which he sees as inimical to building the Party: "Yuh cant judge folks jus by how yuh feel bout em n by how long yuh done knowed em. Ef we start tha we wouldn't have *no*body in the party" (*UTC*, 233). As a corollary, he posits class over and against race: "Ma, Ah done tol yuh a hundred times. Ah cant see white n Ah cant see black. . . . Ah sees rich men n Ah sees po men" (*UTC*, 234).

Refusing the binaries by which Johnny-Boy lives and thinks, Sue critiques his reductive notions of proletarian consciousness: "She knew his faith [in working-class radicalism]; it was deep. . . . But he believes so hard hes blind, she thought" (*UTC*, 233). By characterizing Johnny-Boy's dogmatic Communism as blind faith, Sue parallels it to her earlier use of religion as a crutch rather than a challenge to exploitative conditions; both kinds of idealism obfuscate the realities of systemic racism. For Sue, working-class solidarity cannot be assumed but must be attained.

Such solidarity is exemplified in "Star" by the relationship between Sue and Reva, whose bonds are based on but exceed their shared commitment to organizing the sharecroppers. As the sister of a political prisoner, Reva empathizes with Sue's loss of Sug to the penal system, and they relate to each other's pain not only as comrades but also as women:

[Sue] heard Reva sobbing.
"Hush, honey!"
"Mah brothers in jail too! Ma cries ever day . . ."
"Ah know, honey." (*UTC*, 229–230)

Although Reva is condescendingly cast as a helpless white woman who leans on Sue's maternal strength, there are indications that in the past it was Reva who helped Sue. We are told that Reva's trust and acceptance gave Sue "her first feelings of humanity," "her refuge from shame and degradation" (*UTC*, 229). Because of Reva, Sue has withstood the temptation to cocoon herself in religion, even in the face of virulent racism: "If in the early days of her life the white mountain had driven her back from the earth, then in her last days Reva's love was drawing her toward it, like the beacon that swung through the night outside" (*UTC*, 229). Reva and Sue's mutual support reveals women's subjectivities and experiences as primary sites of working-class solidarity.

An additional basis for Sue and Reva's solidarity is their love for Johnny-Boy. Although Sue receives "the brightest glow her heart had ever known" when she discovers that Reva loves her son, nothing comes of Reva's yearnings, and after Johnny-Boy is captured by the police, Sue acknowledges that they "couldna been together in this here South" (*UTC*, 231, 253). Reva's unrequited love shores up Wright's response to the Southern lynching triangle in which white men protect white women against black rapists. Instead of rehearsing the homosocial model of black and white male workers commonly repudiating the white whore, Wright shows black and white women workers bonding over their love for the black man. He thus reiterates the feminized images of interracial solidarity that arose when Bates joined the Scottsboro mothers in their campaign.

In "Star," however, the militance of women like Janie Patterson and Ruby Bates is domesticated: in representing female solidarity arising out of the domestic sphere, Wright also confines Sue and Reva's relationship within it. Reva is both deified and infantilized by Sue, who then cannot turn to her comrade in her moment of crisis. Evoking patriarchal and racist stereotypes, Wright eschews the opportunity to represent black and white women fighting together. Yet despite these limitations, "Star" refutes the masculinist logic of proletarian struggle that demonizes white women's desire and renders black women invisible. Along with the march in "Fire and Cloud," the relationship between Sue and Reva exemplifies interracial unity in *Uncle Tom's Children*.

More radically, "Star" places the African American mother at the center of the struggle against racialized, capitalist exploitation. Initially marginal to the Party, Sue is not content to remain so. Her conversion to Communism gives rise to a "hate of those who would destroy her new faith" and "quicken[s] in her a hunger to feel how deeply her new strength went" (*UTC*, 225). An opportunity to prove her valor arises when the sheriff and his men invade her home in search of Johnny-Boy. Defying their threats, insults, and blows, Sue exultingly taunts the departing sheriff: "Yuh didnt git whut yuh wanted! N yuh ain gonna nevah git it!" (*UTC*, 240) Enraged by this further act of defiance from an "Anty," the sheriff beats her unconscious. Her weakened state trumps her suspicion of Booker, the newly recruited white Communist, and she gives him the names of the Party members.

Learning too late that Booker is a stool pigeon, Sue is utterly demoralized. She undergoes an existential crisis that arises out of her belief, encouraged by her sons, that she must either retreat to the religion of her earlier days or persist in her radicalism in the face of what appears to be certain defeat: "[C]all and counter-call, loyalty and counter-loyalty struggled in her soul. Mired she was between two abandoned worlds, living, but dying without the strength of the grace that either gave" (*UTC*, 252). But in good dialectical form a synthesis emerges: "The clearer she felt [the struggle] the fuller did something well up from the depths of her for release; the more urgent did she feel the need to fling into her black sky another star, another hope, one more terrible vision to give her the strength to live and act" (*UTC*, 252). Sue recognizes what she has only intuited before, that she can, indeed must, create her own vision of grace out of both her Christianity and her Communism.

Sue's final act of heroism unites the different aspects of her identity that had been rent by the masculinism of the Party or disfigured by the racist and patriarchal regime of the state. Deciding to intervene directly in the crisis wrought by Booker's betrayal, Sue breaks with the sexual division of labor that has opposed the African American mother to the radical worker. She reauthorizes her identity and asserts her own humanity as a self-conscious agent of historical change: "Her whole being leaped with will; the long years of her life bent toward a moment of focus, a point" (*UTC*, 253). Mulling over how to infiltrate Booker's rendezvous with the police, who have by now apprehended Johnny-Boy, she acts on the sheriff's threat to "go lika nigger woman wid [her] windin sheet t git [her] dead son" (*UTC*, 253). Her subversive minstrelsy deceives the police long enough for her to shoot Booker dead before he can betray the comrades, but she herself is fatally wounded. Ultimately, though, Sue is doubly triumphant, preventing the state from getting the comrades' names and controlling the terms by which she has lived and died. As she silently reiterates before dying, "Yuh didnt git what yuh wanted! N yuh ain gonna nevah git it! Yuh didnt kill me; Ah come here by mahself. . ." (*UTC*, 263). And in her death, she is "swallowed in [the] peace and strength" of the star, which now represents her victorious fusion of race- and class-consciousness, Christian and Communist struggle (*UTC*, 263).

In the dialectical framework of *Uncle Tom's Children*, Sue's martyrdom is both testimony to the power of the state and a call to action. Far from an ending, Sue's death marks the emergence of another stage of radical- ism yet to be written. The epigraphic declaration, "'Uncle Tom is dead,'" is reinscribed: "Mammy" is dead as well. Moreover, the revolutionaries have finally "come home to us," to recall the problem that Wright had set out to address in writing the last two novellas. As he shows in "Star," the experi- ences of the mother and domestic worker within the home are integral to conceptualizing radical subjectivity.

Re-viewing Wright and the Politics of Identity

With radically different intentions but something of the same effect, liter- ary studies that perform the much-needed analysis of the gender politics in Wright's work, and of *Uncle Tom's Children* in particular, display the same blindness that prevents the sheriff in "Star" from seeing Sue for what she is. Divorcing Wright's gender ideology from his conception of radical praxis or uncritically rehearsing narratives of his misogyny does not do justice to his work. Furthermore, overlooking the work of radical women to which *Uncle Tom's Children* responded perpetuates the invisibility of African American women, which Michele Wallace sees as "a problem of ideology" but also "the final, and most difficult to combat, stage" of racism.[39]

Through my reading of *Uncle Tom's Children*, I have argued that the ex- periences of African American rural women are central to Wright's literary synthesis of Marxism and black cultural nationalism, as theorized in his "Blue- print for Negro Writing." To achieve this merging of politics and aesthetics, Wright rearticulates contemporaneous discourses of masculinity, womanhood, and working-class militance that rose out of the Scottsboro trials and the work of the Scottsboro mothers, drawing on the activism and insights of women on the Left who challenged the forms of proletarian masculinism that contributed to their marginalization. As literary critics and scholars, we cannot afford to be blinded by anti-Communism any more than by racism. Not only does unques- tioned anti-Communism make for reductive literary and historical analysis, it also perpetuates racism and sexism by assuming that political minorities, such as African American women, had little agency within the Communist Party, and that they could not critically engage Marxism.

Beyond arguing that *Uncle Tom's Children* develops a protofeminist per- spective on revolutionary struggle, I would also contend that this perspective provides an important corrective to limitations in certain strands of feminist analysis that rely on narrowly defined identity politics to uncritically rehearse narratives of Wright's misogyny. The key word here is *uncritically*, for Wright's oeuvre should certainly be critically examined for its representations of women, especially African American women. But to date, these studies miss the mark by assuming that Wright's portraits of women are distorted because of his identity as a black man and, even worse, a black male Communist.

Why shouldn't *Uncle Tom's Children* be considered in conjunction with women's revolutionary writing? Why should revolutionary writing about women and gender be limited by biological essentialism? Paula Rabinowitz's groundbreaking work on (white) women revolutionary writers can help to flesh out these questions. As I mentioned earlier, Rabinowitz asserts that men's proletarian fiction generally instrumentalizes sexuality, marriage, and the family to serve as metaphors for class struggle instead of exploring them as sites of struggle and subject formation. Radical women writers, in contrast, "recognized the female body as one contradictory site of sexual, gender, race, and class conflict in American society. . . . By redefining the narrative of desire as a means by which the female subject entered history, they repositioned both the female intellectual and the working-class woman in literature and history."[40] While important, Rabinowitz's point is limited insofar as she assumes that only (white) women writers can theorize and inscribe female bodies and desire in this way. This assumption prevents us from appreciating the impact of women's activism on male writers such as Wright who ground revolutionary praxis in feminine experiences of labor and desire.

In making this point, I am not simply arguing for Wright's inclusion within certain genres of women's writing but also for the reinterrogation of these generic and ultimately political boundaries that are based on essentialized categories of identity. This, I think, is one of the most fruitful messages that *Uncle Tom's Children* imparts: we need to recognize common concerns formed within specific historical conditions, even and especially when these interests transcend lines of race and gender.

Notes

For their criticism and support in writing this essay, I want to thank Biodun Jeyifo, Dan Won-gu Kim, Barry Maxwell, Raj Patel, Hortense Spillers, Ed White, and Sunn Shelley Wong.

1. Richard Wright, *American Hunger* (New York: Harper & Row, 1977): p. 114; further references are to this edition and will be cited parenthetically as *AH*.

2. Mark Naison, *Communists in Harlem during the Depression* (Urbana: University of Illinois Press, 1983): p. 208.

3. Zora Neale Hurston, "Stories of Conflict," review of *Uncle Tom's Children* by Richard Wright, *Saturday Review of Literature*, 2 April 1938, 32; see also Richard Wright, "Between Laughter and Tears," review of *Their Eyes Were Watching God*, by Zora Neale Hurston, *New Masses*, October 1937, 22, 25. In his discussion of the Hurston-Wright debate and its rearticulation in recent African American literary

scholarship, William Maxwell persuasively argues that the polarization of these two writers, primarily seen as an example of the dominance of black men's over black women's voices, has given rise to its own Manichean allegory in which Hurston (representing race, modernism, Harlem Renaissance, black nationalism, rural folk) is posed against Wright (representing class, naturalism, Chicago Renaissance, Marxism, urban masses). Maxwell's literary history and close readings of Wright and Hurston challenge the oversimplifying tendencies of this polarization (see *New Negro, Old Left: African-American Writing and Communism between the Wars* [New York: Columbia University Press, 1999], pp. 153–157).

4. Trudier Harris writes: "Wright himself was perhaps so blinded by the treatment of males, particularly in relation to Communist ideology, that he failed to see that Bessie could carry out his theme just as effectively" ("Native Sons and Foreign Daughters," in *New Essays on "Native Son,"* ed. Keneth Kinnamon [Cambridge, Eng.: Cambridge University Press, 1990], p. 80.)

5. Sherley Anne Williams, "Papa Dick and Sister-Woman: Reflections on Women in the Fiction of Richard Wright," *American Novelists Revisited: Essays in Feminist Criticism,* ed. Fritz Fleischmann (Boston: G. K. Hall, 1982), p. 395.

6. Nagueyalti Warren, "Black Girls and Native Sons: Female Images in Selected Works by Richard Wright," in *Richard Wright: Myths and Realities,* ed. C. James Trotman (New York: Garland, 1988), p. 70.

7. In 1939, soon after completing *Native Son,* Wright began drafting a novel that was eventually given the working title *Little Sister.* According to Michel Fabre, Wright organized its plot around "three principal themes: the situation of women in the big cities, the working conditions of the domestic help, and the role of religion in the feminine mentality." He never published *Little Sister,* but the next year he attempted another novel about domestics, whose lives and social conditions he thoroughly researched; although he finished at least two versions of this novel, it too never came to fruition (*The Unfinished Quest of Richard Wright,* trans. Isabel Barzun [Urbana: University of Illinois Press, 1993], p. 188).

8. My reading of Wright draws on but differs from earlier scholarship that has reassessed his misogyny, in particular, the work of Paul Gilroy and William Maxwell. In his discussion of Wright's later works, Gilroy argues that we need to recognize Wright's contribution to gender studies through his "inauguration of a critical discourse on the construction of black masculinity" and his "proto-feminist statements" (*The Black Atlantic: Modernity and Double Consciousness* [Cambridge: Harvard University Press, 1995], p. 176). I agree with Gilroy here but find his analysis insufficient on two grounds. First, he equates Wright's misogyny largely with his representations of physical violence against black women, but this is not the only (if the most blatant) way in which his misogyny is manifest. Wright's reliance on stereotypes and his grotesque depictions of female bodies are just as frequent and enact their own kinds of violence against black women. Second, Gilroy does not discuss Wright's construction of black masculinity in relation to his representations of black femininity and sexuality. I have found William Maxwell's rethinking of Wright's notions of the "folk" to be more helpful, and I pursue this line of inquiry by considering the significance of African American, Southern, rural women to Wright's project in *Uncle Tom's Children.* Finally, although Joyce Ann Joyce recuperates Wright's representations of black women, I find her focus on racism instead of, rather than in conjunction with, sexism and patriarchy methodologically problematic. Furthermore, Joyce dehistoricizes "Long Black Song," which she reads

as presenting a transhistorical center of consciousness through Sarah (see "Richard Wright's 'Long Black Song': A Moral Dilemma," *Mississippi Quarterly* 42 [Fall 1989]: 379–385).

9. See Wilson Record, *The Negro and the Communist Party* (Chapel Hill: University of North Carolina Press, 1951); and Harold Cruse, *The Crisis of the Negro Intellectual: A Historical Analysis of the Failure of Black Leadership* (New York: Quill, 1984).

10. See Richard Wright, "Blueprint for Negro Writing," in *The Norton Anthology of African American Literature,* ed. Henry Louis Gates Jr., Nellie Y. McKay et al. (New York: Norton, 1997), pp. 1380–1388; further references to this essay are to this edition and will be cited parenthetically as "B." Alain Locke offers a different but equally compelling assessment of the major trends in African American modernism in his "Retrospective Reviews," published annually in *Opportunity* (1929–1942). In his review "The Negro: 'New' or Newer," Locke rebuts Wright's repudiation of the Harlem Renaissance generation in "Blueprint." Locke, "Dean" of the Harlem Renaissance, subsumes the social protest school of writers within the still unfolding development of the New Negro that he himself had foreseen from the outset (*Opportunity* 17 [January-February 1939]: 4–10, 36–42). Sterling Brown's column "The Literary Scene: Chronicle and Comment"—also published in *Opportunity* (1930–1935)—is another important source of African American cultural critique.

11. Wright's article on Huddie Ledbetter (Leadbelly) for the *Daily Worker* exemplifies his materialist approach to folk culture. When four of the Scottsboro boys were freed, they were feted in Harlem. Huddie Ledbetter contributed to the celebration with songs such as "The Scottsboro Boys Got Here" and "Bourgeois Blues." Wright's profile of the musician praises his artistry and wide knowledge of African American folklore and documents his exploitation by the culture industry ("Huddie Ledbetter, Famous Negro Folk Artist, Sings the Songs of Scottsboro and His People," *Daily Worker,* 12 August 1937, 7).

12. I concur with Barbara Foley, who argues that *Uncle Tom's Children* portrays nationalism as integral to the discourse and agenda of Communism (*Radical Representations: Politics and Form in U.S. Proletarian Fiction, 1929–1941* [Durham, N.C.: Duke University Press, 1993], p. 209). For a different analysis of Wright's evolving thought on Marxism and nationalism, see Cedric Robinson, *Black Marxism: The Making of the Black Radical Tradition* (London: Zed Press, 1983).

13. African American women's specific histories and experiences had a slightly greater presence in a draft of "Blueprint," which presents "Negro women who carry the triple burden of their sex, of their race, and of their class," "the baffled thoughts of that Negro woman social worker who works in the slum areas of her race," and "that . . . Negro girl reading the True Story magazine" as parts of "a landscape teeming with questions and meaning" for the black writer (Richard Wright, "Blueprint for Negro Literature," draft, Richard Wright Papers, 1927–1978, Beinecke Rare Book and Manuscript Library, Yale University, 14; quoted by permission of John Hawkins & Associates. © 2003 by Ellen Wright).

14. Robin D. G. Kelly, *Race Rebels: Culture, Politics and the Black Working Class* (New York: Free Press, 1994), p. 112.

15. See Paula Rabinowitz, *Labor and Desire: Women's Revolutionary Fiction in Depression America* (Chapel Hill: University of North Carolina Press, 1991), p. 83.

16. Richard Wright, *Uncle Tom's Children* (New York: HarperPerennial, 1993). Further references to *Uncle Tom's Children* are to this reissue of the 1940 edition and will be cited parenthetically as *UTC*.

17. Williams, "Papa Dick," p. 409.

18. Miriam De Costa-Willis, for example, argues that Sarah and Sue "cannot be viewed as women of flesh and blood but as symbols of primal forces or as mythic figures who evoke memories of a tribal past" ("Avenging Angels and Mute Mothers: Black Southern Women in Wright's Fictional World," *Callaloo* 9 [summer 1986]: 542).

19. Richard Wright, preface to *Uncle Tom's Children* (unpublished), Richard Wright Papers, Beinecke Rare Book and Manuscript Library, Yale University, 3; quoted by permission of John Hawkins & Associates. © 2003 by Ellen Wright.

20. Richard Wright, "How 'Uncle Tom's Children' Grew," *The Writers' Club Bulletin II*, May 1938 (New York: University Extension, Columbia University), n.p.

21. Wright, preface to *Uncle Tom's Children*, Richard Wright Papers, 5.

22. In "Blueprint," Wright says that "even today there are millions of American Negroes whose only sense of a whole universe, whose only relation to society and man, and whose only guide to personal dignity comes through the archaic morphology of Christian salvation" (1382). For a discussion of Wright's perception of how religion expresses and enables class consciousness, see Thomas Larson, "A Political Vision of Afro-American Culture: Richard Wright's 'Bright and Morning Star,'" in *Richard Wright: Myths and Realities*, ed. Trotman, pp. 147–159.

23. Taylor's political conversion, for example, articulates the Judeo-Christian idea of God's chosen people with the Popular Front symbol of "the people": "Gawds wid the people! N the peoples gotta be real as Gawd t us!" (*UTC*, 210).

24. For the most thorough history of the Scottsboro case, from which I draw, see Dan T. Carter, *Scottsboro: A Tragedy of the American South* (London: Oxford University Press, 1975).

25. For details on the Communist Party's work in Harlem, see Naison, *Communists in Harlem*, pp. 66–69. *The Narrative of Hosea Hudson* vividly presents the impact of *Scottsboro* in politicizing African American workers in the South (see Nell Irwin Painter, *The Narrative of Hosea Hudson: The Life and Times of a Black Radical* [New York: Norton, 1994]).

26. For a succinct analysis of the pivotal role that the Communist Party envisioned for *Scottsboro* in radicalizing African Americans and breaking down divisions between black and white workers, see James S. Allen, "The Scottsboro Struggle," in *American Communism and Black Americans: A Documentary History, 1930–1934*, ed. Philip S. Foner and Herbert Shapiro (Philadelphia: Temple University Press, 1991), pp. 307–318.

27. Maxwell, *Old Negro, New Left*, pp. 137–141.

28. Ada Wright, "Save Their Lives," *Working Woman*, April 1934, 12.

29. Carter, *Scottsboro*, pp. 143–144.

30. J. Louis Engdahl, "A Scottsboro Mother Fights," *Labor Defender*, July 1932, 124. Regarding the exposure of the Scottsboro mothers, Carter writes that "[a]t one time, there were so many 'Scottsboro mothers' traveling through the country that [NAACP executive secretary] Walter White charged fraud." Carter adds that while there may have been a few instances of such duplicity, it was generally unnecessary as most of the Scottsboro mothers were willing and available to tour (*Scottsboro*, p. 143).

31. Rabinowitz, *Labor and Desire*, p. 55. Rabinowitz is actually referring here to the broader Popular Front period beginning in 1935, rather than to the United Front initiated in 1933. However, insofar as the United Front had similar, if more limited, effects in pushing the U.S. Communist Party to form alliances with "bourgeois" organizations, her point about "partisan mothers" applies to the symbols and representations of womanhood that appear in *Working Woman*.

32. For an example of how the image of the sacrificing mother was managed, see "Appeal of Scottsboro Mothers," *Daily Worker*, 21 January 1932; quoted in *American Communism and Black Americans*, ed. Foner and Shapiro, 288. Signed by seven of the women, the document states: "We've been starving all our lives and forced to live from hand to mouth, working for as low as $2.50 a week down here in the South and our boys wanted to go out and find work to help us out. We didn't want to let them go because they are almost only babies."

33. Viola Montgomery, quoted in *Sasha Small*, "Your Son May Be Next!" *Working Woman*, December 1933, 4.

34. Louise Thompson, "And So We Marched," *Working Woman*, June 1933, 6.

35. Mary Heaton Vorse, "Hard Boiled," *Working Woman*, May 1933, 6.

36. Ada Wright and Ruby Bates, "Save Their Lives," *Working Woman*, April 1934, 12. ("Save Their Lives" comprises two separate articles, one by Wright and one by Bates.)

37. Thompson, "And So We Marched," 6.

38. In a letter to Wright, Burnett objected to the ILD reference on the basis that it made the novella "too contemporary or too topical," contending that Wright's story "[had] nothing to do with either [the ILD or the Scottsboro boys] and would gain strength by remaining strictly in its own setting." He also told Wright to edit Sue's interior monologue in the opening scene and her exchange with the sheriff: "I think, from a reader's standpoint, she talks too much and I, for one, got as bored with her as the sheriff did. She over-talks and it seems to me that four or five of her sentences could be cut out and so heighten the sympathy one feels for her" (Whit Burnett to Richard Wright, 27 January 1938, Richard Wright Papers, Beinecke Rare Book and Manuscript Library, Yale University).

39. Michele Wallace notes further: "The fact that [this invisibility] involves conjunctions not only of racism and sexism but also conjunctions of capitalist exploitation and compulsory heterosexuality makes it even more difficult to diagnose" (introduction to *Black Macho and the Myth of the Superwoman* [London: Verso, 1990], p. xix).

40. Rabinowitz, *Labor and Desire*, p. 62.

PETAR RAMADANOVIC

Native Son's *Tragedy:*
Traversing the Death Drive with Bigger Thomas

He [Richard Wright] was, this argument runs, led astray from the realistic
and naturalistic styles of fiction to which his experience in the segregated
South gave rise by the heady influence of friends like Sartre and others
like Blanchot, Mannoni, and Bataille, whose inappropriately cosmopolitan
outlooks poured their corrosive influences on his precious and authentic
Negro sensibility. . . . There is a further suggestion, shared by both those
who exalt and those who have execrated Wright as a protest writer, that he
should have been content to remain confined within the intellectual ghetto
to which Negro literary expression is still too frequently consigned. His
desires—to escape the ideological and cultural legacies of Americanism; to
learn the philosophical languages of literary and philosophical modernism
even if only to demonstrate the commonplace nature of their truths; and to
seek complex answers to the questions which racial and national identities
could only obscure—all point to the enduring value of his radical view of
modernity for the contemporary analyst of the black diaspora.

Paul Gilroy, *The Black Atlantic*

"Bigger, sometimes I wonder why I birthed you," she said bitterly. Bigger
looked at her and turned away.
"Maybe you oughtn't've. Maybe you ought to left me where I was."

Richard Wright, *Native Son*

Arizona Quarterly, Volume 59, Number 2 (Summer 2003): pp. 81–105. Copyright © 2003
Arizona Board of Regents.

What . . . does he who has passed through the experience of this opaque relation to the origin, to the drive, become? How can a subject who has traversed the radical phantasy experience the drive?

Jacques Lacan, *The Four Fundamental Concepts* of *Psycho-Analysis*

Paul Gilroy's *The Black Atlantic: Modernity and Double Consciousness* is praised for offering a new understanding of Western modernity and of the black diaspora, and even for revamping Atlantic studies. Though no less path-breaking, Gilroy's contribution to specific areas within the field of African American literature have not stimulated scholars with the same force. The fifth chapter of *The Black Atlantic*, "Without the Consolation of Tears': Richard Wright, France, and the Ambivalence of Community," from which I have borrowed the above epigraph, shows, if nothing else, that a thorough reassessment of Wright's oeuvre is long overdue. In this article I follow the general thrust of Gilroy's reading of Wright as I try to identify the basis for an alternative to the prevailing interpretations of *Native Son* and, in particular, to show why this novel should be read as a tragedy.

PART I: TRAGEDY
Apologue

In what is perhaps the most revealing article in Henry Louis Gates and Anthony Appiah's 1993 *Richard Wright: Critical Perspectives Past and Present*, Barbara Foley asserts that, as opposed to Theodor Dreiser's *An American Tragedy*, Richard Wright's *Native Son* is "grotesque rather than tragic, and Bigger's fate, emotionally gripping as it may be, is ultimately subordinated to Wright's bitter social commentary" (Foley 194). Foley thus affirms two commonly accepted claims about *Native Son*: first, that this novel bears many parallels with Dreiser's An *American Tragedy*, parallels which are also owed to the ur-text of both novels, Dostoievsky's *Crime and Punishment*. Second, that Wright's novel is a commentary on the social status of black people in the United States. Wright's protagonist's acts are determined, the logic goes, by the social position Bigger Thomas occupies as a black man in a racist American society. On this reading, *Native Son* is an excruciating testimony to the consequences of segregation. As Ishmael Read put it in a recent article, "Richard Wright knew what he was talking about. Not only had he been poor but as a youth worker he got to know many Biggers and, on the basis of this experience, was able to draw a character so convincingly that Bigger has become an archetype for the inner-cities' disaffiliated youth" (Read 169–170).

The problem with which I want to start my re-reading of *Native Son* concerns Foley's understanding of tragedy, which is the basis of her judgment that Wright's novel is an apologue and Dreiser's a tragic narrative. While the reader can identify with Dreiser's main character, Clyde, and feel pity for him, Foley maintains, "Wright directs our pity for his hero primarily toward a conceptual understanding of the social system that destroys him." Foley then concludes, "Wright thus takes the 'story' of Dreiser's tragedy and restructures its 'plot' as an *apologue:* from his unrelenting account of Bigger's outer violence and inner struggle for meaning emerges a powerful indictment of the blighting effects of American racism" (194, emphasis added).

According to Foley, it is the reader's identification with the main character, the reader's feeling of pity for the protagonist, that makes a story into a tragedy. Dreiser's story of crime and punishment is a tragedy and Wright's is an apologue because the reader feels for Dreiser's character (though this feeling requires a deliberation about the system that produces and destroys him). *Native Son* takes us further away from pity in that Wright shifts the focus of his writing from the protagonist to a "conceptual understanding" of the racist system that produced Bigger Thomas. This is the crucial difference that makes Dreiser's novel a tragedy and Wright's an apologue.[1]

Read thus, *Native Son* follows not only the blueprint of Dostoievsky's *Crime and Punishment* but also the most famous apologue in Western literature, Plato's *Socrates' Defense (Apology)*, in the sense that both Wright's novel and Plato's *Apology* can be seen as versions of a crime and punishment story wherein the city or the society is revealed as the true culprit in the hero's downfall. In both works the protagonist is a scape-goat, guilty because he is an anomalous, monstrous product of a certain social order. Since the protagonist's guilt is determined by the inner contradictions of a given political organization, it is also reducible to them. Socrates is sentenced to death as a philosopher in a society that, though it produced the philosopher (as different from the politician, priest, etc.), has no place for his relentless questioning or his system of beliefs. Bigger Thomas is, similarly, sentenced to death in a society which has made him into a "black man" but has no medium for his realization as either black or a man. As Richard Wright puts it in *Black Boy (American Hunger)*, "Though he is an organic part of the nation, he is excluded by the entire tide and direction of American culture" (272).[2]

But, are pity and identification with the protagonist the crux of tragedy, as Foley assumes when she suggests that *Native Son* is an apologue and not a tragic narrative? And, more importantly, should we agree with Foley's assumption that social inequality and its racist organization outweigh the significance of Bigger Thomas's act?

With these two questions we can begin to recast the novel in terms that differ significantly from its commonly accepted interpretations. In this article I will try to show, first, that the notion of fate or necessity is crucial for understanding why *Native Son* is, in fact, a tragedy. Second and more important, I will argue that Bigger Thomas acts against the assumption that anything general (namely, social constraints) can stand in the way of or subsume his singular, that is, constitutive or founding act. In my understanding, Thomas acts in a way that counters and preempts the explanation that American society is the true culprit of his crime—an explanation upon which the novel's positive reviewers (and, for that matter, two of the novel's characters, Jan Erlone and Boris Max) agree. As I will show in some detail below, Bigger Thomas does not kill *because* he is a black man living in a racist society, nor does he kill *as* a black man. His blackness is not the *cause* that predetermines his actions; rather, his blackness is constituted after he is caught for killing a white woman, and the *cause* of his actions can be posited only belatedly, after Thomas performs what the novel calls the "supreme act."

Tragedy

What is essential about the classical, Sophoclean tragic hero is, as Jacques Lacan says in his seminar on ethics, that his or her race is already run (272). The tragic hero cannot change his situation no matter what he does and, when the protagonist becomes aware of the ramifications of his act, he cannot say "I am sorry," "I didn't mean it," "Let me try again." Which means simply that the tragic hero suffers not because of what he has done—he has committed the act necessarily or unknowingly—but because of *who* he or she has become during the tragic drama. This is the fundamental reason the audience identifies with the hero and is, as Lacan says, fascinated by the protagonist.[3] In Sophocles's *Oedipus the King*, for instance, the protagonist kills his father. The crime is, however, not the cause of his tragic fate; in fact, Oedipus kills a stranger, arguably in self-defense, and later marries a woman he believes he has never met before. His guilt, his suffering, his misfortune are all due to the mere fact that he discovers that he is Oedipus, son of Jocasta and Laius, who has killed his father and married his mother. The task of tragedy can therefore be defined as showing that the protagonist is indeed the person named by fate to perform a terrifying crime, deserving the honor of being singled out by necessity in this exemplary, catastrophic way.

The notion of fate, and more precisely, the enactment of what the Ancient Greeks called *atè*, is the condition for the protagonist's tragedy.[4] The audience only has to recognize that the character suffers because of *who* he has become during the course of the play (not because of what he has done) in order to view the play as a tragedy. On this understanding, what matters concerning the tragedy of *Native Son* is that Thomas has an *atè*—that, to put it simply, he is driven or fated to commit a crime, to become a colored man, and to die in the electric chair. The notion that Thomas is fated is present throughout the novel, and comes to the fore in its most critical form after he is caught, in the third part of *Native Son* entitled "Fate." For example, during his conversation with his lawyer, Boris A. Max, Thomas says, "Well, to tell the truth, Mr. Max, it seems sort of *natural-like*, me being here facing that death chair. Now I come to think of it, it seems like something like this just *had* to *be*" (415, emphases added). The same sentiment is given voice when, earlier in his conversation with Max, Thomas says, "Naw; naw. . . . I knew what I was doing, all right. But I couldn't help it. That's what I mean. It was like another man stepped inside of my skin and started acting for me . . ." (407).

What we learn from these statements, besides the fact that Thomas acts under compulsion and constraints, is that Thomas, like a true tragic hero, knows what he has done. Further, he recognizes his fate as his own and accepts the murder of Mary Dalton as his deed. (Thomas is defined by the accidental murder of Mary Dalton in the same sense that Oedipus is defined by the murder of a stranger at the crossroads. In the process of acceptance, spanning the entire plot of Sophocles's *Oedipus the King*, Oedipus acknowledges that his act on the road was not an accident, a mere accident, but that it was a necessary act from which he could not have escaped.)

We now have enough explanation to conclude that (a) because Thomas has an *atè* and accepts his fate, and (b) because pity is a structural characteristic of the novel (not simply a feeling that is provoked in the reader), *Native Son* is a tragedy in the rudimentary sense of this term.

But this conclusion that *Native Son* is a tragedy does not take us very far, since it is by no means certain *how* we are to understand that this "black man," Bigger Thomas, is fated, and that *Native Son* is a tragedy.

Native Son's *History*

Before we can begin to answer these two questions, I will address briefly the history of *Native Son's* negative reception. Essentially, I am now going back to retrace the steps that lead Foley to rehabilitate what she calls the "proletarian novel"—Wright's *Native Son* and Dreiser's *An American Tragedy*—by showing the specific aesthetic principles these works of art follow. The negative critical reception of *Native Son* had its first compelling formulation in James Baldwin's "Everybody's Protest Novel" (1949; *Notes*) and reached an extreme in Harold Bloom's 1987 introduction to *Richard Wright*.

In the third sentence of his introduction, Bloom asserts that Wright is a "son" of Theodore Dreiser who "could not rise . . . even to Dreiser's customarily bad level of writing" (Bloom 1). To illustrate his claim, Bloom cites what he considers to be a poorly written passage from *Native Son*. The passage describes Bigger Thomas after he is condemned to death (*Native* 487–488). According to Bloom, if this passage is taken out of context—if, that is, the protagonist's skin color and background are not known—then the "intense sociological pathos of Wright's narrative" disappears, and there is nothing to support the writing. The reader is left merely with "inadequate rhetoric"

(Bloom 1). The problem with *Native Son,* Bloom says, concluding his analysis of the passage, is "plainly stated, a bad authorial ear" (2).

The passage that Bloom finds inadequate begins: "In self-defense he shut out the night and day from his mind" (*Native* 487). What Bloom fails to see is that even without the social context, without the "sociological pathos" (whatever that means exactly), this passage, which describes Thomas's self-imposed blindness, offers tragic pathos and, thus, an adequate image of an outcast; in fact, an image of *the* outcast. The description is prepared for more than a hundred and fifty pages earlier, at the very first line of the novel's third part, which reads: "There was no day for him now, and there was no night; there was but a long stretch of time, a long stretch of time that was very short; and then—the end" (*Native* 315). After he is sentenced to death, Bigger Thomas, like Oedipus, can no longer look upon the world: "To accustom his mind to death as much as possible, he made all the world beyond his cell a vast gray land where neither night nor day was" (487). A stranger buried in the darkness of his fate, Thomas longs to see the world one last time, just as Oedipus wants to meet his children before he is exiled from Thebes: "the world peopled by strange men and women whom he could not understand, but with those[5] lives he longed to mingle once before he went" (*Native* 487–488). The outcast, however, has no place in the human community and he must sever all remaining ties:

> His mother and brother and sister had come to see him and he had told them to stay home, not to come again, to forget him. The Negro preacher who had given him the cross had come and he had driven him away. A white priest had tried to persuade him to pray and he had thrown a cup of hot coffee into his face. (*Native* 488)

According to Bloom, *Native Son* has a place in the canon of American literature for reasons that can be nothing but political, but James Baldwin has problems precisely with the politics of *Native Son.* Though Baldwin does not value Wright's rhetoric highly either, the crux of his critique of *Native Son* is that the time has passed for novels that take a high moral stance, saying to society, in effect: "This is perfectly horrible! You ought to be ashamed of yourselves!" (*Notes* 9). The criticism that Baldwin levels against "protest novels" is that, whatever their rhetoric, the genre is politically inadequate because these novels relegate all problems and unsettling questions to an impersonal social arena (the "they" frequently mentioned in Wright's novel) and thereby serve to appease the guilty reader's conscience. *Native Son,* thus, names the society responsible for Bigger Thomas's destiny, without telling who this society is or what the "they" stand for. The aesthetics of protest novels is therefore too much, anesthetizing rather than engaging, provoking, or affirming. That is the reason *Native Son,* like other protest novels, is ultimately theological, serving to reassert the age-old ideology according to which "to flee or not, to move or not, it is all the same; [a character's] doom is written on his forehead" (*Notes* 16).

At once radical and too sweeping in its conclusions, Baldwin's exposition of the ideology of protest novels applies to *Native Son* to the extent that this novel is indeed a descendent of Harriet Beecher Stowe's *Uncle Tom's Cabin,* which Baldwin takes to be the founding example of the protest genre. *Native Son* can indeed be seen as a protest novel, but only if it is reduced to representing the racist ideology that its protagonist has internalized. That is, *Native Son* fits Baldwin's description of the protest novel if it is understood to be a story about Bigger Thomas, the every-Negro, which is precisely how the novel's Boris Max, Thomas's lawyer, and Jan Erlone, the Communist fiancé of the murdered Mary Dalton, see Thomas. In order to consent to such a reading, however, we have to overlook Wright's irony in having Max claim that there is something "bigger" than Bigger: "Well, this thing's bigger than you, son. In a certain sense, every Negro in America's on trial out there today" (*Native* 426).

The most obvious problem with Baldwin's critique of *Native Son,* then, is that it identifies Wright's ideology with Max's. Max, however, fundamentally misunderstands the nature of Thomas's crime, believing it to be identical with and reducible to the murder. It is not the murder that makes Thomas feel free, but, as I noted above and as I shall explain in some detail below, Thomas's acceptance of his fate and his decision not to struggle. From Max's perspective, there can be only a half way understanding of what it is precisely that Wright calls Thomas's "supreme act" (for Max, the murder) and of what makes this act supreme, absolute, total, or ultimate (again, for Max, it is the fact that Thomas has killed a young, beautiful, and rich white woman). Anything regarding the significance of the murder for Bigger Thomas, and for Bigger Thomas alone, remains beyond the scope of Max's ideology.

A related problem—more complex psychologically, since it includes Baldwin's ambiguous personal relation with his mentor, Richard Wright—is that the basis for Baldwin's reading of protest novels is a repetition without acknowledgment of Wright's critique of his own first well-known work, titled *Uncle Tom's Children* which is a response to and revision of Beecher Stowe's *Uncle Tom's Cabin.*[6]

From what has been argued above, we can deduce that the crucial problem with Baldwin's critique of *Native Son* is that Baldwin does not allow for the possibility that Wright created a singular character, a radically autonomous, essentially modernist individual who does not follow any universal precept; a character who, in fact, understands that he is expected to internalize a racist ideology and act according to a pre-assigned role, but who refuses to do so, asserting his own imperative instead. When, after the murder, Thomas sees the reflection of "his black face in the sweaty windowpane," he reflects:

> Would any of the white faces all about him think that he had killed a rich white girl? No! They might think he would steal a dime, rape a woman, get drunk, or cut somebody; but to kill a millionaire's daughter and burn her body? He smiled a little, feeling a tingling sensation enveloping all his body. He saw it all very sharply and simply: *act like other people thought you ought to act, yet do what you wanted.* (128)[7]

What we see here is not that Bigger Thomas is a criminal who would "steal a dime, rape a woman, get drunk, or cut somebody," but that he wants to assault nothing less than the philosophical and moral foundation of the system. His rewriting of Kant's categorical imperative should have made Baldwin and other critics at least pause before accusing *Native Son* of social determinism, and ask whether it was possible that *Native Son* was Wright's attempt to radically reconfigure his social space—a necessarily tragic attempt to create a new life. Bigger Thomas is indeed a violent criminal, but not a criminal who breaks the law; he is rather a criminal who—somewhat like the Marquis de Sade's criminals in Jacques Lacan's understanding *(Ethics)*—wants to blot out the entire symbolic order—i.e., the Law with a capital "L."

If Bigger Thomas is not a complex character, and the reader, consequently, does not know him, as Baldwin maintains, this is not because Wright is not "perceptive" enough (*Notes* 27) or because his ideology is simplistic. It is rather because the task of his self-creation requires that Thomas be a one-dimensional character driven and thus defined by his zeal. Bigger Thomas is, in a word, a revolutionary criminal, and revolutionaries are simple people—simple and sharp, as Wright would say (*Native* 128)—who have sacrificed themselves to the fulfillment of their goal, which they have elevated to the level of an absolute. As a revolutionary, Thomas neither accepts nor rejects life, but wants to change it, fundamentally.

Baldwin is correct, however, to say that *Native Son*'s protagonist is a fated, tragic hero, and I will now proceed to explain how we are to understand Thomas's fate and tragedy. In dealing with this question I will argue for an understanding of *Native Son* as a tragedy that differs in every significant detail as well as in its fundamentals from the only published in-depth treatment of this issue, Joyce Ann Joyce's *Richard Wright's Art of Tragedy*. I will also try to show what it is precisely that Baldwin missed in his critique of *Native Son;* namely, that the novel's ideology is, in Nietzsche's sense, untimely. It is an ideology that acts on its time out of its time, striking against what a person *ought to be* in a political and aesthetic sense.

PART II: FATE

To summarize what I've said so far: *Native Son* is a tragedy because its protagonist acts in order to fulfill his fate. His fate is fulfilled in his singular act of self-realization, a revolutionary act (whose nature we will explore in this section) in which Thomas asserts his autonomy over and against the American social order. That an act is singular means that it confirms that a person is a human being regardless of what he has done in his lifetime or, as Lacan puts it in his reading of *Antigone*, irrespective of his history and his individuality. The tragic hero's act affirms what Lacan calls "the unique value of his being without reference to any content, to whatever good or evil [he] may have done, or to whatever he may be subjected to" (*Ethics* 279). The hero confirms, in other words, that his being is not exhausted or fully defined by how he is seen by the American socio-political system that produced him. Based on this understanding, we can say that there is something in *Native Son* that is other than either Thomas's individualistic project or his socially determined behavior. And it is precisely this alterity, this unidentified surplus that is in Thomas—other than "I," other than "a black man"—that is his "being," which is affirmed in the novel.

The understanding of Thomas's act as an affirmation of his singular being will allow for a reading of *Native Son* fundamentally different from the redemptive interpretations of the generation of critics who, working against Baldwin's critique of the novel, claim that Thomas transcends the adversity of his environment through his own efforts. Katherine Fishburn, Valerie Smith, Joyce Ann Joyce, Donald B. Gibson, and others have tried to show that Bigger is not, to borrow Alessandro Portelli's words, "an inarticulate victim of his environment" (Portelli 255), as Baldwin charged, but a hero who achieves freedom through his own doing. In the conclusion to her argument, Joyce Ann Joyce makes a claim characteristic of this entire strain in *Native Son* scholarship, showing it to be based on an unrecognized and untheorized moralistic, anti-modernist understanding of tragedy. She writes: "In its execution of [the] tragic theme, *Native Son* charts Bigger's growth from darkness into light, from innocence into experience, and from ignorance into knowledge" (117). In other words, the suffering of the tragic hero is not in vain; Thomas's efforts lead to his "spiritual awakening" (50), which in turn leads him to an ultimate triumph over the oppressive, racist system. If Thomas triumphs at the end, this is not because of his conscious efforts and calculations, but rather because he fulfills a more difficult task. He accepts that he is driven by a force—by an *atè* in Lacan's terms—that neither he nor anyone around him can control. The only conscious thing he can do is to acknowledge the drive behind his fate and accept his extreme situation.

I should repeat here that the notion of fate as I am using it does not assume that there is a destiny written in advance and that our protagonist is either a mindless pawn in its hands (as Baldwin maintains) or an active, conscious hero who tries to fight it (as Baldwin's critics claim). Literature does not have much use for a notion of fate as written in advance, except perhaps to show how much a protagonist would enjoy (in the sense of Lacan's *jouissance*) such extremely confining circumstances. In my reading of *Native Son*, fate is a way to interpret a life-story belatedly, a way to explain all the events in the life of a character retroactively, based on one critical event or act. For example, it was merely prophesied that Oedipus would kill his father and marry his mother. It is only after the king recognizes that the man he murdered was his biological father and the woman he married was his mother that we can say that he has a fate and that the prophecy was correct. On this understanding, Oedipus's critical act is neither the murder of the father nor his attempt to escape the prophesy, but his recognition and acceptance of who he is. That is why Sophocles's drama follows closely the process of discovery, this last, ultimate, or critical event,[8] and only *informs* us, in a second-hand way, about the prophecy and the murder.

The meaning of Thomas's fate and tragedy depends on how we understand the act he performs: what this act is exactly, and what constitutes its social context. I will begin with the social context and will then focus on the act.

Racism

Thomas lives in a racist society, but there are two qualitatively different racisms in this novel and, therefore, there are two fundamentally different ways to understand what and who a "black man" is in *Native Son*. The first racism, which we could term post–Civil War racism, is epitomized in the rule of the mob, and is a kind of racism that is not considered legal in 1930's Chicago. This is the racism Wright tries to escape in *Black Boy (American Hunger)*; it is present in *Native Son* as a background to the kind of racism that is formulated during the trial, in the last book of the novel where Thomas's fate acquires its final form.

According to the prosecutor's winning argument, Bigger Thomas has jeopardized the very institution of the law—the law that, in Buckley's words, "makes us human" (*Native* 476). Buckley uses Thomas's trial to draw a legal boundary between the human and the inhuman, "us" and "them," a divide that runs along racial lines. During the trial, we see, therefore, how mob rule comes to be replaced by the American judicial and penal systems. After Thomas is sentenced, it is the institution of the law and the apparatus of power it can mobilize on its behalf—not the rule of the mob—that stands between white and black communities, protecting the former from a perceived, or fantasized, threat from, in Buckley's words, "some half-human black ape" who "may be climbing through the windows of our homes to rape, murder, and burn our daughters!" (*Native* 476). Buckley's argument does one more thing: it inverts the historical roles of perpetrator and victim. In his argument, whites suffer precisely those brutalities—rape, murder, and burning—that African American people suffered at the hands of whites during slavery and in its aftermath. The inscription of mob rule and of the supremacist stereotype or fantasy in the law during Thomas's trial is the crucial reason why Buckley does not want to turn Thomas over to the white crowd asking for the black man's blood in front of the courthouse. Though the effect would be, in practical terms, the same, the legal ritual leading to Thomas's execution has a fundamentally different significance and consequences. The trial places the allegedly impartial courtroom at the very center of race relations. The trial thus represents the culminating phase—the phase in which we still live—in the long history of American racism, where the legal sphere becomes the primary site of the regulation and definition of race, as opposed to the social or economic spheres. The force behind the law is no longer the white mob, but the state's apparatus of power: its police, National Guard, military, its courts, prisons, etc.

Thus, that Thomas is a "black man" can be deduced only after Thomas is caught for the Dalton murder and brought to trial, for it is only then that his deed and the new definition of what black men are merge. Only after this event does Bigger Thomas become a "black man" in one of the two senses of the term argued during the trial, either Buckley's supremacist sense ("black men" are inhuman), which wins out, or Max's liberal sense ("black men" are products of a certain society), which will be legally represented years later in the Civil Rights Act of 1964 and the ensuing Affirmative Action programs designed, in the words of the United States Commission on Civil Rights, to "provide redress, however belated, for past practices of racial exclusion."

We can then say that Thomas's rebellion fails at the end of the novel because he is recognized not as the singular being called "Bigger Thomas," but only as a member of a group called "black men" in either Buckley's or Max's sense; and that, therefore, Wright's novel fails because it does not finally affirm its protagonist's struggle to affirm his being. Yet, to judge Thomas in these terms is to assign a specific nature to his act, namely, that his act could have been successfully accomplished in the U.S., and that Thomas had an opportunity to succeed in his self-realization. Since his act is neither an individual project, nor an ego-realization on the order of "be all that you can be"; since, more importantly, Thomas lets himself be caught, we are forced to look elsewhere for the full scope of his singular, tragic act, and for the significance of Thomas's death.

To reduce Thomas to predetermination by a racist society as Baldwin does, or to understand his struggle as an individualistic act is to overlook the fact that Thomas is a revolutionary, radical agent and that this agency, this affirmation of life that transcends his ego, is so essential to him, to who he *is*, that he is willing to die for it.

Escape

Returning to the scene of his crime, Thomas deliberates about running away. He feels "caught up," consumed by a "supreme and meaningful act" and postpones making his decision whether to flee to a later moment (*Native* 131). That moment, as we know from book two of *Native Son*, titled "Flight," never comes, and it seems that Thomas has not found a good reason to run away. We can then say that this native son is also "caught up" in the sense that he has no "away" toward which he can run, no other home but America.

As a tragic hero, Thomas has to show that he is aware that he has the option to flee and thus try to change his fate. But, at the same time, in order to be a tragic hero, he cannot exercise this possibility, and must proceed on his way toward his final doom—just as Oedipus has to hear and disregard Jocasta's plea to call off the search for Laius's murderer. Only by remaining on his path can Thomas affirm his being and, further, it is only if Thomas stays in America that the affirmation of his being can have an impact on America. If he runs away, he would cease to be Bigger Thomas, a native son and the country's illegitimate offspring, and he would give up the possibility of opening the system onto a logic, genealogy, and identity that are radically different from anything the system would or could acknowledge. Only if he stays can he make himself into what he already is, a *native alien* from whom the American system has tried to protect itself ever since, figuratively speaking, the first slave ships arrived on this continent.

What Thomas chooses to do when he postpones his flight can then be described in the following way: he attempts to strike at the system, to blot out its founding assumptions and myths, and, seeking recognition, to show that his being cannot be affirmed in his native land—not even by the most progressive ideology of the day. In order for Wright to show this, Thomas has to let the police catch him.

Once Thomas is caught, we could say that even Richard Wright pulls back from the monster he has created.[9] Beginning on page 490, after Max enters his cell, Wright makes this radical revolutionary—who thus far has rejected everyone around him—believe that he has been understood, and we see Thomas ready to submit to the authority of the benevolent, fatherly Jewish man. But Wright does not give in all the way; Thomas's appeal of the death penalty is refused, and he is left alone in the cell to meet his death, which is both the moment of Thomas's end and his triumph. After he is sentenced, he will die as a radical, and in this final act, in this act that defines all of his other acts, he will become what he is. The radical nature of Thomas's self-annihilating goal, this threatening "no" to both the white and black communities, is the crucial reason Wright occupies an ambiguous place in American and, more importantly, African American literature.

The Act

When Thomas is deliberating flight, the text reads:

> He had some money to make a run for it when the time came. And he had his gun. His fingers trembled so that he had difficulty in unlocking the door; but they were not trembling from fear. It was a kind of eagerness he felt, a confidence, a fulness, a freedom; his whole life was caught up in a supreme and meaningful act. (*Native* 131)

While the first impulse is to identify the supreme act in this sentence as the act of murder, this conclusion would prevent us from facing the radical nature of Thomas's rebellion. The act is also, and in a logical sense firstly, the effect of the murder of Mary Dalton on Thomas. It includes his feelings of fulness and freedom and his transformation from a petty criminal into a person who has dared to commit the supreme act—supreme because he attacks the integrity of the symbolic system supporting the definition of what it means to be an American. Thomas thus sees his rebirth as a part of the act: "Like a man reborn, he wanted to test and taste each thing now to see how it went; like a man risen up well from a long illness, he felt deep and wayward whims" (*Native* 125). He has created a new life out of nothing, *ex nihilo*, and this new being, this supreme act of the being's constitution, is all his own: "He had murdered and had created a new life for himself. It was something all his own, and it was the first time in his life he had had anything that others could not take from him" (119).

The supreme act achieves its full measure once Thomas accepts responsibility for the murder, and this acceptance frees him. Let us look closely at the words that constitute the turning point of the novel. This—and not, as Joyce Ann Joyce claims, the murder of Mary Dalton (Joyce 43)—is the climax of the novel. The murder sets the stage for the unfolding of Thomas's tragic fate, just as the plague, which is a figurative representation of Oedipus's murder of Laius, does in *Oedipus the King*.

> Having been thrown by an accidental murder into a position where he had sensed a possible order and meaning in his relations with the people about him; having accepted the moral guilt and responsibility

for that murder because *it* had made him feel free for the first time in his life; having felt in his heart some obscure need to be at home with people and having demanded ransom money to enable him to do it—having done all this and failed, he chose not to struggle any more. With a *supreme* act of will springing from the essence of his being, he turned away from his life and the long train of disastrous consequences that had flowed from it and looked wistfully upon the dark face of ancient waters upon which some spirit had breathed and created him, the dark face of the waters from which he had been first made in the image of a man with man's obscure need and urge; feeling that he wanted to sink back into those waters and rest eternally. (*Native* 316, emphasis added)

Wright here describes, first, Thomas's thrownness in the world; his being alone in a world without God. To be alone here implies that Thomas has distinguished himself from what Martin Heidegger calls "the they" *(das Man)* in *Being and Time*. It is this "they" that Baldwin, misunderstanding Wright's philosophical idiom, wants to see identified. The point is that "the they" do not have an identity in the terms Thomas is forging.

In this world ruled by accident, Thomas senses a possible order (that is, a certain necessity beyond the system that created him) which it is his task to uncover and establish. This new, possible order would regulate his relation with other people "about him," that is, this order would offer a foundation for revolutionizing existing political relations. An exemplary existentialist hero, Thomas accepts the responsibility for his being in the world and, Wright says, "it" makes him free. Wright's ambiguous "it" here stands for several things, including the murder and the acceptance of responsibility. But more importantly, "it" denotes the state of thrownness—the unacknowledged order of the world, the accident of the murder, but also the accident of his skin color— that Thomas accepts. Now, upon accepting himself, there is nothing left for him to accomplish apart from giving himself up to the law that he has tried to escape.

Thomas is neither submitting to the racist law nor simply surrendering to the police. In refusing to struggle further, he encounters "the essence of his being," that is, his origin—"the dark face of ancient waters upon which some spirit had breathed and created him." In gazing upon his origin (which may or may not be Africa), he wants to return to it. He discovers the drive that he has acted upon, the drive that has driven his fate—to "sink back," that is, to perish—and through this discovery his supreme act is accomplished.

Talking to Max in preparation for the trial, Thomas says: "They kill you before you die" (*Native* 409), and his act is meant to counter this death (this social invisibility), to give himself a new birth, thus shaping a death that is, in Freud's sense *(Beyond the Pleasure Principle)*, his own, and that no one can take from him. For Freud, one's own death is a death to which an organism is "instinctually" lead or driven. Since humans are social organisms, since our "instincts" are socially formed, our "own" death is the death which confirms that which is own-most and proper to the one who dies. For Bigger Thomas, to die his own death would mean to die *as* Bigger Thomas, an autonomous man, in the country which refuses to recognize him as a human being. When Thomas dies on the electric chair, it is the racist court that decides how he dies, but this decision and the manner of his death have nothing to do with the significance of his death, which has been determined through his act. Put simply, after Thomas's decision not to struggle, "they" can take his life, but not his death.

We can then say that Thomas's crimes consist of his self-realization, his acceptance of himself, and his acknowledgment of his fate. These are crimes because, according to the rules of his native land, Thomas is not supposed to define himself in and through an ultimate, singular, tragic act. He is not supposed to be an autonomous, that is, self-legislating radical but a symbol. Now the native alien's criminal fate is fulfilled and now we can say that his mother's prophecy was correct:

> "You'll regret how you living some day," she went on. "If you don't stop running with that gang of yours and do right you'll end where you never thought you would. You think I don't know what you boys is doing, but I do. And the gallows is at the end of the road you traveling, boy. Just remember that." (*Native* 8)

In sum, Thomas's supreme act begins with the accidental murder, is compounded by the accident of his skin color, and climaxes when Thomas accepts the responsibility for what he has done and for who he is, deciding not to struggle any more. Wright's *Savage Holiday* tells a similar story. Once again, the assuming of one's own responsibility is the event around which the entire story turns. Erlskine Fowler, the protagonist of *Savage Holiday*, is Thomas's opposite, a rich white man. "But I would say," Wright comments in a 1956 radio interview with Raymond Barthes, "it does not really matter in *Savage Holiday* whether the protagonist is a rich man or a poor one. What matters is his fear of assuming the responsibilities entailed by his new kind of life, a holiday, i.e., a life deprived of the props and support of a daily task to perform." After thirty years in the same company, Fowler has lost his job, but not his wealth, and with it he has lost what Wright calls his *raison d'être*. Fowler's crime and dilemma are, despite the differences, identical to Thomas's: "His dilemma brings him to be responsible for two deaths—he is accidentally responsible for the death of his female neighbor's son, and he deliberately murders her some time later" (*Conversations* 168).

This is not to say that the accident of skin color has no implications for what happens to Thomas. It has. But it determines primarily how Thomas is seen. For example, Britten, whom Mary Dalton's father hires to investigate her murder, would interrogate Thomas differently, if the latter's skin were white. But what is crucial about and necessary in *Native Son* is that Thomas acts to affirm his being, which is not a function of his identity as a "black man," or to whatever he is subject. In his act, in other words, Thomas separates that which is accidental from that which is necessary—namely, a death which would confirm the singularity of his being. Wright admits this essential humanism of his ideology in a 1955 interview with *L'Express:*

> Writing is my way of being a free man, of expressing my relationship to the world and to the society in which I live. My relation to the society of the Western world is dubious because of my color and race. My writing therefore is charged with the burden of my concern about my relation to that society. The accident of race and color has placed me on both sides: the Western World and its enemies. If my writing has any aim, it is to reveal that which is human on both sides, to affirm the essential unity of man on earth. (*Conversations* 163)

CONCLUSION

In this article I hope to have shown that *Native Son* is a tragedy in the basic modernist understanding of what constitutes a tragedy. That a work is a tragedy means that it demonstrates the life of a character who assumes a singular fate that is realized at the moment of his ultimate demise. Put differently, tragedy shows a human character for what he is in the relation of his being to his origin and death; it reveals what Heidegger called a being-toward-death. If *Native Son* is a protest novel, it is so in the etymological sense of this term—"to protest" derives from the Latin *protestari; pro,* forth, and *testari,* to affirm. *Native Son* is a protest novel in the sense that it affirms (attests to and asserts) the singularity of Bigger Thomas, a violent black criminal and a native alien who is denied the status of native son in the U.S. and who suffers precisely his *being* America's native son.

Native Son thus offers the political and aesthetic alternative—a version of authentic American black literature—that Baldwin calls for and refuses to acknowledge in Wright's novel. *Native Son* is authentic and authentically black if for no other reason than because it attests to the authenticity—that is, the singularity—of (even) Thomas's (criminal) being. Further, the novel is authentic in the sense that it shows that Thomas's act need not be defined by any higher goal, any moral end, besides his own affirmation and autonomy.

What we can fault Wright for is the ideology of the protest, because it is based on Wright's vision of the "essential unity of man on earth" (*Conversations* 163). That is, we can criticize him for his humanism, which may appear to some critics as politically and aesthetically naive and inadequate, and to others as exclusive rather than inclusive, since Wright's female characters are often killed off in violent deaths, thus making it seem that women are not a part of "the essential unity of man" Wright wants to assert. I would, however, hesitate before suggesting that we can explore fruitfully either line of critique. This is because, first, nowhere in his work does Wright assume that there is an essential positive characteristic of the human (even though the protagonist is invariably male). As in *Native Son,* what is human derives from a singular (non)relation with a being's origin and mortality; that is, from Thomas's situation at what Lacan calls the limit of the symbolic.

One might wish that Thomas were constructive rather than destructive in his self-realization, that he might fashion or cultivate rather than create *ex nihilo,* and that Wright were life-affirming rather than obsessed with human passions, monstrosity, origin, and mortality. But these are wishes and imperatives that Wright would have seen as naive and inadequate. To say the least, they were not his desires. In *Native Son,* he created a character who wants the entire system blotted out, and his being affirmed regardless of where he has come from and what he has done.

CODA

I will end this essay with a brief argument against the most recent trend in interpretation of *Native Son,* which suggests that this novel leads to a traumatic impasse since it repeats the trauma of race in America. For instance, Jonathan Elmer writes: "After sixty years, *Native Son* continues to be a problem, continues to pressure us toward conflicting conclusions that share only their unacceptability" (Elmer 792). If for no other reason than because of the history of racism, Elmer seems to be correct when he claims that Bigger Thomas's enactment of a white supremacist fantasy (e.g., that black men are sexually attracted to white women) as well as the stereotypical aspects of his character are compulsive and, therefore, traumatic. We can indeed see the entire trajectory that Thomas traverses—the trajectory I have called Thomas's fate—as a repetition of the history of racism and therefore as a trauma. But, there is also another interpretative possibility, a reading following from my analysis of *Native Son,* which does not negate the historical trauma, but counts it as a given and proceeds beyond what Elmer identifies as a traumatic impasse (using Lacan's concept of trauma as a missed encounter).

Coming to the same issue with two examples other than *Native Son* in mind, we could ask if Oedipus's and Antigone's fates are traumatic. In one obvious sense, yes, both fates are, because they repeat the doom of the Labdacus family. Indeed, Sophocles's tragedies present us with a traumatic impasse of family relations and, more generally, of the human position in the world. But this is precisely a given—assumed by the tragic playwright and his audience—rather than born of the tragedy. We could even say that the Greeks invented Necessity to give a face and name to the cause behind what in modern psychological language is termed trauma. Greek fate is, on this understanding, an acting-out of trauma, and tragedy is a working through the trauma—a catharsis or, in Lacan's translation, abreaction and release from the crisis provoked by the tragic play (*Ethics* 244–246).[10] To the best of my knowledge, there is no critic (including Freud and Lacan) who has seen or would want to see either Oedipus's search for the killer or Antigone's burial of her brother only in terms of the trauma that they repeat. The point has been, rather, to interpret the autonomy of the two characters and explain how and why they go beyond such constraints (traumatic or otherwise). That is, the two plays have been read, correctly, *as* tragedies. I would like to suggest then that, similarly, *Native Son* does not lead us to a traumatic impasse, but, like those two tragedies, begins with that impasse and takes us elsewhere.

With *Native Son* we traverse the symbolic field of post–Civil War America. As it reveals certain fantasies that go into the making of America—white supremacist fantasies, liberal fantasies, African American fantasies—*Native Son* takes us to the limit of the symbolic field and makes the claim that there is a human being who unconsciously enacts these fantasies, fulfills the preset roles, *and* is not defined by them, is not merely the subject of the history he suffers. Where is this elsewhere marked by the limit of the symbolic field? Who or what is this being which is not reducible to the subject of trauma? What, to put it differently, is the subject that emerges, that begins its becoming from the meeting point between these fantasies and the real (in Lacan's sense)?

These questions bring us to the problematic treated at the end of Lacan's 1964 seminar, *The Four Fundamental Concepts of Psycho-Analysis*—the first seminar Lacan delivered after he was excommunicated from the International Psychoanalytical Association. Lacan, now an outsider, an alien of sorts, turns to the four fundamental concepts of psychoanalysis, pursuing the essential psychoanalytic problem of the analyst's desire. At the end of the seminar, talking about transference and counter-transference, Lacan puts the following questions: "What . . . does he who has passed through the experience of this opaque relation to the origin, to the drive, become? How can a subject who has traversed the radical phantasy experience the drive?" (*Four* 273).

The answer to the first question, which we can give based on our reading of *Native Son,* is that he who passes through the experience of the relation to the origin and drive has gone beyond stereotype (beyond those identities his symbolic world holds out to him), and has become a tragic—singular, extreme—character. And the answer to the second question is that the subject who has traversed the radical fantasy experiences the drive as a necessity and consequently his act and his fate as his.

Using psychoanalytic terms, we can say that *Native Son* brings us to the point that Lacan characterizes as the "beyond of analysis" (*Four* 273). It is here that we can grasp the import of Freud's *durcharbeiten*[11] as precisely working through the beyond of analysis (the real) which is, though beyond it, constitutive of analysis. And here in this exploration of the "beyond of analysis," we get a precise Lacanian understanding of what working through *(durcharbeiten)* trauma is supposed to accomplish, namely to cross "the plane of identification"; that is, to force the separation between analysand and analyst (read also as reader and character) and reorient the analysand's (that is, the reader's) desire in such a way that the "experience of the subject is . . . brought back to the plane at which, from the reality of the unconscious, the drive may be made present" (*Four* 274). Or, in Bruce Fink's simpler formulation, the beyond of analysis is where the subject "experiences the drive after his or her fantasy has . . . been radically transformed or removed" (Fink 213). The drive in question is, in Freud's terms, the death drive, and the fantasy in question—the fantasy that Wright wants to identify and expose—is that one can be an American and a Negro before being a human being.[12] In *Native Son* we see Bigger Thomas's attempt to acknowledge the death drive, which is something he can do only as Bigger Thomas (not as a black man)—and has to do *in order* to become Bigger Thomas.

On this reading, *Native Son* recalls us to the revolutionary modernist project to affirm, in Lacan's words, the ineffaceable character of what is summed up in Bigger Thomas's cry at the end of the novel: "But what I killed for, I *am*" (*Native* 501).

NOTES

This article is a result of my conversations with Catherine Peebles about Lacan's ethics seminar and Richard Wright's *Native Son*.

1. It is evident throughout her essay that Foley interprets Sacks's understanding of the difference between narrative tragedy and apologue in terms of identification with the protagonist. The following statement is just one example: "*Native Son*, by contrast [to Dreiser's novel], orders its narration of Bigger's fate to suit the requirement of apologue rather than those of narrative tragedy. Even its title offers a declaration about social reality rather than an invitation to identification and catharsis" (Foley 193–194).

2. In *Native Son*, when he talks to Bigger Thomas before the trial, Boris A. Max says: "They [white, rich Chicago] felt they had you fenced off so that you could

not do what you did. Now they're mad because deep down in them they believe that they made you do it" (415).

3. Though the main example in Lacan's analysis of tragedy is Sophocles's *Antigone,* what he says fits *Oedipus the King* as well. The main difference between the two is that Antigone seems to be, already at the beginning of the play, the kind of tragic hero that Oedipus will become by the tragedy's end, after he learns who his biological mother and father are.

4. *Atè* is for Lacan, as well as for some classicists, the crucial term of Greek tragedy. Hard to translate, *atè* is best approximated by ruin, disaster, misfortune, infatuation, error, or blindness (in a metaphorical sense). In short, *atè* is something in the protagonist that leads him or her to the downfall and, in this narrow sense, it is the cause of what we could call, in *Native Son*'s terms, fate. In addition to Lacan's *Ethics,* see Dawe and Doyle.

5. "Those" is possibly a printing error. The text should instead read "whose."

6. See Wright *How "Bigger" Was Born,* published in the same volume with *Native Son* (531). On Baldwin's oedipal envy of Richard Wright, see Baldwin, "Alas, Poor Richard."

7. *Black Boy (American Hunger)* portrays a similar rebellion against the imperative to do what one ought to do, and a similar attempt at self-realization in the main character, who acts against that imperative. When, for example, young Richard Wright publishes his first story, "Voodoo and Hell's Half Acre," neither his school mates nor his family recognize it as Wright's creation. The school children believe that he is not telling them the truth, and his family's attitude is summed up in Aunt Addie's blaming the "whole thing upon my [Wright's] upbringing." Rejected and misunderstood by his immediate community, Wright felt that he "had committed a crime" in publishing this story (*Hunger* 168).

8. In *The Interpretation of Dreams,* Freud links this process of discovery in Sophocles's tragedy "to the work of a psycho-analysis" (295). I will address this link directly in the final section of my article.

9. For some reasons why Wright censors his portrayal of Thomas, see Richard Wright, *How "Bigger" Was Born* (523).

10. When Lacan links catharsis to abreaction, by the latter term he means, as we read in Laplanche and Pontalis's *The Language of Psycho-analysis,* an "emotional discharge whereby the subject liberates himself from the affect attached to the memory of a traumatic event in such a way that this affect is not able to become (or to remain) pathogenic" (1).

11. Or, in Lacan's French translation of Freud's term (in *Les quatre concepts fondamentaux de la psychanalyse*), "la nécesité de l'élaboration" (246), meaning "the necessity of elaboration."

12. In his 1960 interview with *L'Express,* Wright says, "My color is not my country. I am a human being before being an American; I am a human being before being a Negro, and, if I deal with racial problems, it is because those problems were created without my consent and permission. I am opposed to any racial definition of man" (*Conversations* 201).

Works Cited

Baldwin, James. "Alas, Poor Richard." *The Price of the Ticket: Collected Nonfiction, 1948–1985.* New York: St. Martin's, 1985. 269–288.

————. *Notes of a Native Son.* New York: Bantam, 1968.

Bloom, Harold. *Richard Wright.* New York: Chelsea House, 1987.

Dawe, R. D. "Some Reflections on *Ate* and *Hamartia.*" *Harvard Studies* in *Classical Philology* 72 (1968). 89–123.

Doyle, Richard E. *Ate, Its Use and Meaning: A Study in the Greek Poetic Tradition from Homer to Euripides.* New York: Fordham University Press, 1984.

Elmer, Jonathan. "Spectacle and Event in *Native Son.*" *American Literature* 70 (1998). 767–798.

Fink, Bruce. A *Clinical Introduction to Lacanian Psychoanalysis: Theory and Technique.* Cambridge: Harvard University Press, 1997.

Foley, Barbara. "The Politics of Poetics: Ideology and Narrative Form in *An American Tragedy* and *Native Son.*" *Richard Wright: Critical Perspectives Past and Present.* Ed. Henry Louis Gates and Anthony Appiah. New York: Amistad, 1993: 188–199.

Freud, Sigmund. *The Interpretation of Dreams.* Trans. James Strachey. New York: Harper, 1998.

————. *Beyond the Pleasure Principle.* Trans. James Strachey. New York: Norton, 1989.

Gilroy, Paul. *The Black Atlantic: Modernity and Double Consciousness.* Cambridge: Harvard University Press, 1993.

Heidegger, Martin. *Being and Time.* Trans. John Macquarrie and Edward Robinson. San Francisco: Harper & Row, 1962.

Joyce, Joyce Ann. *Richard Wright's Art of Tragedy.* Iowa City: University of Iowa Press, 1986.

Lacan, Jacques. *On Feminine Sexuality, The Limits of Love and Knowledge.* Trans. Bruce Fink. New York: Norton, 1998.

————. *The Ethics of Psychoanalysis.* Trans. Dennis Porter. New York: Norton, 1988.

————. *The Four Fundamental Concepts of Psycho-Analysis.* Trans. Alan Sheridan. New York: Norton, 1981.

————. *Les quatre concepts fondamentaux de la psychanalyse.* Paris: Seuil, 1973.

Laplanche, Jean and J.-B. Pontalis. *The Language of Psychoanalysis.* Trans. Donald Nocholson-Smith. New York: Norton, 1974.

Nietzsche, Friedrich. *Untimely Meditations.* Trans. R. J. Hollingdale. New York: Cambridge University Press, 1997.

Portelli, Alessandro. "Everybody's Healing Novel: *Native Son* and Its Contemporary Critical Context." *Mississippi Quarterly* 50 (1997). 255–266.

Read, Ishmael. "Bigger and O. J." *Birth of a Nation'hood: Gaze, Script, and Spectacle in the O. J. Simpson Case.* Ed. Toni Morrison and Claudia Brodsky Lacour. New York: Pantheon, 1997. 169–196.

Sacks, Sheldon. *Fiction and the Shape of Belief: A Study of Henry Fielding, with Glances at Swift, Johnson, and Richardson.* Berkeley: University of California Press, 1964.

Sophocles, *Oedipus the King. The Three Theban Plays.* Trans. Robert Fagles. New York: Penguin, 1984. 155–251.

The United States Commission on Civil Rights, *Statement* on *Affirmative Action. Clearinghouse Publication* 54 (October 1977).

Wright, Richard. *Black Boy (American Hunger): A Record of Childhood and Youth.* New York: Harper, 1998.

————. *Native Son and How "Bigger" Was Born.* New York: Harper, 1998.

————. *Conversations with Richard Wright.* Ed. Keneth Kinnamon and Michel Fabre. Jackson: University Press of Mississippi, 1993.

———— *Savage Holiday.* New York: Avon, 1954.

QIANA J. WHITTED

"Using My Grandmother's Life as a Model": Richard Wright and the Gendered Politics of Religious Representation

> My grandmother had deep-set black eyes with over-hanging lids and she had a habit of gazing with a steady, unblinking stare; in my later life I've always associated her religious ardor with those never-blinking eyes of her[s], eyes that seemed to be in this world but not of this world, eyes that seemed to be contemplating human frailty from some invulnerable position outside time and space.
>
> —Richard Wright ("Memories of My Grandmother" 7)

Silent and fearless, an Indian maiden drowns herself rather than break a mysterious vow—this is the essence of Richard Wright's first short story, written on his knees during a time of prayer. Each day his grandmother pleaded with him "to pray hard, to pray until tears came," so frustrated was she with her grandson's rebelliousness, his willful religious doubts, and feeble attempts at Christian devotion (*Black Boy* 119). Wright consented to the older woman's wishes, like many of his own characters in the years and novels to come, with much apprehension and dismay. Convinced that his prayers were empty words that "bound noiselessly against the ceiling," he manipulated the daily hour of private reflection toward his own creative ends. After failing to write a hymn, the thirteen year old put aside his Bible,

The Southern Literary Journal, Volume 36, Number 2 (2004): pp. 13–30. Copyright © 2003 by the *Southern Literary Journal* and the University of North Carolina at Chapel Hill Department of English.

121

turned to his studies in Native American history, and found his own voice in imaginative prose (*Black Boy* 120).

"I had never in my life done anything like it; I had made something, no matter how bad it was; and it was mine," Wright remarks in his 1945 autobiography, *Black Boy* (120). Cloistered in his room, Wright chose not to commune with his grandmother's god, and yet the moment retains a special reverence in light of his career as a writer, poet, and essayist. The Indian maiden's narrative is poorly written, he admits, and lacks a unifying plot or conflict.[1] Nevertheless, the story is made sacred through his account of its creation in *Black Boy*. It is a cultural marker as significant as the library card that gave the youth his first glimpse into the insurgent power of the written word. The unrefined tale reminds us that in his life, as in his writing, Richard Wright wrestled unceasingly with his faith.

While religion is consistently portrayed as the enduring core of black folk culture in Wright's work, the Mississippi-born writer typically surveys the liturgical landscape over the shoulders of skeptics and unbelievers. His narrative choices in works such as *Uncle Tom's Children* (1938), *Native Son* (1945), *The Outsider* (1953), and the unfinished novel, *Tarbaby's Dawn*[2] emphasize the declining efficacy of black Christian theism in modern times of crisis. Wright also stresses the betrayal of elders, particularly mothers, whose exhortations to believe act as a hindrance to his young protagonists' full understanding of manhood, human dignity, and race pride. As a result, Wright's literary meditations on the black church act as signposts of his own struggle for transcendence, even as they underscore the material angst and fragmentation of his characters.

Black Boy makes this connection explicit through the troublesome birth of his first short story. Likewise, in the unpublished essay, "Memories of My Grandmother," Wright attributes the primary inspiration for works like "The Man Who Lived Underground" to his maternal grandmother, Margaret Bolton Wilson. Signifying upon the planar concept of the believer who lives "*in* the world but not *of* the world," Wright's short story features a black male protagonist named Fred Daniels who eludes police capture for a murder he did not commit by hiding in the tunnels and caves of an urban sewer system. From a subterranean vantage point, Daniels surveys the actions "aboveground" like a ghost one moment, and a god the next, hovering in the margins of human-ness. This, Wright insinuates, is how his grandmother used her religion to survive in a strange and hostile world. He believed that she was tethered to a similar sense of "psychological distance," eschewing reality for the dark passageways of the mind where time stands still. Wright explains:

> The idea—or, if you prefer to call it, the concept—back of THE MAN WHO LIVED UNDERGROUND is half as old as my

life and has slept somewhere within my heart since my childhood, awakening now and then to baffle me, to startle me, to amuse me, to fill me with new insight into myself and my environment. The whole idea is centered around the ardent and volatile religious disposition of my grandmother who died in Chicago in 1934. My grandmother lived her religion day by day and hour by hour; *religion* was her *reality*, the sole meaning in her life. The inconsistencies of her behavior were the subject of much agonizing thought and feeling on my part during at least one-half of my life; indeed, it was my grandmother's interpretation of religion—or perhaps I should say that it was my religious grandmother's interpretation of life—that actually made me decide to run off from home at the age of fifteen.

("Memories of My Grandmother" 1)

Black Boy attributes Wright's departure from the South to a variety of sources—his mother's illness and his father's abandonment, the vicious racism of southern whites, and the poverty and cultural depravity of his surroundings. But Wright's previous musings in "Memories of My Grandmother" depict an alternate view, a desperate flight from religious persecution. The grandson who was once so beleaguered by Wilson's religious fanaticism now claims to have exorcised these memories in print as an adult. Wright further insists that "The Man Who Lived Underground" deciphers the puzzling doctrine, contradictions, and ephemeral joys of his grandmother's theology in a way that illuminates the spiritual complexity of African Americans in general. Out of his critique of her belief system, Wright tells us that he fashioned an agenda that would shape his fictional renderings of African American faith:

My concern with depicting the religious impulses among Negroes —using my grandmother's life as a model—did not in any degree accur [sic] to me all at once. The vague desire would well up and subside many times throughout a period of years; but always I'd push the thought aside, feeling that I had not yet found the form of action that would do justice to the principle involved, that would bring out in bold outline the functional pattern of response and reflex that lay at the back of her religious disposition.

("Memories of My Grandmother" 4)

Observations such as these make "Memories of My Grandmother" an invaluable essay. Two drafts of the piece are currently housed at the Beinecke Rare Book and Manuscript Library at Yale University.[3] Although the essay is not dated, Wright probably wrote it after "The Man Who Lived

Underground" was completed in 1941 (Fabre 239). Wright received similar pressure from his mother, Ella Wright, to join her church and accept God as his savior, yet the unpublished piece maintains that his grandmother is the one whose religious orientation fascinated and disturbed him the most. With this in mind, my reading of "Memories of My Grandmother" will scrutinize Wright's reflections of Margaret Bolton Wilson in relation to his well-known autobiography, *Black Boy*. How, I ask, can the personal reflections detailed in "Memories of My Grandmother" intensify our critical analysis of gender and religion in Wright's work? I will further examine the way in which Wright develops the story of Fred Daniels in "The Man Who Lived Underground" against his own ongoing struggle to understand his "religious grandmother's interpretation of life." Do the images, rhetorical concepts, and narrative structures in the tale meet the ideological objectives Wright set for the piece? And how should readers reckon with the author's mission to demystify the religious attitudes of all African Americans through the memory of a single, elusive female figure?

Such an examination deepens our awareness of a complex African American religious literary tradition, one vital and vigorous enough to incorporate the strains of humanist dissent that rise to a fever pitch after World War I. Wright takes a prominent place among a number of black artists, including Nella Larsen, Walter White, Langston Hughes, James Baldwin, Carolyn Rodgers, Alice Walker, Ernest Gaines, and Randall Kenan, who feature theistic and nontheistic religious perspectives in their work. The existence of this community of writers refutes Wright's own insistence that "despite our proud boast that we are a religious people, we have but little literature dealing with religious emotion per se" ("Memories of My Grandmother" 2). Although he was convinced that there was no god—not in the Black Belt of Chicago, not in the Jim Crow South—that could effectively address the needs and desires of twelve million black voices, the subject matter of Wright's fiction never strayed far from the doors of the church.

In *Black Boy*, the accounts of Wright's upbringing define Granny primarily as an "archetypal oppressor."[4] Well-intentioned but adversarial attacks and militaristic campaigns are the key to her relentless proselytizing. As a result, Margaret Bolton Wilson looks favorably upon her grandson only once in *Black Boy*—when he "sees" an angel during revival services at their Jackson, Mississippi church. After hearing the elder describe Jacob's angelic visions from the book of Genesis, he whispers, "You see, granny, if I ever saw an angel like Jacob did, then I'd believe" (117). Here young Wright hopes to assuage his grandmother's concern for his soul, but his "if . . . then" theorem of repentance also serves another purpose. Any faith that he embraces will require "infallible evidence" and, in his mind, angels cannot thrive in the "dread, fear, hunger, terror, and loneliness" beyond the church doors (115). Like the bizarre pulp fiction serials that he reads at night, Wright regards the "cosmic tales" of his grandmother's religion as elaborate fantasies created to satisfy the needs of a willing audience (102). Believing that he would never actually see an angel, Wright uses the Old Testament story to articulate a clear rationale for his unbelief.

But Granny fails to hear his "if." She believes in the power of visions, as do the church elder and the rest of the congregation. She misinterprets Wright's challenge and assumes that the young boy has, in fact, already witnessed a vision of God. After service she shares her grandson's miraculous awakening with the elder. His response to the boy—"She says that you have seen an angel"—forces Wright to stammer aloud, "No . . . N-nooo, sir! No, sir!" and when questioned repeatedly, he admits: "But I didn't see *anything*" (117–118). Indeed, Wright underestimates the serious implication of his suggestion which, lost in translation, becomes "an obscene act" that rouses their hopes "wildly high":

> Granny rushed to me and hugged me violently, weeping tears of joy. Then I babbled, speaking with emotional reproof, censuring her for having misunderstood me; I must have spoken more loudly and harshly than was called for—the others had now gathered about me and Granny—for Granny drew away from me abruptly and went to a far corner of the church and stared at me with a cold set face. I was crushed. I went to her and tried to tell her how it had happened.
>
> "You should't've spoken to me," she said in a breaking voice that revealed the depths of her disillusionment. (119)

The elder is disappointed, but Granny is even more disgraced by her grandson's apparent recklessness. His action, intended to ease her worry, has only magnified his impiety. Over two decades later, Wright would remember the mistake in *Black Boy* as the incident that brought his grandmother "the greatest shame and humiliation of her entire religious life" (116).

Wright recounts this same mistranslation in "Memories of My Grandmother." This time he prefaces the incident with the suggestion that he and Granny had previously agreed upon rudimentary guidelines for belief, conversion, and church membership. Wright reasons, "When she would ask me what real objections I had, I would tell her that I had to see something before I would join [the church]. She had to accept my explanations, because she had told me that she had not joined until she has *seen* something" ("Memories of My Grandmother" 5). Biblical accounts of Jacob, in particular, would have resonated with Wright's insistent yearning to "see something." In four separate instances, the Old Testament figure not only beholds angels in his dreams, but hears the voice of a heavenly messenger warning him against danger.[5] Once again Wright tells his grandmother: "[I]f I ever saw an angel like that man did, I'd join the church," but in this version, his fictional self is not overcome with emotion and uncontrollable outbursts; Wright does not "babble." Instead, he sharply corrects the older woman and publicly counters her unrealistic hopes with an appeal to logic:

> "You *did* tell me you saw an angel," my grandmother said. "You told me during service . . ."
>
> "No'm," I said hastily, burning with embarrassment, ashamed that so many people were listening. "I told you that *if* I saw one I'd join church . . ."
>
> The elder smiled. My grandmother was angry.
>
> "You did tell me!" she said stoutly.
>
> Church members began to laugh.
>
> "Granny, you didn't understand," I said.
>
> My grandmother walked away, hurt. For a week there was coolness between us. Such was the atmosphere in which I spent my most sensitive and formative years. (6)

In *Black Boy*, Wright blames these supposedly nonsensical expectations on the fundamental character of his Granny's religion. He is "crushed," we are told, by her anger and coldness. But the same scene in "Memories of My Grandmother" does not emphasize the youth's blunder as much as it underscores a willful irrationality on the part of the grandparent. So focused is Granny on converting Wright that she fails to listen, to hear his vulnerability in a private, confessional whisper. Her authority thusly compromised, Wright uses her embarrassment to make her appear foolish before the elder and the laughing church members. Granny is the one who is chastised like a child in this version; she is "crushed." Wright details this misunderstanding as a crucial turning point in the way he viewed his grandmother. Her faith became a signifier of weakness to him, an unstable guide for negotiating reality and answering questions of ultimate significance.

In the essay, "How Bigger Was Born," Wright argues that black responses to white oppression have historically ranged "from outright blind rebellion to a sweet, otherworldly submissiveness" (438). While the essay's five nameless Bigger Thomases—reckless, defiant, and all relatively young—personify the former response, "Memories of My Grandmother" demonstrates how Margaret Bolton Wilson epitomizes the latter. She is Wright's emasculating prototype of surrender in both secular and religious forms. Furthermore, her old age, as a former slave, anchors her image in spaces and times past. Though most black women during this time belonged to Baptist or Methodist churches—as in the case of Wright's own mother—he uses Granny's fundamentalist devotion to the Seventh-Day Adventists to encompass nearly all African American religions. The denomination is known for its evangelical conservatism and literal readings of the Bible as a revelation of God. The church's name, for example, is derived from the Fourth Commandment to observe the seventh day as the Sabbath-rest in preparation for the return of Christ, or "Second Advent."[6] In *Black Boy,* the Seventh-Day Adventist commitment to healthy living can be found, to offer one example, in Granny's refusal to serve pork, veal, fish without scales and spines, and other foods considered harmful. Wright learns to navigate around many of these practices—he stomachs his grandmother's peanut roast and is eventually allowed to run errands on Saturday for extra money. But in "Memories of My Grandmother," he expresses unmitigated dissatisfaction with Granny's slavish allegiance to "sacred time" and the way in which her faith "encompasses and regulates every moment of living."[7] Wright states:

> A man who worships in the Seventh-Day Adventist Church lives, psychologically, in a burning and continuous moment that never ends: The present is ever-lasting; the past is telescoped into *now;* there is no future and at any moment Christ may come again and then the anxious tension of time will be no more.
>
> ("Memories of my Grandmother" 2)

Using his grandmother's life "as a model" for his literary representations of religion becomes particularly problematic, however, when we begin to consider the doctrinal variations of Protestant denominations and the diversity of African American churches, North and South. The nation also witnessed a growing number of black Catholics, Muslims, Jews, and smaller black sects after World War I and the Great Migration, especially in northern cities like Chicago where Wright made his home after 1927. The political activism and moral leadership of African Methodist Episcopal bishops Daniel Alexander Payne and Henry McNeal Turner in the 1800s extended far into the next century as AME churches continued to distinguish themselves as social progressives against segregation, racial violence, and black economic and educational disparities. Likewise, the National Baptist Woman's Convention had met regularly for over four decades when Wright penned "The Man

Who Lived Underground." This auxiliary of the National Baptist Convention participated in foreign missionary work, established a training school for women in Washington D.C., spoke out against disfranchisement, encouraged black migration from the South, and called on African American leaders to "teach [black people] how to make their religion a real, potent factor in race regeneration."[8]

But Wright was not concerned with qualifying his rendering of the black folk church with these exceptions. He was consciously writing in the shadow of "Green Pastures" and popular caricatures like Florian Slappey, the black private detective and Alabama migrant whose antics were celebrated in the *Saturday Evening Post* in the 1920s and 1930s.[9] Wright's greatest dilemma centered around finding a form that would accurately portray the nuances of African American religion without succumbing to "local color" stereotypes:

> I do not mean *literary* form, but form of *action*, a contour of *movement*, a ritualistic scheme whose dynamics would lay bare the inner but not the outer processes of religion. The primitive forms of religious life among the masses of Negroes in America are all too well-known: the shouting, the singing, the moaning, the fainting, and the rolling . . . I suppose my grandmother indulged in more than her share of these during her lifetime, but these external manifestations, in my opinion, did not indicate the true structure of her religious personality.
>
> ("Memories of My Grandmother" 3)

Wright claims instead that he accessed his grandmother's "religious personality" through a network of cultural products. In music, the erratic juxtaposition of images in blues songs, unified abstractly through mood, corresponds with Granny's "ability to tie the many floating items of her environment together into one meaningful whole" (13); in film, Hollywood's "invisible men" adventures resonate with her stories of invisible angels hovering in the sky (14); in art, the creative detachment of Surrealism is suggestive to Wright of his grandmother's "enforced severance" from reality (23); and finally, in literature, he credits Gertrude Stein's "Melanctha" for awakening within him a new respect for the language of his people. Upon reading the story, Wright states: "My mind was swept back over the years to the days when I lived in Mississippi, to the thousands of times when I'd heard my grandmother speak to me and I began to hear the intonation of her voice, the rhythm of her simple, vivid sentences" (20). To further tap into the inner processes of his grandmother's religion, Wright would invoke her "steady, unblinking stare" and the familiar discourse of sensory deprivation—blindness, deafness, numb flesh, and an indistinguishable blur between sleeping and waking—in the short story, "The Man Who Lived Underground."

In conceptualizing the idea of "sweet, otherworldly submissiveness," Wright distills his grandmother's religious life to the patterns and symbols that we find fixed in nearly every southern black female character in his work. Consider Mrs. Thomas' desperate appeals for Bigger's soul in *Native Son*, or the way in which Cross Damon describes his mother's "tainted" love in *The Outsider:*

> Though she had loved him, she had tainted his budding feelings with a fierce devotion born of her fear of a life that had baffled and wounded her. His first coherent memories had condensed themselves into an image of a young woman whose hysterically loving presence had made his imagination conscious of an invisible God—Whose secret grace granted him life—hovering oppressively in space above him.
>
> (*The Outsider* 22)

What, then, does Wright hope to accomplish by inverting these gendered representations of the black woman as religious zealot through the male protagonist of "The Man Who Lived Underground"? Recalling the short story in an extended draft of "Memories of My Grandmother," Wright tells us that he was not concerned about his main character's gender, just as long as he was able to capture his grandmother's "way of looking" and what made her "tick" (53). Yet Wright's fictional account of Fred Daniels' otherworldly withdrawal into a sewer establishes a troubling kinship with his memories of Granny. Although the black man initially denounces traditional Christian beliefs and practices in the short story, he inevitably succumbs to a "womanly" fear of an aboveground life that "baffles" and "wounds."

At the start of the tale, Daniels opens the sewer cover and enters the purgatorial realm for protection. But he discovers a strange sense of power betwixt worlds. He makes a new home, ironically, in a cave beside a church, initially mistaking the song floating through the brick wall for a "siren."[10] He listens and watches the church service, which he describes as "abysmally obscene" through a crack above the wall (24). Throughout the story, Daniels will leave to explore other tunnels and hiding places underground, but he always returns to this dirt cave beside the church. With each instance, an increasing sense of timelessness overtakes him. "How long had he been down here?" (25) "Was it day or night now?" (35) "How long had he slept? Where was he?" (59). Such questions indicate Daniels' uneasiness as he becomes less and less aware of the world moving aboveground. In fact, the church on the other side of the brick wall is an apt parallel for his liminal condition. He, too, would have to "kill time" in order to survive.[11]

Daniels' other voyeuristic encounters underground have similar themes. He compares the choir's song to the "nothingness" of a dead infant floating in the sewer, an embalmed body on an undertaker's table, and a theater filled with moviegoers, desensitized by the flickering images (30). When Daniels finds a passageway to a jewelry store, he spies an employee opening a safe and decides to use the privileged information to steal the contents. Afterwards, he surrounds himself with pilfered money and diamonds only to discover that such treasures are worthless, robbed of their significance in the leveling darkness of the cave. Such a realization is deeply liberating for Daniels: "He had triumphed over the world aboveground! He was free! If only people could see this!" (54). At the height of his euphoria, however, Wright's protagonist is forced to reckon with the world of man. He watches in horror as the store security guard is accused and beaten for his crime. When the innocent guard commits suicide, Daniels is shaken by the startling implications of his actions; no longer a voyeur, the invisible man is dabbling with omnipotence. He re-emerges from the sewer on the brink of insanity, eager to "confess" and share his revelations from the lion's den below.

It is at this point that Daniels' kinship with the church worshipers comes full circle. Early on in the narrative, he makes an explicit connection between the Christians and his own flight from persecution: "A vague conviction made him feel that those people should stand unrepentant and yield no quarter in singing and praying, yet *he* had run away from the police, had pleaded with them to believe in *his* innocence" (25). What disturbs Daniels most about the church members is the strain of guilt and unworthiness that he hears in their message. Their songs fatalistically repent for "some dreadful offense which they could not remember or understand" (61). After returning aboveground, Daniels wants to assuage their guilt by sharing his new insight from the cave below. The church, therefore, is his first destination. He tries to tell the gathered congregation about his awakening, but he is violently turned away. Having risen from a sewer netherworld, strangers recoil from his filthy clothes, gaunt face, "red and glassy" eyes, and strange laughter (66–68).

Daniels returns to the police station next, where his words and thoughts shift erratically between the murder he was previously accused of committing and his recent transgressions underground. So desperate is Daniels to make the police officers believe in his newfound vision that he takes the white men to the sewer opening and tries to lure them inside:

> They did not believe him now, but they would. A mood of high selflessness throbbed in him. He could barely contain his rising spirits. They would see what he had seen; they would feel what he

had felt. He would lead them through all the holes he had dug. . . .
He wanted to make a hymn, prance about in physical ecstasy, throw
his arm about the policemen in fellowship. (80)

In the police car, Daniels begins to sing a familiar tune in anticipation of
the connection he hopes to make with the officers. But in keeping with
Wright's previous works, the words Daniels whispers—"*Glad, glad, glad,
oh, so glad / I got Jesus in my soul*"—signal a troubling transference from the
world of "concrete externals" to a distant plane of reality ("The Man Who
Lived Underground" 80; "Memories of My Grandmother" 7). Puzzled, but
strangely curious, the white men allow Daniels to lead them to the sewer.
They watch in silence as he "placed his hands on the rim of the hole and sat
on the edge" before going through (82).

This time, however, Daniels is accustomed to the stench, his feet balance easily in the turbulent water. Wright revisits the moment of his main
character's life-altering transformation, extending the religious metaphor in
order to portray Daniels now as missionary, a conveyance between two planes
of living. His actions transform the edge of the sewer into a mourner's bench
that offers the hope of true metanoia for the nonbelievers above. Like an
evangelist at a revival, Daniels begs and pleads repeatedly with his charges on
the other side—"Come on, you-all!" (83). But the officers are not adolescents,
hampered by inexperience and doubt. These men are not bound to Daniels by
family ties or communal allegiances. Nor do they share a racial history; they
are armed white police officers who stand symbolically over Daniels' head in
the sewer. Without these connections, the narrative suggests that the officers
are unaffected by the rantings of "that crazy nigger" (83). Daniels, on the
other hand, becomes increasingly vulnerable, unwittingly laughing and smiling. He fails to convince the men to take the first step down the metal rung
ladder and at the conclusion of the tale, an officer fires into Daniels' chest and
kills him.

Posthumously published in the collection *Eight Men*, "The Man Who
Lived Underground" is an abridged version of a 150-page novel that was
rejected by several publishers before first appearing as a short story in the
anthology *Cross Section* in 1944.[12] The theme of police brutality and injustice
is particularly well-developed in the piece, as are the existential implications
of "invisibility" among oppressed classes and ethnic groups. Wright is at his
strongest in the narrative when weaving the intricate liminal metaphors of
his protagonist's sewer existence between worlds. But Wright privileges
form over substance and his religious goals for the work, stated clearly and
succinctly in "Memories of My Grandmother," are never fully realized in
Fred Daniels' story. For instance, we are given little indication that Daniels
has experienced a Christian awakening, despite the messianic overtones that

surround his return aboveground and his subsequent death. Any relationship that he may have had with the church ended the moment God-fearing hands tossed him down the brick steps of the sanctuary. Perhaps Wright intended to demonstrate that Daniels, with his expulsion, bears a closer resemblance to Jesus than either the deacons or the repentant choir, for "no prophet is accepted in his own country."[13]

But appropriating the language of the spirituals and affixing clichés to the main character ("he wanted to make a hymn, prance about in physical ecstasy") only forces the reader to engage superficial understandings of deep religious convictions. Even as Daniels is pushed literally and ideologically outside the church, Wright continues to rely on the outward symbols, words, and gestures associated with black Christian worship to indicate his character's neurosis and detachment from society. As a result, his efforts to chart the complex constellations of his grandmother's religion are obscured by the very "external manifestations" he sought to avoid. What are we to make, for example, of the notion that Wright's metaphor for his grandmother's guiding devotion, "the true structure of her religious personality," is a *sewer*? Surely this is not the way the elderly woman described the touchstone of her inner peace during long conversations with her grandson. Here and throughout his writing career, he remained convinced that her religious impulses were mired in absurdity, steeped in the stench and refuse of an underground tomb.

Indeed, Wright's troubling fictional characterizations of black women are virtually inseparable from his attitude toward religion. Like Helga Crane in *Quicksand,* who was initially drawn to the black southern church because of its anesthetizing power, the women in Wright's work turn to religion for its sense of dependency (on God, on the male preacher) that allows them to "deliberately stop thinking" (*Quicksand* 116). Religion as Wright understands it—with his frequent references to its warmth, softness, and analgesic qualities—constitutes their entire response to the world around them. Even those who renounce Christianity, as Sarah Hunter does in *The Outsider,* are unable to resist the "faith of their childhood" in times of crisis (553). Significant problems arise when mothers who are themselves suspended in an infantile state, teach this way of being to their adolescent sons. The resulting discomfort and anger of these young men can often be attributed to what Claudia Tate shrewdly identifies as Wright's "urtext of matricidal impulse" that stresses "the son's perception of maternal betrayal and his reactions of initial ambivalence and subsequent hostility" (Tate 96). Wright spends much of "Memories of My Grandmother" discussing how his religious upbringing had a profound, and often unsettling, impact on his life and work as an adult. He speculates, for example, that "it may be that a man goes through life seeking, blindly and unconsciously, for the repetition of those dim webs of conditioning which he learned at an age when he could make no choice" (17). *Black*

Boy demonstrates that Wright faced a similar set of obstacles with his own mother, Ella Wright, who labored to convert her son after Granny failed.

When we consider "The Man Who Lived Underground" in this context, the sewer as tomb can be read figuratively as a *toxic womb*. Wright portrays the underground cave as a maternal space that nurtures false comfort through fear and frenzied detachment. The defensive posture, irrationality, and arrested sensory awareness of the story's protagonist are, in actuality, gendered patterns of behavior that mimic what Wright believes is a female way of looking at the world. Wright uses the nested enclosure to combine the desperation of black flight with the emasculating "conditioning" of black religion. Psychologically confined to the sewer/womb, Daniels easily misinterprets his surroundings and, like Wright's own grandmother, fails to see, hear, or fully understand his social reality. He is unable to elude the fatalism embedded within the pejorative female imagery of the church's "siren" songs.

Conversely, Wright represents creativity, self-awareness, and religious skepticism as gestures of masculine assertiveness. For characters like Bigger Thomas who fight to declare their humanity in an oppressive society, religion is their "first murder" (*Native Son* 284). Even the preacher in Wright's short story "Fire and Cloud" stops humming spirituals when he decides to protest for the rights of the poor. But Daniels does not experience a comparable awakening or a lasting sense of self-realization. He dies pathetically and, trapped in the otherworldly womb, he becomes another infant corpse decomposing in the sewer water.

In his autobiography, Wright recalls the creation of his first short story as a transformative moment in which he refused to be bound by his grandmother's siren-like religious obligations. He got up off his knees and began to write. And he would continue to assert his own identity in this way, even when alienated by his family and friends. Indeed, Wright's way of bridging the spiritual and temporal gaps between himself and his grandmother came primarily through his art. The act of writing was, as Tate notes, "therapeutic" for Wright; he described it as a profoundly sensual experience and "a kind of significant living" (Tate 109; "How Bigger Was Born" 457). It was under the aegis of research and material-gathering that he made an effort to understand his grandmother's way of life, but only, it should be noted, after both had relocated to the North and the elderly woman, baffled by the urban terrain, was forced to depend on him for rent. Wright explains:

[A]fter having read MELANCTHA, I began to engage my grandmother in long conversations merely to hear her express herself, in order that I could revel in the way she talked, the way that MELANCTHA had enabled me to understand. Then my grandmother died suddenly and *I had to depend entirely upon*

*my memory to reconstruct her innumerable conversations, speeches
of endearment, admonishments, longing, horror, anger, fear, threats,
exhortations.*

("Memories of My Grandmother" 20, emphasis added)

Wright's work is obsessed with new and immediate ways of seeing, with filling in ideological blind spots and shifting the reader's attention, often through startling acts of violence, on the *terra firma* of racism and poverty throughout the world. But we cannot ignore how Wright further inscribes these ways of seeing with gendered religious dimensions. Consider, for example, the two sons in his short story "Bright and Morning Star" who, in their effort to "convert" their Christian mother to a more progressive Communist ideology, "ripped from her startled eyes her old vision" of resignation and humility (225). For Wright, being *in* the world but not *of* the world is unacceptable madness for black men in times of disfranchisement, lynching, and Jim Crow. He constantly explores alternative endings and options through his fiction, having failed to wipe the scales from his own grandmother's eyes before her sudden death.

To be sure, Margaret Bolton Wilson cannot encompass the gamut of African American spirituality, but it is crucial to our investigation of Wright's work to understand the many ways in which his *memory* of her serves as the primary point of reference for the religious characterizations, symbols, and expressions on belief and unbelief in his writing—particularly when he makes the claim that such depictions represent "the American Negro" ("Memories of My Grandmother" 2). A complex network of social experiences, institutional relationships, and moral choices that were specific to her race, gender, region, and class influenced his grandmother's faith. In a segregated society that normalized the inhumanity of blacks and the silence of women, she chose to define herself through a sense of moral superiority. And as a former slave, she may have had access to a wellspring of racial wisdom beyond prayers and hymns that her grandson was not prepared to explore. For while Wright details the abuses he suffered as a youth within her southern church community, he does not expend the same critical energy mining the historical and cultural processes that shaped her patterns of behavior. Instead, her spiritual hopes and desires are invoked as obstacles to his male characters' identity.

The strengths and silences of "Memories of My Grandmother" reveal more about Wright's struggles with God, with racial belonging and manhood, than they do about his maternal "model." This literary autoanalysis could be read, taught, and scrutinized against all of his novels and short stories, but must be given special critical attention alongside "The Man Who Lived Underground." Indeed, Wright believed that his life and his literature shared a unique reciprocity and he steadfastly encouraged his readers to embrace this interconnectedness through essays, interviews, and personal reflections. "Memories of My Grandmother" should be appended to Fred Daniels' tale, supplementing the reader's immediate perceptions in much the same way that the essay "How Bigger Was Born" now greets readers after the final page of *Native Son*.[15]

NOTES

1. Could Wright have been attempting to capture his grandmother's devotion to God in his story about the Indian maiden's willingness to sacrifice her life for an unspoken oath? Or perhaps there are echoes of the author's own anxieties about his impending baptismal rites in his character's unflinching immersion in a "watery grave" (*Black Boy* 120)?

2. Originally titled, *Tarbaby's Sunrise: A Folk-Saga*, Wright's unfinished novel, *Tarbaby's Dawn* was rejected by numerous publishers and in 1940, he turned the final chapters into the short story, "Almos' a Man" for *Harper's Bazaar* (Fabre 135).

3. Unless otherwise stated, the quotes from "Memories of My Grandmother" in this article refer to shorter edited typescript.

4. Robert Stepto, *Behind the Veil: A Study of Afro-American Narrative* (Urbana: University of Illinois Press, 1979): 141.

5. In Jacob's dream at Bethel, he sees angels ascending and descending on a stairway to heaven (Genesis 28.12); when his father-in-law, Laban, tries to cheat Jacob, an angel advises him to leave and return to Canaan (Genesis 31.11); Jacob is also reassured by God's presence through the appearance of angels on his return journey (Genesis 32.1) and wrestles with a heavenly messenger later that night (Genesis 32.24-31).

6. Saturday is regarded by Seventh-Day Adventists as the Sabbath. Frank S. Mead and Samuel S. Hill, *Handbook of Denominations in the United States*, 11th ed. (Nashville: Abingdon Press, 2001): 36.

7. Religious scholar Mircea Eliade characterizes "sacred time" as a break in the historical present in which human existence is defined by a desire to return to a paradisaical state. Such religious nostalgia can lead to ceaseless repetition of beliefs, customs, and patterns of behavior and thus, can "appear to be a refusal of history." Eliade's theory resonates with Wright's perception of the black church as a space where congregants struggle to apply an outmoded belief system to an ever-changing modern landscape. Mircea Eliade, *The Sacred and The Profane: The Nature of Religion* (New York: Harper & Row, 1957): 90; "Memories of My Grandmother" 2.

8. Nannie H. Burroughs, "Report of the Work of Baptist Women," *Journal of the Twentieth Annual Session of the Woman's Convention Auxiliary to the National Baptist Convention, Held with the Second Baptist Church, Indianapolis, Indiana Sept. 8–13, 1920, African American Religious History: A Documentary Witness*, ed. Milton C. Sernett (Durham: Duke University Press, 1999): 380.

9. In "Memories of My Grandmother," Wright remarks that his reluctance to write about black religion stems, in part, from the fear that readers will associate his depiction with the bucolic stereotypes of "Green Pastures," the award-winning Broadway play that was made into a film in 1936. Wright protested the depiction of Florian Slappey in a 1945 interview for *The Sunday Star*. Coit Hendley, Jr., "Richard

Wright Stresses Realism in Dealing with Fictional Stereotypes," *The Sunday Star* [Washington] 11 November 1945: C-3, C-7, *Conversations with Richard Wright,* eds. Keneth Kinnamon and Michel Fabre (Jackson: University Press of Mississippi, 1993): 83.

10. "But the faint sounds tantalized him; they were strange but familiar. Was it a motor? A baby crying? Music? A siren?" (23). Wright's description of the strange and "tantalizing" sounds being mistaken for a "siren" can be read as a reference to the mythological Sirens—beautiful sea nymphs who, according to Greek legend, lured men to their deaths.

11. "The Man Who Lived Underground" 27. This same sense of timelessness can be found in *Native Son* as Bigger attempts to evade the police by hiding in the abandoned buildings on Chicago's South Side. Recall Bigger's confusion as he awakens to the singing and shouting of a nearby church service and wonders, "What time was it? He looked at his watch and found that it had stopped running" (252).

12. Fabre 241-242. The original version of "The Man Who Lived Underground" is included among the Richard Wright papers at Beinecke Rare Book and Manuscript Library, Yale University.

13. Luke 4.1–30 describes Jesus' early return to Nazareth and his cold reception in the local synagogue by the worshipers who refused to accept him as the fulfillment of the Lord's prophecy. In response, the people in the synagogue, "rose up, and thrust him out of the city, and led him unto the brow of the hill whereon their city was built, that they might cast him down headlong" (Luke 4.29).

14. Claudia Tate, *Psychoanalysis and Black Novels: Desire and the Protocols of Race* (New York: Oxford University Press, 1998): 96.

15. "How 'Bigger' Was Born" has been appended to *Native Son* since 1942. Current editions continue to follow the novel with the essay. Keneth Kinnamon, "How *Native Son* Was Born," *Richard Wright: Critical Perspectives Past and Present* (New York: Amistad Press, 1993): 111.

Works Cited

Fabre, Michel. *The Unfinished Quest of Richard Wright,* 2nd ed. Urbana: University of Illinois Press, 1993.

Larsen, Nella. *Quicksand and Passing.* 1928. New Jersey: Rutgers University Press, 1986.

Wright, Richard. *Black Boy/American Hunger.* 1945. New York: HarperCollins, 1998.

———. "Bright and Morning Star," *Uncle Tom's Children.* 1938. New York: HarperCollins, 1993.

———. "Fire and Cloud," *Uncle Tom's Children.* 1938. New York: HarperCollins, 1993.

———. "The Man Who Lived Underground." *Eight Men.* 1961. New York: HarperCollins, 1996.

———. "Memories of My Grandmother." Richard Wright Papers. Yale Collection of American Literature, Beinecke Rare Book and Manuscript Library.

———. *Native Son.* 1940. New York: HarperCollins, 1998.

———. *The Outsider.* 1953. New York: HarperCollins, 1993.

———. *Tarbaby's Dawn.* Richard Wright Papers. Yale Collection of American Literature, Beinecke Rare Book and Manuscript Library.

CEDRIC GAEL BRYANT

"The Soul Has Bandaged Moments":
Reading the African American Gothic in Wright's "Big Boy Leaves Home," Morrison's Beloved, *and Gomez's* Gilda

> When you go out to hunt monsters, take care that you do not become one. And when you look into the abyss, remember that the abyss looks back at you.
>
> —Friedrich Nietzsche, *Beyond Good and Evil*

> The Soul has Bandaged moments—
> When too appalled to stir—
> She feels some ghastly Fright come up
> And stop to look at her—
>
> —Emily Dickinson, #512

Alluding to Henry James, Nathaniel Hawthorne, and Edgar Allan Poe in his introduction to *Native Son*, Richard Wright invokes the American gothic tradition. Wright's "How 'Bigger' Was Born" concludes with the chilling announcement, "And if Poe were alive, he would not have to invent horror; horror would invent him." *Native Son*, with its invocation to James, Hawthorne, and Poe; its searing critique of the American Dream come-a-cropper; and the arrival of Bigger Thomas—like some rough beast out of Yeats's "Second Coming"—was an unprecedented literary and cultural event.

African American Review, Volume 39, Number 4 (Spring 2003): pp. 39–52. Copyright © 2005 Cedric Gael Bryant.

Conjuring Poe is an act of repetition and revision, Wright seems to know, that acknowledges the literary significance of 19th-century gothic horror in American culture and its immeasurably more terrifying modern reality in the ordinary lives of contemporary Americans. Wright's use of the phrase "invent horror" ironically conveys the differences between 19th-century literary imagination and 20th-century social reality by implying that modern institutions exert far greater influence in socially constructing (or *inventing*) the horror of racism and economic determinism. The terror of the modern-moment allowed Wright, as Joseph Bodziock puts it, "to bore into the white American psyche and find the anxieties and terrors that dwelled there. The American gothic replaced the social struggle of the European gothic with a Manichean struggle between the moral forces of personal community order and the howling wilderness of chaos and moral depravity" (33).

The 1938 publication of Wright's short story "Big Boy Leaves Home" and, later, *Native Son* in 1940, are benchmarks in the evolution of the African American gothic tradition that extends back to early 19th-century slave narratives and forward to Toni Morrison's *Beloved* (1987) and Jewelle Gomez's *The Gilda Stories* (1991).[1] These writers and texts represent a significant Africanist presence—as *producers* of, and not simply as *subjects* in, the prevailing modes of gothic and grotesque narrative discourse in American literature and culture, a fact that has not been sufficiently explored.[2] "Big Boy Leaves Home" was the lead story in the collection *Uncle Tom's Children*. Later, when the collection was revised and reprinted in 1940, Wright added his polemical essay "The Ethics of Living Jim Crow," to preface the five stories comprising the volume. In each edition, "Big Boy Leaves Home" is pivotal in its narratological relation to both Wright's introductory essay and to the four other stories. Wright's story is a metonym for the cultural critique and narrative strategies that African American writers throughout the second half of the twentieth century develop and deploy through gothic discourse.

"Big Boy" is divided into five concise sections that begin with the combative but harmless verbal game of put-downs, or "signifying," that Buck, Bobo, Lester, and Big Boy play; it terminates with Big Boy hidden in a secret compartment beneath the driver's seat of a truck speeding northward. The primary sites of gothic intervention occur in sections two and four. The central events in section two analogize the "mirror stage," or gaze, in Jacques Lacan's construction of ego development (Clark 450). In Lacan's radical revision of Freud's early childhood stages of psychosexual development, the mirror stage marks the crucial period when the individual's nascent sense of self is "mirrored" or oriented in the intimidating presence of another who, in turn, elicits aggressive reactions of self-preservation in the self. Consequently, this period is one of intense anxiety in which the individual develops against the potentially dominating influence, or gaze, of powerful "others." Lacan's gaze, and the equally important forms of the gaze expressed in the passages from Nietzsche and Dickinson quoted above, form a central idea and motif in African American gothic literature.

"Big Boy Leaves Home" deploys the gaze to perform transgressive acts that dramatically critique the "ethics of living Jim Crow" and the gothic horror of resisting those "ethics." In section two, the "swimming hole" reserved for whites only demarcates a separate and unequal racial division and can be breached only by defiant movements through a construction of space that is physical, emotive, and ideational. To reach any of the three kinds of space, the boys must climb "over a barbed-wire fence and enter a stretch of thick woods" (23) delimited by the intimating sign "NO TRESPASSIN" (25). Once there, the swimming hole evokes both fear and desire in the teenagers, emotions that the "gothic," in Judith Halberstam's definition, produces in the reader. Emotionality forms a crucial part of a "technology of subjectivity," that "produces the deviant subjectivities opposite which the normal, the healthy, and the pure can be known.... The production of fear in a literary text (as opposed to a cinematic text) emanates from a *vertiginous excess* of meaning.... Within Gothic novels ... multiple interpretations are embedded in the text and part of the experience of horror comes from the *realization that meaning itself runs riot*" (Halberstam 2, italics added).

Fear and desire are yoked together in the heated exchange between the boys in "Big Boy Leaves Home" when they reach the water and in their consciousness of what the "idea" of trespassing means:

> They came to the swimming hole.
> "Ah ain goin in," said Bobo.
> "Done got scared?" asked Big Boy.
> "Naw, Ah ain scared. . . . "
> "How come yuh ain goin in?"
> "Yuh know ol man Harvey don erllow no niggers t swim in this hole."
> "N jus las year he took a shot at Bob fer swimmin in here," said Lester.
> . . . "See that sign over yonder?"
> "Yeah."
> "Whut it say?"
> "NO TRESPASSIN," read Lester.
> "Know whut tha mean?"
> "Means ain no dogs n niggers erllowed," said Buck.

Having already performed physical and emotive transgressive acts, the friends commit the one that is irrevocable by defiantly jumping into the water. This moment, in which the boys read race in the "NO TRESPASSIN" sign, is full of significations, as Buck clearly implies in the answer he constructs: "no dogs n niggers erllowed" expresses their full awareness and defiance of the convoluted logic in the "ethics of living Jim Crow."

However, the moment when their collective consciousness and the text become "gothic," in Halberstam's sense—when it "emanates from a vertiginous excess of meaning"—occurs later when, virtually naked, the boys are shocked by the presence of a "white woman, poised on the edge of the opposite embarkment" (29). Big Boy's terrified announcement that "'It's a woman! . . . A *white* woman!'" captures the full, vertiginous excess of meaning and locates this moment within a racialized gothic discourse. Sematically, Big Boy's horrified response opens a space between the words "woman" and "white," then collapses it, with emphasis, into a single terrifying idea, "*white* woman," which, semiotically, expresses a vertiginous proliferation of irrevocable meanings that each boy immediately understands: their lives are in mortal danger, and the "crime" they have committed is punishable in unspeakable ways—beatings, public humiliation, adjudicated fines and/or imprisonment, and greater still, "their" crime summons the specter of family suffering, loss of property, and death. Lynching, itself a semiotic sign of vertiginous excess, given its myriad forms—including whipping, shooting, castration, immolation, drowning, and hanging—is a violent abridgement of "due process" under the Constitution.[3] The pyrotechnic combination of meanings that this scene evokes is also located in the reader, who *knows* what the characters know and, consequently, participates in the production of gothic meaning. Transfixed, locked in each other's gaze, in this moment "multiple interpretations" abound and both characters and readers are "embedded in the text and part of the experience of horror comes from the realization that meaning itself runs riot" (Halberstam 2).

Each character in this scene is almost paralyzed with fear, and the only movement possible is akin to the slow-motion effect of walking underwater. The white woman who "stands twenty-five feet away" and has "her hand over her mouth" (30) also stands between the teenagers and their clothes. In a sense, she is paralyzed by a fearful conjunction of historically codified racial myths—the inviolate white female and the bestial black male, on the one hand, and the Jim Crow laws and customs that both prescribe and proscribe her responses to black men, on the other; she is cast into the historically-determined role of victim/ victimizer. Blackness and whiteness are constructed within Wright's text as transhistorical or absolute ideological categories, which gothic discourse, as Teresa A. Goddu argues, attempts to "disrupt" and deconstruct (4–5). Thus, both Bertha, already abstracted as "white woman," and the "black boys" are powerless to act outside of the separate or conflated roles of victim/ victimizer. Each is locked, in Frederic

Jameson's phrase, in "the prison-house of language" and behavior inscribed in American racial ideology and the history of lynching.

When Big Boy takes cautious steps toward the white woman to get his clothes, Bertha yells at him to "go away!" but her own movements are limited to a few backward steps, "her eyes wide, her hand over her mouth" (30) into the tree "where [the boys'] clothes lay in a heap" (30). For the terrified white woman, this is Dickinson's "bandaged moment,"

When too appalled to stir—
She feels some ghastly Fright come up
and stop to look at her—.

For her, the "ghastly Fright" that materializes is semiotic: its sign is the sudden appearance of four naked, young black men and its gothic signification is fear and desire, complex emotional responses that keep Bertha from advancing or fully retreating. The trope here of the paralyzing gaze is reversible because while Big Boy takes cautious, slow-motion steps toward his clothes, so long as the "ghastly Fright" stands there looking at him, he, too, is "too appalled to stir"—to make the movement that would accomplish his aim. Only the "CRACK" of Jim Harvey's rifle shatters this frozen moment, breaking the mutual gaze in mutual gaze in which the characters are locked, and returning them to real time.

This moment of gothic cathexis has its corollary in "Book One: Fear" of Wright's *Native Son* as Bigger Thomas stealthily tries to deliver Mary Dalton, who has passed out from drugs and alcohol, to her bedroom without being discovered. The mansion of the rich, philanthropic Dalton family becomes the archetypal haunted house where, in Stephen King's commentary on horror fiction, "universal forces collide" (267). The catalytic, binary forces in this scene from *Native Son* are fear and desire, whiteness and blackness, privilege and poverty. Each pair of binaries is embodied in the complex exchange of emotions between Bigger and Mary. For Bigger, "something urged him to leave at once, but he leaned over her, excited, looking at her face in the dim light, not wanting to take his hands from her breasts" (73). This scene, however, reaches the zenith of gothic possibility when Mary's blind mother appears in the doorway to Mary's bedroom, triangulating the action and accentuating the tension in the last two binaries: whiteness and blackness, privilege and poverty. When Bigger sees Mrs. Dalton, his terror follows from a vertiginous excess of reasons to fear her and to dread his situation, trapped as he is between two terrifying symbols of whiteness and femininity. Mrs. Dalton's sudden appearance freezes him with terror, and she becomes literally a "ghastly Fright" that locks him in her blind gaze. Through the irony in the text, Wright signifies on several interdependent gothic tropes: the gaze, paralysis, and supernatural or ghostly terror: Bigger "turned and a *hysterical terror seized him,* as though he were falling from a great height in a dream. A *white blur* was standing by the door, *silent, ghostlike. It filled his eyes and gripped his body.* It was Mrs. Dalton. *He wanted to knock her out of his way and bolt from the room*" (85, italics added).

Despite Bigger's sense of "falling from a great height" and his desire to "knock [Mrs. Dalton] out of his way and bolt from the room," he stands by Mary's bed—"too appalled to stir"—with his hand over her mouth, transfixed by the gaze of the "white blur" that he fears will discover him. That Mrs. Dalton is blind only enhances and ironizes the gothic gaze by extending it to Bigger's other senses as well, primarily audition and tactility, each of which has the capacity to produce paralysis: "He knew that Mrs. Dalton could not see him; but he knew that if Mary spoke she would come to the side of the bed and discover him, *touch* him" (85, italics added). As in "Big Boy Leaves Home," race and gender are gothicized. They elicit fear and desire and a "vertiginous excess of meaning" where physical space and psychic space collide, transgressing culturally constructed "ideas" of what is permissible—traditional, normal, and/or natural—and, therefore, *not monstrous.* In conventional gothic discourses, which African American literary texts repeat and revise, "monstrosity," by definition, is a "deviation from the natural order; unnatural" and "abnormally formed; malformed" (*OED* 1351). This pivotal scene in *Native Son* depends on a form of doubling (of characters) and repetition (of plots and situations) to produce the gothic effects that inform Wright's social critique. What occurs in the two narrative spaces—Mary's bed and her bedroom doorway—confirms the semiotic logic that links blackness with monstrosity in the cultural mythology and racial politics that the novel explores. Conversely, Bigger fears discovery by a second instance of physical contact with Mrs. Dalton that has the power, indirectly, to inflict pain and suffering on him. Bigger could lose his job and the income his family desperately looks forward to; be arrested for a vertiginous array of false charges stemming from his compromised position (a poor, young black man hired to chauffeur found in his wealthy employer's daughter's bedroom); and, at the very least, be made to feel shame and a further erosion of his self-esteem.

And yet, in these crucial moments of gothic intervention for both Bigger and Big Boy, in their respective texts, there are what culture critic bell hooks calls "spaces of agency" that open up, "wherein we can both interrogate the gaze of the Other but also look back . . . naming what we see" (116). Bigger grasps clumsily for such agency through his transparent scheme to throw the blame for Mary's disappearance onto the novel's Communists and through his convoluted logic, in the final scene, that locates both self-vindication and affirmation in the violent deaths of Mary and Bessie Mears. In contrast, the spaces for agency that materialize for Big Boy in sections four and five employ a "critical gaze" that is not only rebellious, but also " 'looks' to *document*, one that is *oppositional*" (hooks 116, italics added). As Trudier Harris notes, "from Big Boy's limited perspective, we witness the end of the chase as it culminates near his hiding place in a kiln on the hill where Bobo is burned" (106), lynched by the mob before he can safely reach Big Boy. Although a "limited perspective," the *act* of seeing is fully invested in agency through the documentary evidence of lynching, of human rights violations, that Big Boy carries with him on his exodus north. Like the gothic interventions in *Beloved*, the "festival of violence" (Tolnay and Beck x–xi) that Big Boy witnesses is "not a story to pass on" (Morrison 274), but nevertheless *must* be a story that Wright tells.

"Imagine the terror," bell hooks says, remembering childhood lessons learned about black female spectatorship, "felt by the child who has come to understand through repeated punishments that one's gaze can be dangerous. The child who has learned so well to look the other way when necessary.... Afraid to look, but fascinated by the gaze. *There is power in looking*" (115, italics added), hooks's assertion of an "oppositional gaze" that empowers the one being objectified and subjugated—who, in southern vernacular, engages in "reckless eyeballing"—revises the Lacaruan construction of the "mirror gaze" discussed above. The power that results from daring to look, as Big Boy does in Wright's story, is a vehicle for social change and critique that comported well with Wright's agenda of communist propaganda—witnessing, public testimonials (on street comer soapboxes and before congressional committees), newspaper editorials, "speaking the unspeakable," in Morrison's words:

> "There came a roar. Tha mus be Bobo; tha mus be Bobo. . . . In spite of his fear, Big Boy looked" (54)

and,

> "He stared hard trying to find Bobo. His eyes played over a long dark spot near the fire. Fanned by wind, flames leaped higher. He jumped. That dark spot had moved. Lawd, thas Bobo; thas Bobo. . . . " (56)

and finally,

> The flames leaped tall as the trees. The scream came again. Big Boy trembled and looked. The mob was running down the slopes, leaving the fire clear. Then he saw a writhing white mass cradled in yellow flame, and heard screams, one on top of the other, each shriller and shorter than the last. The mob was quiet now, standing

still, looking up the slopes at the writhing white mass gradually growing black, growing black in a cradle of yellow flame." (57)

Beyond doubling and repetition and the gaze, both Book One of *Native Son* and "Big Boy Leaves Home" play on an important vampire motif through the ways that the central scenes in these texts construct inviolable spaces, *thresholds* that cannot be crossed—literally the Dalton mansion (Bigger stays in the chauffeur's quarters over the garage) and Mary Dalton's bedroom—and ideological spaces, such as the racial mythologies that delimit the physical space between Big Boy and Bertha. These thresholds are inviolable, psychically or literally marked "NO TRESPASSIN"; the monstrous "other" cannot enter uninvited. What is impermissible in these texts is codified in transhistorical, ideological "norms" concerning race and sexuality. To violate or transgress them as do Wright's characters, uninvited by patriarchal, that is, by either white male privilege *or* white female authority, is a monstrous act precisely because it destabilizes the myth of a naturally hegemonic social order.

Trespassing prohibited literal or ideological space is a central gothic motif within African American literature that signifies on vampirism—both repeating and revising it—particularly gothic literary conventions, cultural constructions initiated with Bram Stoker's publication of *Dracula* in 1897. However, in contrast to Wright's "Big Boy Leaves Home" and *Native Son*, Toni Morrison's *Beloved* appropriates *Dracula* to gothicize the horrors of slavery and, more importantly, to defamiliarize the assumptions of 18th- and 19th-century rationalist discourse that elided blackness from essentialist arguments about what it means to be—and not be—fully human. In "Literary Theory and the Black Tradition," Henry Louis Gates, Jr., expresses the difference that race made in the "Age of Reason":

> . . . the creation of formal literature could be no mean matter in the life of the slave, since the sheer literacy of writing was the very commodity that separated animal from human being, slave from citizen, object from subject. Reading, and especially writing, in the life of the slave represented a process larger than even 'mere' physical manumission, since mastery of the arts and letters was Enlightenment Europe's sign of that solid line of division between human being and thing. (24–25)

Three pivotal, polemical moments in *Beloved* perform the "reading" about which Gates is generalizing between human and animal, object and subject as inviolable ideological boundaries, then trespass against them through challenges that disrupt their fixed, transhistorical status: schoolteacher's "lessons" to his nephews about the irreducible differences between Sethe's, and all black people's, animal and human "characteristics" (193); and Paul D's insistence that Sethe's killing her own baby is a savage act that obviates reason, the irreducible 18th-century "sign" of human superiority: " 'You got two feet, Sethe, not four'" (165).

But the narrative space that most crosses the "threshold" between animal and human and disrupts these inviolable ontological categories also transforms Sethe into a creature with wings, claws, and a "beaked face" that "flew" to the barn, "snatching up her children like a hawk" (157), when she sees schoolteacher coming to take her and her children back to Sweet Home and to slavery. Running to the woodshed with her children—"all the parts of her that were precious and fine and beautiful"—Sethe enters a temporary "safe place" where she can hide and be alone long enough to punch a hole "through the veil" big enough to "drag" her children "out, away, over there where no one could hurt them" (163). The woodshed is a liminal "safe place" that is violated by the *uninvited* presence of schoolteacher and the other white men who enter it. Seeing the two boys. Bugler and Howard, bleeding, "lying opened-eyed in sawdust," and the baby at Sethe's breast—whose blood pumps "like oil in her hands" and whose face has to be held "so her head would stay on" (251)—schoolteacher "beat his hat against his thigh and spit" to punctuate his disgust. The "lesson" that this wasteful scene teaches, schoolteacher stresses, when you "overbeat" an "animal"— "beyond the point of education" (148)—is that "you just can't mishandle creatures and expect success" (150). Sethe's humanity is challenged, contested through the authorial narrative voice, and the characters themselves, especially schoolteacher and Paul D, who compare her to a predatory bird, a horse, and hounds.

Sethe herself hears the "wings"—"little hummingbirds [that] stuck their needle beaks right through her headcloth into her hair and beat their wings" (163)—that destabilize and blur the boundary between animal and human, and make her appear a monstrous mother. This, then, is a decidedly gothic moment that, as Theresa A. Goddu notes about the peculiarly American form of this genre, is "obsessed with transgressing boundaries" (5). Sethe's insistence, " 'I took and put my babies where they'd be safe'" (164), not only defies most definitions of "reason," but the murder of her own child collapses the either/or binary between animal and human into the both/and of monstrous motherhood. This destabilizing act at the very least compels both the characters in the novel and Morrison's readers to review and perhaps to revise normative ideas of what it means to be animal, human, white, black, mother, and/or monster. The novel's ability to conjure the unspeakable in these textual places depends, in part, on vampire mythology, as it does when the authorial narrator describes the monstrous nature of the Ku Klux Klan: "Desperately thirsty for black blood, without which it could not live, the dragon swam the Ohio at will" (66). The historical figure of Vlad Tepes, on whom Bram

Stoker based his novel, was a 15th-century Romanian prince whose name, like his father's, Vlad Dracul, meant both "devil" and *dragon*. Both the family crest and coins minted by the father during his lifetime bore the sign of the Dragon. "Dracula" literally means "son of the dragon" or "son of the devil" (McNally and Florescu 22). Morrison's monstrous metaphor, therefore, alludes to Stoker's text and to vampire mythology generally through the double reference to blood consumption and to Dracula.[6]

Halberstam persuasively argues that the vampire Dracula is a "technology of monstrosity" and that Stoker's Dracula is a "machine text" that "generates particular subjectivities," forms of otherness that his body and the text distill, including race, sexuality, gender, and class. Dracula is the essence of otherness, as Halberstam suggests, "a monster and man, feminine and powerful, parasitical and wealthy; he is repulsive and fascinating, he exerts the consummate gaze but is scrutinized in all things, he lives forever but can be killed. Dracula is indeed not simply a monster but a technology of monstrosity" (88). The technology, or gothic economy, that Dracula embodies is both figurative and fixed discursively within the 1890's Victorian "hegemonic ideal of bourgeois" womanhood, femininity, and class that Stoker's novel both challenges and reaffirms. In *Beloved*, Sethe is a technology of monstrosity "against whom," as Halberstam asserts of Dracula, "the normal and the lawful, the marriageable and the heterosexual can be known and quantified" (89). By murdering her own child and embracing the pariah-status that ensues, Sethe defines by negation the same Victorian hegemonic ideals that Dracula destabilizes.

Like Linda Brent in Harriet Jacobs's slave narrative, *Incidents in the Life of a Slave Girl* (1861), paradoxically subject to but not protected by the codes governing the "cult of true womanhood" in the runeteenth century, Sethe exalts in the appropriation of powers and privileges codified in masculinity and whiteness. Like Sethe, Linda Brent reasons that killing her children is preferable to surrendering them to slavery: "I thought to myself that, God being my helper, they should never pass into [my master's] hands. It seemed to me I would rather see them killed than have them given up to his power" (80). And later, Brent muses, "As I held [my daughter] in my arms, I thought how well it would be for her if she never waked up; and I uttered my thought aloud" (87). Both Linda Brent and Sethe can speak, and in Sethe's instance *do* speak, the unspeakable because each, like Dracula, occupies a liminal space that challenges "normalcy," "lawfulness," and "marriageability." And Dracula, Sethe, and Linda Brent all embrace the power at the margins unapologetically, defiantly. Brent apostrophizes:

> But, O, ye happy women, whose purity has been sheltered from childhood, who have been free to choose the objects of your

affection, whose homes are protected by law, do not judge the poor desolate slave girl too severely! If slavery had been abolished, I, also, could have married the man of my choice; I could have had a home shielded by the laws . . . but all my prospects had been blighted by slavery. (54)

Sethe, however, is made more monstrous than Linda Brent by the difference between *thinking* and *doing* the unspeakable, and by the intoxicating freedom of her act, which transforms, *shape shifts*, her into something "new," as Paul D says, that lies outside all the familiar social constructions of normal, human, mother, woman, lawful, blackness, and whiteness:

> This here Sethe was new. . . . This here Sethe talked about love like any other woman; talked about baby clothes like any other woman, but what she meant could cleave the bone. This here Sethe talked about safety with a handsaw. This here new Sethe didn't know where the world stopped and she began. Suddenly [Paul D] saw what Stamp Paid wanted him to see: more important than what Sethe had done was what she claimed. It scared him. (164)

What Sethe "claims" is her whole, expansive self and all that her body produces: "I was *that* wide" (162). The repeated pronouns "I," "me," "my," and "we," stress the new "something" Sethe has become, the self-birth her monstrous act conceives:

> I did it. *I* got *us* all out. Without Halle too. Up till then it was the only thing *I* ever did on *my* own. Decided. And it came off right, like it was supposed to. *We* was here. Each and every one of *my babies* and *me* too. I birthed them and *I* got them out and it wasn't no accident. *I* did that. *I* had help, of course, lots of that, but still it was *me* doing it; *me* saying *"Go on,"* and *"Now."* *Me* having to look out. *Me* using *my* own head. But it was more than that. It was a kind of selfishness *I* never knew nothing about before. It felt good. Good and right. *I* was big, Paul D, and deep and wide and when *I* stretched out *my* arms all *my* children could get in between. *I* was that wide. (162, italics added)

As the proliferation of personal pronouns suggests, the claims Sethe makes about her own body and agency are all-consuming. And it is this *wideness*, this self-consumption—"'Love is or it ain't. Thin love ain't no love at all'" (164), Sethe says—that terrifies Paul D and transforms Sethe into a monstrous "new" thing. *Beloved* is, in fact, a veritable gothic grammar comprised of nouns and verbs conjugated in ways that both repeat and revise traditional gothic ideas, such as "haunting" and "possession" of the spirit; the enslaved, chattel body; and the "body" of the text.

This African American gothic grammar also extends to slavery and blackness the play on "consumption and production" that Halberstam argues forms a capitalist "gothic economy" in *Dracula*. *Beloved* typifies such black revision. Gothic novels and monsters are 19th- and 20th-century tropes for class struggle, particularly the rise of and assault on middle-class sexual conventions, desires, and fears. As Halberstam notes,

> gothic novels, in fact, thematize the monstrous aspects of both production and consumption—[Mary Shelley's] *Frankenstein* is, after all, an allegory about a production that refuses to submit to its author and *Dracula* is a novel about an arch-consumer, the vampire, who feeds upon middle-class women and then turns them into vampires by forcing them to feed upon him. (12)

Beyond his blood lust, Dracula is a symbol of a dying, that is, bankrupt, aristocracy, and in Stoker's novel he hoards gold, refusing to allow it to circulate freely back into society where his wealth would "transfuse" a burgeoning middle-class economy. Instead, Dracula "consumes" the middle class, becoming, as Halberstam notes, "an image of monstrous anticapitalism, one distinctly associated with vampirism. Money, as the novel suggests, should be used and circulated and vampirism somehow interferes with the natural ebb and flow of currency just as it literally intervenes in the ebbing and flowing of blood" (102).

The institution of slavery in the nineteenth century is a powerful, multileveled play on consumption and production with its own unique kind of "gothic economy," which *Beloved* revises through Sethe's efforts to "consume" the "product" of slavery, her own children, that law and custom mandate as chattel property. Thinking of killing her own children, Linda Brent notes: "they must 'follow the condition [i.e., the enslavement] of the mother'" (*Incidents* 42). Chattel slavery is a monstrous gothic economy precisely because, *de jure,* it made the slaveowner a machine, a producer of property, profits, and pleasure bound by no other strictures than supply and demand and lust. The unassailable right to "consume" his human property and profits in almost any manner imaginable is what differentiates masters from slaves. Sethe's desperate efforts to kill her children challenge both the legal *and* linguistic authority implicit in what are, in other contexts, reversible terms (producers and consumers) and human arrangements (freedom and enslaved). Sethe's act, therefore, is not only a monstrous theft of her own body and her children's, but it is made more monstrous by the equally great offense of *claiming* language—the proliferation of first-person pronouns aforementioned and the radical re-definition of "safe" and "safe place" (163, 164)—that undermine the proposition that "definitions belonged to the definers—not the defined" (190).

Through these challenges to legal and linguistic authority, Sethe *writes* herself into a text in which literacy is claimed by everyone white, including Amy Denver, the fugitive white girl fleeing the horrors of indentured servitude who nonetheless can read and translate the violence lacerated on Sethe's back as a chokecherry tree in "full bloom" (79). Amy's "reading" is an irreducible interpretation that cannot be erased or altered, a metaphor as dead as the cable-thick, insensate welts of skin on Sethe's back. Paul D touches them, sorrowfully responding, " 'Aw, Lord, girl'" (17). Literally, neither Paul D nor Sethe can read or write and cannot use the power of literacy to dislodge the authority of Amy Denver's chokecherry tree imagery. Amy's irrepressible, the-glass-is-half-full optimism, is Emersonian in its rejection of absolute evil and unshakable belief in a principle of correspondence.[5] Whether Sethe accepts the idea that everything in nature mirrors itself and embodies its own opposite—beauty in ugliness, good in evil, for example—she has no power to change what is written. She can only *right* the wrongs done to her by enlarging the space where the culturally constructed "truth" about what it means to be a black female slave mother can accommodate other possibilities that both *juxtapose* and *oppose* the definitions of the "definers" without necessarily eradicating them.

In *Beloved,* black characters struggle against being subjects, commodified by custom, law, and language within a (con)text controlled by white others, particularly schoolteacher and Amy Denver, who, despite vastly different motivations, are "definers" whose "definitions" appropriate black voices. The "measuring string," chalk, and pages with columns for differentiating Sethe's animal and human "characteristics" (190–192) are the reading and writing instruments that schoolteacher particularly, and the institution of slavery generally, uses. These tools are corollaries of the "writing machines"—pencil, primitive dictaphone, journals, and letters—used by Jonathan Harker, Dr. Seward, and Lucy Westenra to write Dracula into a text in which he has no first-person voice (Halberstam 90–91). Like Sethe, who is both "penned and penned in"[6] by schoolteacher's writing and Amy Denver's "reading," Dracula is trapped, safely contained, within the authorial agency of the principle narrators. The words, by and large, used to describe him are not *his* words, and, like Sethe, he is powerless to change them, despite the terror he embodies.

Beloved, however, unlike *Dracula,* is gothic precisely because it succeeds in speaking the unspeakable about the haunting effects of slavery on the human psyche and the desperate attempts that dehumanized persons make, as Morrison puts it, to survive "whole" in a world "where we are all of us, in some measure, *victims of something*" (Bakerman 40). Monstrosity *is* the unspeakable—institutional slavery, inhuman bondage in manifest forms against people on the basis of race, sexuality, gender, class—but it is also, in African American literature, the *response* that is spoken, that "claims" a retaliatory, self-affirming monstrous difference, as Sethe does and as Bigger Thomas does at the conclusion of *Native Son*. Embracing both the accidental killing of Mary Dalton and the brutal murder of his girlfriend Bessie Mears, Bigger says to his horrified attorney. Max: "Maybe it ain't fair to kill, and I reckon I really didn't want to kill. But when I think of why all the killing was, I begin to feel what I wanted, what I am.... I didn't want to kill! ... But what I killed for, I *am!*... What I killed for must've been good!" (428–429). Bigger repeats this last statement twice, as if first to state a newly comprehended fact and then to affirm it, emphatically. All that Max can to do in response to Bigger's declaration of monstrosity is grope "for his hat like a blind man"; he cannot comprehend the black man he is seeing for the last time. At this moment in the text Max is like Paul D, confronted, incredulously, with Sethe's monstrous shapeshifting into something "new"—and terrified of it.

As Jewelle Gomez states about her own vampire novel *The Gilda Stories*, what African American gothic texts frequently do is "remake mythology" ("Recasting" 86); that is, they revise monstrosity. Writing the African American gothic, then, allows monstrosity to do exactly what Dracula cannot do, given the modes of textual, authorial control that Bram Stoker imposes on the narrative: dominate, take over the page. "Recasting the mythology" of the vampire, Gomez writes, into a black, lesbian, fugitive slave politicizes a nexus of issues, including sexuality and race, and pushes the "boundaries outward for women, lesbians, and writers" (85). Like Sethe, Gomez's lesbian vampire Gilda is identified with issues of "power, isolation, recreating family, fulfilling desire, maintaining honor, [and] sharing" (86)—all central themes in Gomez's novel. The authority that Sethe appropriates by her own vampire acts of consumption—"I was *that* wide"—subsumes each of these central elements as well. Like Gilda, who has survived slavery, attempted rape, and the death of two *blood* mothers—her biological mother and an older vampire also named Gilda, who "makes" her through the ritual "sharing of the blood"—Sethe is empowered by the desire to reconstitute the family that slavery takes from her. Doing so is a matter of honor, of pride, as the tone of her explanations to Paul D (162, 164) and her *defense* to Denver and Beloved make clear: "The best thing she was, was her children. Whites might dirty *her* all right, but not her best thing, her beautiful, magical best thing—the part of her that was clean" (251). As all vampire texts do, Sethe's defense involves a play on blood, on multiple kinds of *sharing*, including passing on her story to her daughters, Denver and Beloved.

In *Beloved*, there is a particular kind of trope or play on blood involving sharing and theft (a form of consumption) figured in the trinity formed by baby's blood, money, and mother's milk. The first two elements signify on *Dracula* and vampire mythology through their associations with capitalist forms of consumption and the "gothic economy" that Halberstam explores. The institution of slavery's economic dependence on human commodification and its unimpeachable hegemony over black bodies—the savage forms of punishment and control codified by law and custom—are corollaries to Halberstam's commentary on Victorian fears about social class and capital. This blood play in Morrison's novel lays particular stress on the theft of women's bodies and the loss of reproductive authority, which *aborts* a woman's choice to nurture, to *share* what slavery's commodification of the feminine steals: a mother's milk and the *natural* right it implies to protect the lives one creates. "And they took my milk'" (17), Sethe repeats twice to Paul D to emphasize that the act of being held down while one of "the two boys with mossy teeth," sucks her breast and their "book-reading teacher" watches, "writing it up" is as humiliating as, if not worse than, the "cowhide" that the nephews use to beat her (70).

Monstrosity, then, is measured by the extent to which an act deviates from social constructions of what is "natural," "normal": the greater the distance, the more monstrous. This moment that erupts from Sethe's "rememory" of Sweet Home grossly perverts and violently disrupts the natural bond between mother and child and is the catalytic experience, for the black community, that transforms Sethe into a monstrous mother. Having been robbed of her mother's milk, Sethe believes that she has only desperate expressions of love to offer. Accordingly, the gothic epicenter of the novel is the earlier scene in the barn at Sweet Home where the first monstrous theft of mother's milk occurs: it makes the later scene in the woodshed of the house on Bluestone Road both possible and *necessary,* and it transforms Sethe into a creature with wings, an animal with "four feet."

Monstrosity, Morrison's gothic novel argues, can be qualitatively differentiated by the complexly layered cultural circumstances involving ideology and power, race and sexuality, *definitions* and *definers,* rather than the transhistorical abstractions that prejudice and privilege engender. African American literature situated within gothic discourse opens up discursive spaces in which revisions of identity are possible and geographies of the imagination can be remapped. Within these narratives, the "gothic" becomes a recuperative, revisionary idea that makes monstrosity not only a fixed, paralyzing moment of horror, but also a catalytic space where agency and progress, hope and being are possible—as they are for Big Boy, and Gilda, and Sethe and Paul D in the closing pages of their respective texts. Finally, for each of them, "The Soul," as the third stanza of the poem that begins this essay proclaims, *also* has

moments of Escape—
When bursting all the doors—
She dances like a Bomb, abroad.
And swings upon the Hours[7]

Big Boy speeding North carrying the ocular, documentary evidence of unspeakable human rights violations; Gilda walking south toward the companions with whom she will build a brave new world; and Sethe and Paul D, who, like Big Boy and Gilda, "need some kind of tomorrow," and have found their "best thing" in themselves and each other: all transformed by the terror and the beauty of gothic possibility into *Bombs dancing abroad*.

Notes

1. See especially Winter's persuasive study of cross cultural forms of feminine resistance and authorial agency between 19th-century British gothic writing and the African American slave narrative tradition.

2. For example, although the introduction to a recent collection of American literature, *American Gothic: An Anthology 1787–1916* (1999), announces that "in assembling this volume of readings, the intention has been to show the breadth of the gothic tradition in the nineteenth century" (2), the editor omits altogether the African American slave narrative tradition.   Consequently, he elides slave narratives' seminal relation to the "breath" of gothic discourse. Still more oddly, in an introduction that defines the American gothic as "a literature of opposition" in which "taboos [concerning race, gender, sexuality, and class] are often broken, forbidden secrets are spoken, and barriers are crossed" (1), no mention is made of the 19th-century authors—particularly Frederick Douglass, Harriet Jacobs, and Harriet E. Wilson—who explore American society and its complex institutional practices in precisely the provocative terms quoted. What accounts, partly, for the elision of the slave narrative tradition here is the editor's restriction of race as a subject category in gothic texts by white writers—with the exception of selections by Charles Chesnutt and the "Frankenstein" section (xiv) of Paul Laurence Dunbar's novel, *The Sport of the Gods* (1902). Perhaps too the editor's criteria reflects the problematic middle-ground that the slave narrative occupies between fiction and autobiography and, consequently, the difficulty of including the latter in an anthology of short fiction, poetry, and excerpts from novels—although, interestingly, a section from Mark Twain's autobiographical narrative, *Life on the Mississippi* meets the criteria for inclusion. The effect, then, if not the intent, is that the slave narrative tradition specifically and African American writers generally are not represented as producers, as "doers of the word," who were, in fact, aesthetically and politically invested in 19th-century gothic discourse.

3. Dray stresses that "since early in the eighteenth century, before the founding of the American republic, due process has been understood to include a clear accusation of charges stating what law the accused has violated, a court made up of competent authorities, the right to confront one's accuser in a trial held under proper proceedings, and the right to be freed unless found guilty. So fundamental is it to our notion of justice that the Founding Fathers embedded it squarely in

the Fifth Amendment to the Constitution, which avows that 'no persons . . . shall be deprived of life, liberty, or property, without due process of law' by the federal government" (18).

4. My contention here is not that Morrison was aware that "dragon" in this historical-literary context carries references to vampires and to Dracula specifically. I *do* contend, however, that these significations are an irreducible part of the rich, intertextual life of her novel, which, like all myth-centered material, transcends time and space.

5. In the third chapter of his essay on "Nature," titled "Beauty," Emerson writes: "There is no object so foul that intense light will not make beautiful. And the stimulus it affords to the sense, and a sort of infinitude which it hath, like space and time, make all matter gay. Even the corpse hath its own beauty" (1110–1111). Nature reveals itself through the limitless reflective relation between the phenomenal, outer world and cognition that together create a "correspondence." Emerson writes, "Every appearance in nature corresponds to some state of mind, and that state of mind can only be described by presenting that natural appearance as its picture" (1115).

6. This beautiful play on words is borrowed from Gilbert and Gubar's discussion of phallocentrism and 19th-century female creativity in *The Madwoman in the Attic*. The play on "pen," penis, and the patriarchal biases against creative women that reduced them to subjects within male-authored texts and gave them marginal access to publishers and publication is one of many powerful tropes Gilbert and Gubar use to explore the "anxiety of female authorship" (12–13).

7. I am indebted here to Winter's brilliant reading of Dickinson's poem # 512 as a feminist trope for power and confinement in the nineteenth century.

WORKS CITED

Bodziock, Joseph. "Richard Wright and Afro-American Gothic." *Richard Wright: Myths and Realities.* Ed. C. James Trotman. New York: Garland, 1988: 27–42.

Bakerman, Jane. "The Seams Can't Show: An Interview with Toni Morrison." Taylor-Guthrie, 30–42.

Clark, Michael P. "Jacques Lacan." *The Johns Hopkins Guide to Literary Theory and Criticism.* Ed. Michael Groden and Martin Kreiswirth. Baltimore: Johns Hopkins University Press, 1994: pp. 450–454.

Crow, Charles L., ed. *American Gothic: An Anthology 1787–1916.* Malden, MA: Blackwell, 1999.

Emerson, Ralph Waldo. "Nature." *American Literature 1820–1865.* Vol. B. *The Norton Anthology of American Literature.* Ed. Hershel Parker. New York: Norton, 2003: 1106–1134.

Davis, Christina. "An Interview with Toni Morrison." Taylor-Guthrie, 223–233.

Dickinson, Emily. "The Soul has Bandaged Moments—." *The Poems of Emily Dickinson.* Ed. Thomas H. Johnson. Boston: Little, Brown, 1955: 250.

Dray, Philip. *At the Hands of Persons Unknown: The Lynching of Black America.* New York: Random House, 2002.

Gates, Henry Louis, Jr. *Figures In Black: Words, Signs, and the "Racial" Self.* New York: Oxford University Press, 1987.

Gilbert, Sandra, and Susan Gubar. *The Madwoman in the Attic.* New Haven: Yale University Press, 2000.

Goddu, Teresa A. *Gothic America: Narrative, History, and Nation.* New York: Columbia University Press, 1997.

Gomez, Jewelle. *The Gilda Stories.* New York: Firebrand, 1991.

——. "Recasting the Mythology: Writing Vampire Fiction." *Blood Read: The Vampire as Metaphor in Contemporary Culture.* Ed. Veronica Hollinger. Philadelphia: University of Pennsylvania Press, 1997: 85–92.

Halberstam, Judith. *Skin Shows: Gothic Horror and the Technology of Monsters.* Durham: Duke University Press, 1995.

Harris, Trudier. *Exorcising Blackness: Historical and Literary Lynching and Burning Rituals.* Bloomington: Indiana University Press, 1984.

hooks, bell. *Black Looks: Race and Representation.* Boston: South End Press, 1992.

Jacobs, Harriet A. *Incidents in the Use of a Slave Girl, Written by Herself.* 1861. Ed. Jean Fagan Yellin. Cambridge: Harvard University Press, 1987.

King, Stephen. "Horror Fiction." *Danse Macabre.* New York: Berkley, 1981: 241–358.

McNally, Raymond T., and Radu Florescu. *In Search of Dracula: The History of Dracula and Vampires.* New York: Houghton Mifflin, 1994.

Morrison, Toni. *Beloved.* New York: Knopf, 1987.

Nietzsche, Friedrich. *Beyond Good and Evil: Prelude to a Philosophy of the Future.* Trans. Walter Kaufmann. New York: Vintage, 1989.

Parker, Betty Jean. "Complexity: Toni Morrison's Women." Taylor-Guthrie, 60–66.

Stoker, Bram. *Dracula.* 1897. Norton Critical Edition. Ed. Nina Auerbach and David J. Skal. New York: Norton, 1997.

Taylor-Guthrie, Danille, ed. *Conversations with Toni Morrison.* Jackson: University Press of Mississippi, 1994.

Tolnay, Stewart E., and E. M. Beck. *A Festival of Violence: An Analysis of Southern Lynchings, 1882–1930.* Urbana: University of Illinois Press, 1995.

Winter, Karl J. *Subjects of Slavery, Agents of Change: Women and Power in Gothic Novels and Slave Narratives, 1790–1865.* Athens: University of Georgia Press, 1992.

Wright, Richard. "Big Boy Leaves Home." *Uncle Tom's Children.* 1938. New York: HarperPerennial, 1993: 17–61.

——. *Native Son.* 1940. New York: Perennial Classics, 1998.

JEFFREY ATTEBERRY

Entering the Politics of the Outside: Richard Wright's Critique of Marxism and Existentialism

> But if a selfish West hamstrings the elite of Asia and Africa, distrusts
> their motives, a spirit of absolutism will rise in Asia and Africa and will
> provoke a spirit of counterabsolutism in the West. In case that happens,
> all will be lost. We shall all, Asia and Africa as well as Europe, be
> thrown back into an age of racial and religious wars, and the precious
> heritage—the freedom of speech, the secular state, the independent
> personality, the autonomy of science—which is not Western or Eastern,
> but human, will be snuffed out of the minds of men.
>
> —Richard Wright, *White Man, Listen!*

Richard Wright issued an invitation to the Western world to enter a political terrain that it has historically and ideologically foreclosed, in one way or another, as outside politics. His invitation went unheeded. The West today, if not the world, can only hope that such an invitation will be extended once again, but will we know how to read the invitation if and when it arrives? Do we even have the courage to read it, much less accept it? Perhaps the best preparation for facing such questions would be to revisit the original invitation. In 1956 Wright addressed the First International Congress of Black Writers and Artists, an event sponsored by *Présence Africaine* and organized by Alioune Diop.[1] The invitation in Wright's lecture, "Tradition and Industrialization" (later published in *White Man, Listen!*), appears near

MFS: Modern Fiction Studies, Volume 51, Number 4 (Winter 2005): pp. 873–895. Copyright © Purdue Research Foundation.

the end and was printed originally in all caps as if to avoid the possibility of being overlooked: "The West, in order to keep being Western, free, and somewhat rational, must be prepared to accord to the elite of Asia and Africa a freedom which it itself never permitted in its own domain" (100). The force of this "must" may, even still today, not sound like much of an "invitation," but political invitations of this sort, especially when coming from the disenfranchised, are rarely festive affairs; they are "invitations" in contrast to the fearful alternatives. Wright knows perfectly well, however, that, for these very reasons, the invitation will be ignored, if not scornfully rejected. "Oh, I'm asking a hard thing and I know it," he confesses (100). The hard things still bear asking.

That such an invitation would be issued by Wright in Paris in 1956 is far from a coincidence. Paris during the mid-twentieth century was the cultural and political capital of the black Atlantic. Colonized peoples from across the globe for some time had been arriving at the metropole and were fashioning in Paris itself the very political space that Wright was inviting the West to enter. Against the backdrop of the Algerian War for Independence, international congresses were being held, conferences were organized, and journals were published. Such an environment should be considered "political" in both a practical and theoretical sense. Recently, Jacques Rancière has suggested that "The essence of politics is *dissensus*. Dissensus is not the confrontation between interests or opinions. It is the manifestation of a distance of the sensible from itself. Politics makes visible that which had no reason to be seen, it lodges one world into another" (par. 24). The increasingly physical appearance of the colonized world in the space of Paris at the heart of the metropole may be considered just such a lodging of one world within another. The colonized world made itself manifest, began to appear, quite materially to the world of the colonizer which had heretofore carefully controlled the form of that appearance by policing the "distance of the sensible from itself." Rancière's recent description, however, is only a tenuous sign that the metropole has begun, perhaps, to recognize the political space that Wright had invited it to enter, forty-five years earlier.[2]

Much of Wright's lecture was devoted to describing the space that the West was being invited to enter, for he knew that the West would not recognize this space, even though it had been forcefully shaping that space, materially and ideologically, for hundreds of years. This lecture was not, however, his first attempt at such an endeavor. A few months before, Wright published *The Color Curtain*, an extended commentary on the Bandung Conference of 1955. In March of that year, representatives from twenty-nine African and Asian countries met in Indonesia in an effort to advance decolonization and to confront collectively the attendant problems of such a process. Among these problems was how to avoid becoming inscribed within the emerging

dichotomies of the cold-war period. As such, the Bandung Conference laid
the groundwork for what would become the Non-Aligned Movement. The
first and longest chapter of *The Color Curtain,* entitled "Bandung: Beyond
Left and Right," serves as an introduction to the colonial world. The chapter
uses a common questionnaire to construct biographical and political profiles
of a number of individuals from across Africa and Asia. The text perfor-
matively acts as the kind of personal introduction that often accompanies
invitations. The subtitle to the chapter, moreover, already gestures toward the
geopolitical positioning of these "outsiders," for they are situated "beyond"
or outside the hegemonic dichotomies that were shaping the global political
space. Wright emphasizes that the identities of these "outsiders" are political
in their very formation. Similarly, Wright begins "Tradition and Industrialization" by outlining the social and historical forces behind the formation of
his own identity. In doing so, he explains the political tenor of his own subject position as it intones his invitation. Wright presents himself as a black
American who, as such, is in a unique position to issue this invitation which
is, in fact, directed specifically to the *white* West. Wright explains that "my
position is a split one. I'm black. I'm a man of the West. These hard facts are
bound to condition, to some degree, my outlook. I see and understand the
West; but I also see and understand the non- or anti- Western point of view.
. . . Hence, though Western, I'm inevitably critical of the West" (78–79).
Recalling Du Bois's notion of double-consciousness, Wright avers that his
position as an African American places him in a position that affords him
knowledge of both the West and its "outside." Wright implicitly argues
throughout the lecture that African Americans, as in the West but not of it,
are well situated to act as guides into the emerging political space because,
historically, their subject positions have long been shaped by the very same
forces that are currently producing these spaces on a global scale.

   Indeed, throughout his lecture, Wright describes a world that has been
Westernized through colonialism and imperialism and which remains, nonetheless, not of the West. The political space of a decolonized world is one in
which regions that had previously been designated by the West as "outside" the
political, economic, and juridical spheres come to exert an immanently transformative pressure on those very spheres. As the distance between metropole and
periphery began to collapse, it became increasingly difficult for the metropole
to pretend that the peripheries were not integral to the economic, social, cultural spaces of the center. Today, as globalization and neoimperialism continue,
this recognition has taken the form of a political and economic integration that
positions these outsides as "excluded interiors." Economically, these former
outsides appear simply as particular markets within the ostensibly universalized
circuits of global exchange. Politically, they have been incorporated within the
body of the United Nations as placeholders in the General Assembly, while

remaining outside the chambers of the Security Council where true executive power is wielded. In short, a total subsumption of the outside has occurred that has in no way altered the basic structural relationship between inside and outside. On the contrary, Wright had invited the West to enter the politics of the outside, and the movement of this entrance would require an opening on the inside that would fundamentally alter the very relationship between inside and outside.

An open and revised relationship between inside and outside powers Wright's politics of the outside. In the years before "Tradition and Industrialization" and *The Color Curtain,* Wright had begun to clear the way in *The Outsider* for entering the politics of the outside by interrogating the basic framework structuring the relationship of inside and outside. When it was initially published in 1953, *The Outsider* was widely read as reflecting Wright's critical turn from communism to existentialism. A few decades later, however, once critics began to examine closely Wright's engagement with existentialism, the ambivalence of that relationship began to emerge, and *The Outsider* increasingly seemed to be a somewhat implicit critique of existentialism as well.[3] In what follows, I will argue that both of these critiques are intimately related in Wright's *The Outsider.* In particular, the rigor of Wright's critique of Communist Party practice leads directly and necessarily to a theoretical critique of existentialist philosophy insofar as existentialism reproduces, on a fundamental level, the basic ideological structures that underwrite and program the political practices of the Communist Party. The specific ideological structures that bind communism and existentialism together are articulated in the philosophical tradition through the categories of "the particular" and "the universal." Just as the political space of Bandung was situated "beyond left and right," the politics of the outside have to be situated beyond the particular and the universal.

By 1953, Wright's criticisms of Communism were no secret, having been publicly aired nine years early with the publication of "I Tried to Be a Communist" in *The Atlantic Monthly,* and anyone who had read the earlier piece would inevitably recognize the fictional recreation in *The Outsider* of its more emblematic scenarios. In both works, Wright dramatizes the dictatorial power of the Communist Party over the human concerns and personal affairs of its members. Through the experiences of the protagonist Cross Damon, as well as those of Bob Hunter, Wright hones his criticism of Communist practice by focusing on the relationship between African Americans and the Communist Party. In doing so, Wright's novel highlights the tensions between African Americans and the Party, a relationship that had been historically and politically structured according to the theoretical relationship between tactics and strategy. The politics of race as they played out within organized Communism, however, do not constitute an isolated theme in the novel. The race politics of Communism appear in *The Outsider* as a symptom of more fundamental structures and racialized features of Western ideological culture. Consequently, in his critical portrayal of the political relationship between African American and the Communist Party, Wright's critique opens upon the fundamental categories of Western thinking as they were being taken up and redeployed by the most prominent European thinkers of his day, the existentialists.

In *The Outsider*, the protagonist Cross Damon is introduced to the Communist Party by Bob Hunter, a Pullman porter who has been trying to unionize the other porters. During the lengthy scene of this initial encounter, Hunter is firmly informed by Jack Hilton, a white member of the Party establishment, that he must immediately cease his organizing activities. Dismayed, Hunter inquires as to why, and the only answer that he gets is, "The Party is not obliged to justify its decisions to you or anybody" (247). A heated argument ensues, and the attitudes of the Party toward questions of race are quickly clarified. Hilton demands that Hunter obey the Party's decision and proceeds to threaten him if he doesn't do so. Hilton flatly declares,

> If you don't, then the Party will toss you aside, like a broken hammer, and seek another instrument that will obey. Don't think that you are indispensable because you are black and the Party needs you. Hell no! The Party can find others to do what it wants! Is this asking too much? No. Why? Because the Party needs this obedience to carry out its aims. And what are those aims? The liberation of the working class and the defense of the Soviet Union. (248)

In this speech, the basic tenets structuring the relationship between the Party and its African American members are expressed in the clearest of terms. Hilton tells Hunter that he is no more than "another instrument," a "hammer," for doing the work of the Party. Moreover, the ultimate aims of the Party are the "liberation of the working class and the defense of the Soviet Union." Racial justice per se is clearly not understood as a stated objective. Rather, issues of race politics are conceived as means to these declared ends. Precisely because Hunter's racial identity makes him an ancillary instrument, a mere means to an end, the Party declares that he is far from "indispensable" ; other means can and will be found, as Hilton's abrupt termination of Hunter's organizing activities already indicates.

In Wright's presentation of this scene, questions of race politics are understood as tactical problems that are systematically and strategically subordinated to class and Soviet politics. While it is true that the Communists were one of the few political organizations of the time interested in "the negro question," that investment was understood by the Communists themselves as purely tactical. Ever since the Fourth Congress of the Communist International in 1922 and its adoption of "Theses on the Negro Question" at the behest of the Negro Commission, the Communists openly recognized the tactical importance of race politics, particularly as it involved blacks in the New World, in the struggle against capitalism. The first thesis clearly stated, "The Fourth Congress considers it essential to support all forms of the black movement which aim either to undermine or weaken capitalism and imperialism or to prevent their further expansion" (Adler 331). The practical subordination of race politics to class politics is grammatically inscribed into this proclamation by the restrictive clause qualifying that "forms of the black movement" are to be supported. The thesis does not proclaim unconditional support for all forms of "the black movement"; rather, the proclamation declares Party support for only those movements that are deemed to advance the fight against capitalist imperialism. The adoption of this position is in line with the historical trend of the Third International to organize political activity across the globe under the strategic control of the Soviet state, in contrast to the isolated and relatively uncoordinated tactics of the Second International. As a historic and political document, "The Theses on the Negro Question" is truly quite significant insofar as it politically recognized the connections between colonialism and racialism and cleared the way, in the United States and elsewhere, for the active involvement of the Communist Party in the political struggle for racial justice. As long as the relationship between tactics and strategy was open to constant negotiation, the Communists' recognition of the struggle for racial justice afforded blacks their own tactical opportunity to form alliances with the Communists in the pursuit of their own political objectives.

Under Stalin, however, the subordination of tactics to strategy became an ever more rigid buttress for the party dictatorship. Negotiations over how the relationship between tactics and strategy should direct political action were increasingly suppressed; correspondingly, politics within the Third International became progressively more depoliticized. On the international level, the activities of Communist Parties around the world became tactically secondary to the strategic aims of the Soviet Union, which held itself forward as the point at which the most decisive blow to global capitalism was being delivered. Moreover, because of the racialized structures of power within each nationalist Party, this trend further manifested itself in the instrumental domination and subordination of blacks and their political concerns. While the Communists presented blacks with a political opportunity, it remained "a *white* man's Party," as Bob Hunter's wife forcefully declares (257). As a white man's party, the concerns of blacks were tactically taken up, in accordance with the first thesis on the "negro question," only when they were understood to serve the larger strategic interests of the white industrial working class, which was understood to be the authentic and universal political subject.

These dynamics directed the racial politics of the Communist Party in every Western nation, and it is within this context that Wright's opposition to the Party must be understood, for his position reflects a larger political struggle within and around the Communist Party. Within the racialized domain of Western Communism, the tactics/strategy paradigm dictated that the political concerns of the white, industrialized worker constituted the Party's central concern, while the political struggles of blacks were deemed to be outside that core interest.

Examples of protest and resistance from black activists are legion. In 1933, for instance, Claude McKay would express his "concern about the Communists capturing the entire colored group by cleverly controlling such organizations as the so-called National Negro Congress" (228). This charge is especially pointed when one recalls that Claude McKay, as one of the more prominent members of the Negro Commission at the Fourth Congress, was largely responsible for the adoption of "The Theses on the Negro Question." McKay forcefully asserted the need for black independence in any alliance with the Communists on the political basis of the theses, writing that "Experience since the Emancipation should have taught the various colored leaders that it is a mistake to deliver the colored people over to any one political party" (229).[4] While McKay had always maintained some distance between himself and the Party establishment, others such as Aimé Césaire had aligned themselves with the Party in the most official manner possible. Césaire not only had great institutional prominence with the Communist Party, as the mayor of Fort de France and as a deputy of the French Parliament, but he also had had a close association with Richard Wright since their collaborative founding of *Présence Africaine* in 1946. Césaire's famous 1956 "Letter to Maurice Thorez," in which he passionately explained the reasons for his resignation from the Party, helps frame the theoretical stakes at work within this general struggle and Wright's own stance within it. Indeed, the timing of the letter's publication must be marked here, for it was originally published on October 24, 1956, just over a month after Césaire had participated in the International Congress of Black Writers and Artists where Wright delivered his lecture "Tradition and Industrialization."

In his letter, Césaire lays out a stringent critique of the tactic/strategy paradigm as it determined the political position of blacks within the Party. From the very beginning, Césaire contrasts his struggle with the privileged struggle of the French Communist Party. He writes, "the fight of colonized peoples against colonialism, the fight of colored peoples against racism, is much more complex—indeed, it's of a completely different nature than the fight of the French worker against French capitalism, and it cannot be considered a part or a fragment of that fight" (8–9).[5] On the one hand, Césaire makes absolutely no distinction between the fight against racism and colonialism, underscoring the way in which these two social and ideological structures have become mutually supportive. On the other hand, he insists that this fight differs in nature from that of the French proletariat and, therefore, cannot and should not be reduced to "a part or a fragment of that fight." In refusing to be "a part or a fragment," Césaire rejects the racialized logic of tactical subordination to strategy, a point that he makes even more explicit when he describes his political activity as guided by "a will that does not confuse alliance with subordination" (10). Through the dominance of their strategic concerns, which remain racialized in their Eurocentric orientation, the Communists systematically perverted a political alliance into a relation of subordination. As such, Césaire declares, "the very anticolonialism of the French Communists bears the mark of the colonialism which it fights" (13). The structures of subordination on which colonialism is based are reproduced within the structures of the Party itself, through the political theory of strategy and tactics. On this basis, both European colonialism and Western Communism alike have systematically constructed a racialized ordering of the inside and the outside.

The reproduction of these structures occurs so readily because, at a fundamental level, the ideologies of both colonialism and communist strategy, as historical products of the West, depend on the same basic conceptual apparatus. A key component of that apparatus has been the concept of the "universal" as it has been structurally opposed to the "particular." Césaire anticipates and forestalls the reactionary implementation of this very specific apparatus of capture when, at the end of his letter, he affirms, "I'm not entombing myself within a strict particularism. Nor do I want to lose myself in a fleshless universalism. There are two ways of losing oneself: through walled segregation in the particular or through dissolving into the 'universal.' My conception of the universal is one of a universal rich with all that is particular, rich with all the particulars, the deepening of all particulars in their coexistence" (15). The relationship between the particular and the universal constitutes an integral component of Western thought as an ideological apparatus of capture. It has long programmed the global hegemony of Western capitalism, whether it takes the historic form of colonialism or its present "globalized" form. Quite simply, the racialized deployment of these categories by the West has systematically determined the concerns of the white West as "universal," while those of the nonwhite periphery are taken as "outside" the universal in their "particularity." With the Communists, the racialized subordination of the particular to the universal is simply filtered through the tactic/strategy paradigm.

During the Stalinist regime, this subordination became increasingly rigid in its practical application. It was also explicitly theorized by Stalin in order to justify his own political maneuvering. In his formulation of relationship between tactics and strategy, Stalin repeatedly emphasizes the particularity of tactics as opposed to the implicitly universal dimension of strategy. He explains that "Strategy strives to win the war, or to carry through the struggle, against tsarism let us say, to the end; tactics, on the contrary, strive to win *particular* engagements and battles, to conduct *particular* campaigns successfully, or *particular* operations, that are more or less appropriate to the concrete situation of the struggle at each given moment" (169; emphasis added). By emphasizing the particular character of tactics, Stalin was able to consolidate the power of his own strategic position as General Secretary of the Central Committee. Césaire foresees the deployment of the particular as a category against him, and he can anticipate this maneuver so well because of its ideological consistency and its programmatic predictability. As Césaire knows, the Party response would inevitably be that his adherence to his "particularistic" racial concerns are the result of strategic shortsightedness that reveal a more general failure to grasp the political struggle on a more "universal" level. His concerns for racial justice are considered, precisely as racial, matters of purely "particular" interest to the Party and the "universal" political struggle in which it is engaged. In responding in advance to such a charge, Césaire aims to disable the machinery behind it by refusing to accept the binarism of the particular/universal pair. Rather, in entering on an alternative political course, he proclaims the need for a thorough reconceptualization of their relationship.

Contemporary political theory is still grappling with the problem laid out by Césaire. Within recent years, the category of the "universal" has been a central topic for many political theorists from all across the political spectrum. On the one end, there are those, such as Jürgen Habermas and John Rawls, who variously continue within a Cartesian tradition and thus posit "rationality" as the universal basis for political order. On the other end, there are those, such as Judith Butler, Ernesto Laclau, and Étienne Balibar, who seek to reconceptualize the basic structures of political subjectivity itself through a rigorous and dynamic rearticulation of the relationships between particularity and universality.[6] These latter theorists participate in a larger trend on the left that takes the overcoming of the metaphysics of subjectivity as the necessary theoretical condition for an effectively resistant mode of political thinking. In this context, for instance, Hardt and Negri's recent proposals to replace the categories of particularity and universality altogether with those of singularity and commonality attest, if nothing else, to a desire within contemporary political theory to transfigure its basic ontological ground.[7] At this level, Heidegger arguably constitutes the horizon of contemporary political theory insofar as it was Heidegger who, with *Being and Time*, introduced *Dasein* as that being in terms of which the basic categories of human subjectivity are to be rethought. Of course, Heidegger's engagement with National Socialism has raised many legitimate concerns among some theorists and philosophers, who accept the central importance of radically rethinking subjectivity but question the viability of Heidegger's philosophy and its terms to accomplish that task in a politically responsible way.

The trenchant critiques of Aimé Césaire's "Letter to Maurice Thorez" were, in many ways, anticipated by Richard Wright's *The Outsider*. Moreover, Wright articulates his critique within a conceptual framework of existentialism that is plainly Heideggerian. As such, Wright's work merits much more attention from contemporary political theorists. Given the intellectual milieu of Paris in which Wright wrote *The Outsider*, it should come as no surprise that he would approach the practical and theoretical issues raised by Communist politics through a narrative discourse that is marked by existentialism. In addition to his active involvement with *Présence Africaine*, Wright, as is well known, had a prominent position in the existentialist circles of Jean-Paul Sartre. As early as 1945, the inaugural issue of *Les Temps Modernes*, for example, included Wright's short story "Fire and Cloud" as its very first piece of literature. It was preceded in the layout only by Sartre's presentation of the journal. *Les Temps Modernes* would later publish a serialized translation of *Black Boy* in 1947. During this same period, *Les Temps Modernes* was also introducing Heidegger to the French public through essays by Sartre, Simone de Beauvoir, Maurice Merleau-Ponty, and Emmanuel Lévinas.[8] The intensity of Wright's intellectual engagement with existentialist philosophy during this period is legendary. According to Wright biographer Michel Faber, Wright's existentialism was based largely on his reading of Heidegger, and he discussed Kierkegaard, Nietzsche and Heidegger with Heidegger's renowned student, Hannah Arendt.[9]

Nevertheless, for many critics, Wright's engagement with existentialism has been judged as "ill-digested" and this judgment serves to justify many of the negative evaluations that have been passed on the novel.[10] Unfortunately, such negative judgments have tended to be made in the absence of any rigorous examination of Wright's relationship to existentialist discourse. As such, these evaluations seem hasty if not ill-conceived. In general, these assessments problematically presume that any deviations from existential orthodoxy attest to some degree of misunderstanding. Moreover, these judgments are grounded in the implicit positing of European existentialists as the authoritative model by which the supposedly inauthentic novelist on the outside must be judged. This model of judgment, which is basically the classical form of judgment in the Western philosophical tradition, is once again supported by the same categories of the particular and the universal.[11] Judgments that the existentialist features of Wright's narrative are "ill-digested" entirely miss the point that Wright is concerned with undermining the very structures that underwrite such judgments, especially in their racialized formulations.

In Wright's work, as Paul Gilroy understands it, "the tension between the claims of racial particularity on one side and the appeal of those modern universals that appear to transcend race on the other arises in the sharpest possible form" (147). Wright's work—and *The Outsider* specifically—should be taken as a thorough critique of the very structures that make such tensions appear to be irresolvable or, rather, a critique of the ways in which the categories of the particular and the universal program a cultural and ideological resolution of their fundamentally aporetic structure through racialized mappings of the inside and the outside. In engaging existentialist discourse, especially in its Heideggerian guise, Wright avails himself of the most rigorous attempt within the rarified confines of European philosophy to undertake a similar project. In this regard, it is worth repeating, with Gilroy, that Wright "was not straining to validate African-American experience in their European terms" (171). If anything, Wright's use of existentialism may strike some as "ill-digested" precisely because he refuses to incorporate this discourse in its entirety since, in Wright's estimation, it ultimately fails to carry out its critique in a fashion that is sufficiently radical.

Recalling Césaire's statement that "there are two ways of losing oneself," the story of Cross Damon represents the dangers presented in the path of "walled segregation in the particular." If Cross's encounter with Communism stages the dangers of "universalism," his solitary "outlaw existence" and his ultimate fate highlight the dangers that haunt any retreat into particularism (224). The form that Cross's particularism takes should be understood against the background of Heidegger's *Being and Time*. Cross's personal library replicates the existentialist cannon, and District Attorney Ely Houston tells Cross in the end that "Your Nietzsche, your Hegel, your Jaspers, your Heidegger, your Husserl, your Kierkegaard, and your Dostoevsky were the clues" (560). The inclusion of this list at the end of the novel explicitly confirms that Cross is to be read as an existentialist figure. The specifically Heideggerian character of his existentialism is dramatized through the central plot device of the narrative. Cross fakes his own death in a way that can be read as an allegorical treatment of what Heidegger calls an "authentic being-toward-death" (§53, 260).[12] Throughout most of the novel, Cross Damon acts under the assumed identity of Lionel Lane, an identity that he comes to adopt after it is mistakenly believed that Cross has died in a subway accident. Immediately on hearing his reported death, Cross "felt dizzy as he tried to encompass the totality of the idea that had come so suddenly and unsought into his mind, for its implications ramified in so many directions that he could not grasp them all at once." In confronting his "death," Cross has an "intuitive sense of freedom" that is rooted in the fundamentally open possibility that is his existence (105). This rush of possibilities that seize Cross and that Cross decides to seize on resonates quite dramatically with Heidegger's description of the pure possibility of Dasein to which authentic being-toward-death is attuned.

In *Being and Time*, "being-toward-death" names the immanent possibility of death as that which discloses Dasein as an open field of possibilities.

An "authentic" being-toward-death, however, does not grasp this open field of possibilities as being lost in the world of chance, but understands death as essentially and always its "ownmost possibility *[eigenste Möglichkeit]*." Dasein thus grasps itself in its "non-relational" and essential solitude, thereby freeing itself for its own death in a way that frees it from "clinging to whatever existence one has reached" (§53, 263). In much the same way, Wright's character understands and takes the possibility that has been freed for him through the "possibility" of his own death. What's most important to mark here, however, is simply the fact that Wright's narrative quite clearly situates Cross Damon within a trajectory that is mapped out by Heidegger's *Being and Time*. The path that Cross assumes, with its violent decisions and tragic end, resounds as a critique of Heidegger's being-toward-death as the primordial means by which existence relates to itself. At the very beginning of the book the reader is told that Cross's "problem was one of a relationship of himself to himself," which is nothing more than the problem or the question which Heidegger says Dasein essentially is (10).[13] The manner in which both Cross and Heidegger pursue this problem forms the fundamental object of Wright's critique in *The Outsider*.

Much like Hardt and Negri today, Heidegger begins *Being and Time* by offering his existential analytic of Dasein as a radical displacement the category of the "universal" in approaching the question of self-relation. Dasein does not, Heidegger promises, relate itself to itself through the mediation of the universal. In the opening section of *Being and Time*, Heidegger clearly establishes that the "'universality' of being" is the basic metaphysical "prejudice" that needs to be dispelled in order to retrieve the question of being (§1, 3). Here Heidegger frames his project as the radical overcoming of metaphysics through the proper retrieval of the question of being, a question that has been obscured by the simultaneous assertion that "'Being' is the most 'universal' concept," and Aristotle's recognition that "The 'universality' of being 'surpasses' the universality of genus" (§1, 3). In short, the category of the "universal" as it applies to the question of being makes being "the most obscure concept of all." As such, Heidegger abandons the category of the universal immediately. The being of Dasein is not to be approached through any 'universal' concept of being; rather, "we shall call the very being to which Dasein can relate in one way or another, and somehow always does relate, existence *[Existenz]*" (§4, 12). Heidegger thus situates the "truth" or "essence" of Dasein not in any form of "universal" being, which would be the classic metaphysical gesture, but in "existence," which has traditionally been conceived as pertaining to the domain of the particular. In positing Dasein as the being whose analytic properly retrieves the question of being, Heidegger replaces the "universal" as a category for the analysis of being with the category of existence. Heideggerian existentialism then, as an attempt to find another terrain on which being itself is to be understood, may be taken as an anti-universalism that is not necessarily an anti-essentialism. Heidegger's Dasein is essentially characterized as having its essence, not in some universal being that would transcend its being-there, but in its very existence.

Although Heidegger's analytic of Dasein attempts to overcome the universal/particular relationship as a fundamental ontological structure, the categories surreptitiously return to encode his distinction between the "authentic" and the "inauthentic." After introducing the "universal" as a category pursuant to the classical metaphysics that his "fundamental ontology" strives to overcome, Heidegger avoids using the term. It returns, however, in his crucial analysis of "the call," the interpretation of which provides the basis for determining whether or not Dasein has assumed an "authentic" existence. The call, according to Heidegger, is not to be confused with the "conscience" of the "they," which "pretends to recognize the call in the sense of a 'universally' binding voice" (§57, 278). The appeal to the "universal" here is the mark of inauthenticity. The use of scare quotes around the word "universal" here is, of course, meant to suggest its usage by the "they." On this level, Heidegger himself is not using the term, but mentioning it. Nevertheless, the force of the universal as a concept cannot be so easily contained or distanced. Heidegger's deployment of the universal and the particular to structure the distinction between the inauthentic and authentic understanding of the call comes to the fore when he writes that "the call does not give us to understand an ideal, universal potentiality-of-being; it discloses it was what is actually individualized in that particular Dasein" (§58, 280). The call is not offered as evidence of any universality; to the contrary, it underscores the primordial particularity of Dasein in its nonrelational existence. The authentic relation to the call discloses Dasein as isolated or "segregated," as Césaire might say, within the walls of its particular existence. The authentic experience of this nonrelational solitude takes the existential form of "guilt."

The foregoing sketch outlines those elements of Heidegger's existentialism that inform Wright's narrative at many of its most crucial moments. While Heidegger eschews the terms "universal" and the "particular," it is far from clear that he has not merely inverted their hierarchical relationship and then reinscribed them under the sign of the "inauthentic" and the "authentic." Moreover, the racialized inscriptions of the "authentic" and "inauthentic" have proven to be just as pernicious as those of the "universal" and the "particular." Wright's turn to existentialism may well have been motivated in part by his rejection of Communism, but existentialism is by no means embraced in *The Outsider* as a simple, viable alternative. As early as 1949, in fact, Wright had already declared that "I am not an 'existentialist'" ("Richard

Wright" 137). Indeed, through Cross Damon, the existentialist particularism of Heideggerian Dasein is revealed to be no less dangerous than Communist universalism. Throughout the novel and against the backdrop of a menacing politics of universalism, Wright contests the political implications of Dasein's authentic individuation as nonrelational by opposing guilty-being and being-toward-death with a thought of the promise that resounds with a fundamental affirmation of innocence.

Cross Damon's assumption of his own being-toward-death is, in an appropriately Heideggarian manner, immediately accompanied by a sense of guilt. The sense of endless possibility that is unleashed in his being-toward-death overwhelms him, as mentioned already, and "he suddenly felt like a criminal" (105). Before Cross has actually committed any crime, the sense of being a criminal seizes him, much in the same way that being-guilty precedes any factical guilt of Dasein. This sense of being a criminal colors Cross's new relationship with himself, a relationship marked by a complete dissociation from his previous social existence. Cross's own being-toward-death confronts him with the nonrelational character of his existence. In assuming this path, he is thrust into an isolating particularism that ultimately will alienate himself from himself more completely than ever. Cross quickly realizes that "He had to break with others and, in breaking with them, he would break with himself. He must sever all ties of memory and sentimentality, blot out, above all, the insidious tug of longing. Only the future must loom before him so magnetically that it could condition his present" (114). The break with others that is required by seizing on his "death" results in a break with himself because, as Cross is beginning to realize, the self is nothing when secluded within the total particularism of being-toward-death. From this point on, Cross struggles with "his non-identity which negated his ability to relate himself to others" (195). The criminal extent of this inability to relate to others, the violent force of its strict impossibility, forces itself on Cross in the most factical of ways when he kills Joe Thomas, an old friend whom Cross unexpectedly encounters and who recognizes Cross, thus threatening to ruin his plans. The murder of Joe Thomas merely confirms the degree to which, because of his resulting inability to relate to himself and others, "he had been deprived of the will to make decisions" (149). Rather than discovering a new found freedom, as Cross had hoped, his severance from society results in the most servile subjection to the contingent necessities of his existence.

Cross had, in resolutely seizing on his own being-toward-death, hoped to "work out a new destiny" (108). Instead, through his non-identity and his self-alienation from others, Cross finds himself exposed to the constraints of what Heidegger would call his thrownness. In beginning to craft his new identity, Cross quickly realizes that to "begin his new life he would relive something he knew well, something that would not tax too greatly his inventive powers. He would be a Negro who had just come up fresh from the Deep South looking for work" (111). The new identity that Cross desires to craft, if it is to be believed by others, must adhere to the highly racialized codes of behavior that are enforced by society. Before Cross assumes the identity of Lionel Lane, he has to perform various stereotypical roles. While his death might have liberated him in an immediate sense from his previous identity, it also subjects him ever more rigorously to the constrictions of his social existence. Indeed, it highlights the degree to which his identity as "Cross Damon" had always already been shaped in response to those very same prescriptions. These conditions are dramatically staged in the scene where he gets Lionel Lane's birth certificate from the clerk's office. To ensure his success, Cross decided that he would approach the clerk in "the role of a subservient negro" (214). The shining success of this performance leads Cross to reflect that he now

> knew exactly what kind of man he would pretend to be in order to allay suspicions if he ever got into trouble. In his role of an ignorant, frightened Negro, each white man—except those few who were free from the racial bias of their group—he would encounter would leap to supply him with a background and an identity; each white man would project out upon him his own conception of the Negro and he could safely hide behind it. (217)

Stripped of any identity of his own, being cut off from any meaningful social relations to others, Cross finds that his possible identity becomes determined by the structure of social relations as they are shaped by racialized hierarchies of power. Initially, here, Cross believes that the projection of this identity on him will provide a kind of cover behind which he "could safely hide." This cover, however, also outlines the surface of his fundamental exposure to his being with others. His search and need for a cover is precisely what will deliver him over to the Communist maneuverings of Gil Blount. In being told about Gil, Cross reflects that in "all his cudgeling of his brain to find some disguise for his outlaw existence, he had never seriously considered Communism. But why not?" (224). The cover that he believes will be offered by the Communists turns out, however, to be the cause of his very undoing.

Cross believes that he can use the Communists, just as they will attempt to use him, because he adheres to his belief in an identity that can be crafted in and through the withdrawal from his social relations with others. His hope that he can hide behind the Communist cover reveals his existentialist belief that his death has freed a self to hide in the first place, a "self" whose immediate relationship to itself as self would form the core of his authentic identity. Here, Cross, once again, proves himself to be a faithful Heideggerian, for Dasein is introduced as "always mine *[je meines]*" (§9, 41). This character of always-being-my-own-being or *Jemeinigkeit* is precisely what is assumed in the authentic being-toward-death. The extreme particularism of the self that results from such a withdrawal, however, hands Dasein over, like Cross himself, to "a possibility that it inherited and yet has chosen" (§74, 384). Heidegger's existentialist particularism, in brief, becomes socialized as a fatality in which the individual is given over to the historical destinies of a community. At the crucial moment in which Heidegger rearticulates Dasein with the "universal" realm of the they, Dasein's ownmost possibility immediately becomes that of the community itself. At this moment, Heidegger argues that "if fateful Dasein essentially exists as being-in-the-word in being-with others, its occurrence is an occurrence-with and is determined as *destiny*. With this term, we designate the occurrence of the community of a people. . . . The fateful destiny of Dasein in and with its 'generation' constitutes the complete, authentic occurrence of Dasein" (§74, 384).[14] Having decided not to address directly the articulation between the particular and the universal, Heidegger's thinking at this pivotal point of articulation finds itself divested of the means to forestall the metaphysical mechanism by which the "universal" of a "community" is filled with a particular content.[15] In positing a nonrelational moment in the individuation of the particular, the particular content that is "fated" to fill the universal continues, moreover, to be determined by historical and social forces that remain unaffected by this moment of articulation.

As evidenced both in the "strategy" of the Comintern and in Heideggerian existentialism, this moment of articulation is the moment of the political itself that both the Party and Heidegger depoliticize, which of course is the most reactionary political maneuver of all. The former immobilizes the dynamics of this articulation through a strict logic of subordination, while the latter short-circuits those dynamics by insisting on the nonrelation between authentic Dasein and the inauthentic Mitsein of the community. The unthought relation of the "between" in this "non-relation" produces the depoliticized character of this political (re)articulation. Thus, Cross Damon repeatedly asserts that Communism and Fascism are only superficially different. These similarities are situated, according to Cross, on "pre-political ground" (488). In describing this ground as "pre-political," Cross is not conceding the "de-politicizing" gesture of both, but articulating an important distinction between the depoliticized and the pre-political. The fundamentally relational structure of being is its prepolitical ground, strictly speaking, insofar as relation itself is the very ground of the political. The depoliticizing gesture of disarticulation, on the other hand, disavows this pre-political ground. It thus forecloses terrain on which the formation of particular identities takes place and posits, instead, a nonrelational identity that preexists the moment of articulation. Wright's parable instructs its readers, however, that the formation of effective political identities does not take place independently of the moment of articulation between the self and society. The effective identity of political agents is formed along the edge, the clifflike margin, of this articulation.[16] Their individuation, precisely as political agents, takes place through the activity of this articulation, a dynamic process which characterizes politics as such and which, consequently, engages both the agents and the society in a reciprocal transformation.

In experiencing the unfolding of his own fate and seeing how, in taking the path that he has chosen, his fate is intimately linked to the destiny of men like Bob Hunter, Cross Damon comes to realize that his position as an "outsider" is by no means isolated and nonrelational. During the brief interval in the narrative when Cross Damon is between identities, when he has adopted the transient and ungrounded identity of "Addison Jordan," Cross hypothesizes that "Maybe man is nothing in particular.... Maybe that's the terror of it. Man may be just anything at all" (175). Such a declaration is practically an existentialist cliché, no doubt, and it encapsulates quite succinctly the "being-the-ground of a nullity" which Heidegger calls the being-guilty of Dasein (§58, 285). The force of Cross's experience as Lionel Lane will lead him to revise, however, or at least supplement, his hypothesis. With his dying words, Cross attests to the insufficiency of his prior formulation; he testifies that "Alone man is nothing.... Man is a promise that he must never break" (585). By the end of the novel, Cross has come to realize that he, in fact, had broken a "promise" in assuming his death and thus isolating himself from the network of social relations. Wright, throughout the final chapter of *The Outsider*, offers the illocutionary speech act of the promise as a performative model for thinking the political moment of articulation between personal identity and a community, between the particular and the universal.

In faking his death, Cross had necessarily broken his ties to others. The moment of recognition comes when he learns that District Attorney Ely Houston knows Cross is guilty of four murders, but cannot prove it and decides to let him go free. At this moment, Cross realizes that he "had broken all of his promises to the world and the people in it, but he had never reckoned on that world turning on him and breaking its promise to him too! He was not to be punished! Men would not give meaning to what he had done!" (573). Cross had broken off his relations with the world, but even in severing all relations, he had counted on his retreat having some meaning. His insistence on attaching a meaning to his protest depended all along on the one-sided nature of his withdrawal, but now the "ludicrous nature of his protest came to him and he smiled wryly at his self-deception" (573). His protest would have meaning only insofar as the world kept its promise to him, the simple promise to give meaning at all. What binds the individual and society together, what they have in common, is meaning or sense. They do not share a given or particular meaning, however; nor does this promise proclaim the content of any "universal" meaning. Rather, the promise of sense itself conditions the possible positing of any such meaning. The communicability of meaning holds forth the very promise of the political.

The promise, therefore, continually lays out the prepolitical ground; and, in this sense, by extending his invitation, Wright was also making a promise. Thus, Wright's lecture "Tradition and Industrialization" begins with an attempt to reopen communication and to clear the way, once again, toward politics. The first sentence, in fact, describes a political world in which "a legion of ideological interests is choking the media of communication of the world today" (74). When the media of communication become saturated with ideological interests, the possibility of an effective political position—a position whose relationship to the political field would not be determined in advance—becomes increasingly difficult to articulate. The first necessary gesture for entering the politics of the outside, according to Wright, would be to recover the prepolitical ground which has been depoliticized through the ideological positing of "absolute objectivity of attitude." "First of all," as Wright says, "let us honestly admit that there is no such thing as objectivity" (77). Objectivity, here, names the relation between a subjective position and events or objects which are, in some sense, deemed to be "outside." Absolute objectivity would posit the existence of a transcendent outside which is determined as being absolved of all relation. The fate of Cross Damon stages the tragically illusory character of understanding the outside in such terms. Rather than being outside all relation, the "most rigorously determined attitude of objectivity is, at best, relative" (78). Wright is not simply advocating an absolute relativism in place of absolute objectivity. He is articulating the most rigorous conception of objectivity by emphasizing its relational character. Absolute objectivity paradoxically negates the essentially relational character of objectivity by positing an outside that is absolved of all relation. Objectivity, in its most rigorous determination, is determined in relation to the outside. The outside with which it enters into relation, however, cannot be determined absolutely, which is the mistake of absolute objectivity. While absolute objectivity is the error of determining the outside absolutely, there is an absolute outside. What makes the outside "absolute" is not its lack of a relation, but the sheer impossibility of determining it absolutely.

The outside is that which can never be completely enclosed; nor can it be completely expelled, insofar as such an expulsion would denegate its relation to the inside. These have been the historical errors of neoimperialism and colonialism, respectively, in relating to the outside. Rather, the outside is an immanent field of difference among which determined positions emerge. The outside is not a determined space or position, but the positionality of position as such. The universal and the particular, along with their political doppelgangers, strategy and tactics, serve as structural indices of thought that coordinate conceptual positions. Entering the politics of the outside, as Richard Wright would have us do, not only requires an engagement with those spaces, both geopolitical as well as biocultural, which have been positioned as "outside." It entails a restructuring of the relationship to the outside as such so that the "outside" represents neither any particular political position nor even the universal space of politics itself. In the politics of the outside, the "outside" represents nothing other than that which cannot be represented within politics. Entering the politics of the outside would expose politics to the force of difference, the resistance of the outsider, which the politics of representation remains unable and unwilling to recognize.

Notes

1. For a detailed discussion of this particular congress, in addition to a highly informative discussion of the general historical context, see Bennetta Jules-Rosette.

2. The sign is "tenuous" because Rancière, like so many others, still never mentions the historical period of decolonization as an example, preferring to stick with the "classic" examples from ancient Greece and the European Marxist tradition.

3. See for example, Michel Fabre ("Richard Wright") and Amritjit Singh.

4. For more on the historical and biographical context of these statements by McKay, see Cooper, 330–333.

5. All translations of this text are my own.

6. The bibliography here would be extensive. A few of the key texts in the past decade would include Butler et al's *Contingency, Hegemony, Universality,* Laclau's *Emancipation(s),* and Balibar's *Politics and the Other Scene.* It should also be noted that the trends that I outline in the remainder of this paragraph extend not only to the "poststructuralists" of this list, but also to "postcolonialists" such as Gayatri Spivak and Dipesh Chakrabarty. See the former's *A Critique of Postcolonial Reason* and, particularly, the latter's *Provincializing Europe,* which is explicitly indebted to Heidegger in exploration of themes that "could be considered 'universal' to structures of political modernity" (19).

7. Hardt and Negri develop this argument throughout *Multitude* which attempts to address the many questions, raised by their book *Empire,* concerning their conception of political agency and subjectivity. The difficulties posed by such a "substitution" are too complex to examine in depth here. Nevertheless, it should perhaps be pointed out that such a substitution cannot take place simply through a change in vocabulary. The philosophical challenge behind such a substitution can be measured, however, by the stubborn persistence of this vocabulary. Throughout *Empire,* for instance, as they are beginning to formulate the features of what they call "the common" in *Multitude,* they have recourse to a very Hegelian vocabulary of the "concrete universal" (362).

8. For an in-depth history of Heidegger's reception in France, see Dominique Janicaud.

9. See Fabre (*The Unfinished Quest* 299, 374).

10. James Tuttleton has written that "In Paris he became a spokesman for the American colony of blacks (and for African blacks in Paris), and he founded

and joined many literary and liberal political organizations. The Existentialism of Sartre and Camus was then all the rage, and Wright began to read in the philosophy of Heidegger, Husserl, and Jaspers. This Existentialism, in ill-digested clumps, unfortunately mars his novel *The Outsider*" (169). Tuttleton's assessment continues a line of critical reception that began with the initial appearance of *The Outsider* in 1953 and Arna Bontemp's casual dismissal of Wright's "roll in the hay with existentialism" (106).

11. For Antonin Artaud's rigorous demolition of these categories, especially as they pertain to the structure of judgment, see my "Reading Forgiveness and Forgiving Reading: Antonin Artaud's *Correspondance avec Jacques Rivière.*" Here would be a crucial site for exploring Robin D. G. Kelly's suggestion that "it is hard to comprehend some of his [Richard Wright's] most radical political impulses without surrealism" (181). Incidentally, Wright donated a manuscript to a benefit auction held for Antonin Artaud in 1946 on his release from the psychiatric facility at Rodez where he had been institutionalized for nine years.

12. All citations of *Being and Time* will be given by section number followed by the number of the German pagination which is reproduced in the margins of most available English translations.

13. "Dasein is a being that does not simply occur among other beings. Rather it is ontically distinguished by the fact that in its being this being is concerned *about* its very being. Thus it is constitutive of the being of Dasein to have, in its very being, a relation of being to this being" (§4, 12).

14. The historical and political interpretation which the National Socialist would give to the destiny of the German community finds itself inscribed most immediately within Heidegger's thought at this specific moment. First published in 1927, Heidegger's thinking in this passage would assume a historically more ominous tone in his 1935 lectures published as *An Introduction to Metaphysics* where he writes, for example, that the German nation "is the most metaphysical of nations. We are certain of this vocation, but our people will only be able to wrest a destiny from it if *within itself* it creates a resonance, a possibility of resonance for this vocation, and takes a creative view of its tradition" (38).

15. Although this is not the place to do so, a rigorous examination should be done here of how a dialectical maneuver reminiscent of Hegel's dialectic of sense-certainty discernibly at work in Heidegger's disarticulation surreptitiously returns to program this moment of re-articulation. In addition to attending more closely to section 51 of *Being and Time*, such an analysis would also have to work through Heidegger's lecture course *Hegel's Phenomenology of Spirit*.

16. The phrase "clifflike margin" is from Wright's *White Man, Listen!*, which is dedicated to "the lonely outsiders who exist precariously on the clifflike margins of many cultures."

Works Cited

Adler, Alan, ed. *Theses, Resolutions and Manifestos of the First Four Congresses of the Third International.* London: Ink Links, 1980.

Atteberry, Jeffrey. "Reading Forgiveness and Forgiving Reading: Antonin Artaud's *Correspondance avec Jacques Rivière.*" *Modern Language Notes.* 115 (2000): 714–740.

Balibar, Étienne. *Politics and the Other Scene.* London: Verso, 2002.

Bontemps, Arna. "Review of *The Outsider.*" *The Critical Response to Richard Wright*. Ed. Robert J. Butler. Westport: Greenwood, 1995: 105–107.

Butler, Judith, Ernesto Laclau, and Slavoj Žižek. *Contingency, Hegemony, Universality: Contemporary Dialogues on the Left*. London: Verso, 2000.

Césaire, Aimé. *Lettre à Maurice Thorez*. Paris: Présence Africaine, 1956.

Chakrabarty, Dipesh. *Provincializing Europe: Postcolonial Thought and Historical Difference*. Princeton: Princeton University Press, 2000.

Cooper, Wayne. *Claude McKay: Rebel Sojourner in the Harlem Renaissance*. New York: Schocken, 1987.

Fabre, Michel. "Richard Wright and the French Existentialists." *The Critical Response to Richard Wright*. Ed. Robert J. Butler. Westport: Greenwood, 1995: 111–121.

——— . *The Unfinished Quest of Richard Wright*. Trans. Isabel Barzun. 2nd ed. Urbana: University of Illinois Press, 1993.

Gilroy, Paul. *The Black Atlantic: Modernity and Double Consciousness*. Cambridge: Harvard University Press, 1993.

Hardt, Michael and Antonio Negri. *Empire*. Cambridge: Harvard University Press, 2000.

———. *Multitude: War and Democracy in the Age of Empire*. New York: Penguin, 2004.

Heidegger, Martin. *An Introduction to Metaphysics*. Trans. Ralph Manheim. New Haven: Yale University Press, 1959.

———. *Being and Time*. Trans. Joan Stambaugh. Albany: State University of New York Press, 1996.

———. *Hegel's Phenomenology of Spirit*. Trans. Parvis Emad and Kenneth Maly. Bloomington: Indiana University Press, 1988.

Janicaud, Dominique. *Heidegger en France*. 2 vols. Paris: Albin Michel, 2001.

Jules-Rosette, Bennetta. *Black Paris: The African Writers' Landscape*. Urbana: University of Illinois Press, 1998.

Kelly, Robin D. G. *Freedom Dreams: The Black Radical Imaginary*. Boston: Beacon, 2002.

Laclau, Ernesto. *Emancipation(s)*. London: Verso, 1996.

McKay, Claude. *The Passion of Claude McKay: Selected Poetry and Prose, 1912–1948*. New York: Schocken Books, 1973.

Rancière, Jacques. "Ten Theses on Politics." Trans. Rachel Bowlby and Davide Panagia. *Theory & Event*. 5.3 (2001): 33 pars. 21 Feb. 2005. <http://muse.jhu.edu/journals/theory_and_event/v005/5.3ranciere.html>.

Singh, Amritjit. "Richard Wright's *The Outsider*: Existentialist Exemplar or Critique?" *The Critical Response to Richard Wright*. Ed. Robert J. Butler. Westport: Greenwood, 1995: 123–129.

Spivak, Gayatri Chakravorty. *A Critique of Postcolonial Reason: Toward a History of the Vanishing Present*. Cambridge: Harvard University Press, 1999.

Stalin, Joseph V. "Concerning the Question of the Strategy and Tactics of the Russian Communists." *Works*. Volume 5. Moscow: Foreign Language Publishing, 1953: 163–183.

Tuttleton, James W. "The Problematic Texts of Richard Wright." *The Critical Response to Richard Wright*. Ed. Robert J. Butler. Westport: Greenwood, 1995: 167–172.

Wright, Richard. *The Outsider*. 1953. New York: Perennial, 1993.

——— . "Tradition and Industrialization." *White Man, Listen!*. New York: Doubleday, 1957.

——— . "Richard Wright, the Black Dostoevski." Interview with Ramuncho Gomez. Trans. Kenneth Kinnamon. *Conversations with Richard Wright*. Ed. Kenneth Kinnamon and Michel Fabre. Jackson: University Press of Mississippi, 1993.

ROBERT BUTLER

The Loeb and Leopold Case:
A Neglected Source for Richard Wright's Native Son

> But we have had many, many such cases to come before the courts of
> Illinois. The Loeb and Leopold case, for example. . . . Shall we deny this
> boy, because he is poor and black, the same protection, the same chance
> to be heard and understood that we have so readily granted to others?
> (Boris Max addressing the judge in *Native Son*, 376).

Richard Wright, who had strong appetites for detective fiction and
film noir movies, had a life-long fascination with criminal behavior and its
causes.[1] When explaining some of the "sources" (43) of *Native Son* in "How
'Bigger' Was Born," he began by describing how Bigger was modeled in
certain ways on five young black men from his childhood and adolescence
in Mississippi who were rebellious lawbreakers whom he both admired and
feared. Each was the product of an unjust social system, and Wright envied
their ability to lash out against a segregated world that frustrated many of
their most human impulses. But Wright also drew away from these figures
since their violent behavior brought them to terrifying ends; each wound
up as dead, incarcerated, or insane. These five prototypes for Bigger paid
a substantial price for violating the taboos of a repressive society, but each
also left a lasting imprint on Wright's consciousness, becoming a kind of
photographic "negative" ("How 'Bigger'" 440) that would be developed in
Native Son.

African American Review, Volume 39, Number 4 (2005): pp. 555–567. © 2005 Robert
Butler.

177

Throughout his life Wright's fascination with rebellious lawbreakers would catalyze some of his most important work. Novels such as *Native Son, The Outsider,* and *Savage Holiday* as well as stories such as "The Man Who Killed A Shadow," "Down by the Riverside," and "The Man Who Lived Underground" focus on central characters forced into criminal behavior either by a repressive society or the macabre compulsions of their inner-most nature. At several points in his career Wright carefully studied actual criminal behavior and incorporated his findings in his creative writings. His work with teenage gangs in New York and Chicago helped to shape certain aspects of *Native Son* and *Black Boy* and resulted in his writing *Rite of Passage,* a nouvelle about juvenile delinquency. The Robert Nixon case, in which a young black man from Chicago murdered a white woman by crushing her skull with a brick, took place in 1938 when Wright was halfway through the composition of *Native Son* and stirred his imagination deeply. His careful study of the news accounts, which Margaret Walker mailed to him over a year's time, played an important role in Wright's construction of Bigger's character, and Wright inserted several of these news accounts from the Chicago papers into the novel. In the same way, Wright became strongly involved both as a person and a writer in the case of Clinton Brewer, a black man serving a life sentence for stabbing to death a woman who had refused his offer of marriage, and this crime became a source for *Savage Holiday,* written late in Wright's career and dedicated to Brewer.[2]

The Loeb and Leopold case, which Wright followed in the Jackson, Mississippi, newspapers when it erupted as "the crime of the century" in 1924 (Rowley 153), was another source that Wright used consciously in his fiction. He made elaborate use of it in *Native Son,* which he was just beginning to imagine when public interest in the case was rejuvenated in 1936: the year that Loeb was brutally murdered in prison.[3] When Wright was half-finished with the first draft of *Native Son* in November 1938, he visited Margaret Walker in Chicago, and the two researched what he thought necessary to complete the novel. They not only visited Ulysses S. Keys, Nixon's lawyer, and went to the Cook County Jail where Nixon was incarcerated, but they also made a trip to a Chicago library where Wright searched for books on the Loeb/Leopold case. As Walker observed in *Richard Wright: Daemonic Genius,*

> The next day we went to the library and, on my library card, checked out two books we found on the Loeb/Leopold case and on Clarence Darrow, their lawyer. The lawyer's defense of Bigger in *Native Son* was modeled after Darrow's defense. Wright took so long to send those books back that I wrote him a hot letter reminding him that I had not borrowed those books permanently! He finished *Native Son* early in the spring of 1939 and wrote to

me that he never worked so hard before in all his life, often staying
up till 3 A. M. (125).

Although much has been written on Wright's use of the Nixon case in
Native Son, very little attention has been paid to his use of the Loeb/Leopold
murder and trial even though they played a more prominent role in the shaping of Wright's masterpiece.[4] A careful examination of *Native Son* and the
Loeb/Leopold case reveals previously unexamined parallels between the two,
from which we can perceive sharp ironies that arise from Wright's powerfully inversive imagination. The Loeb/Leopold case, therefore, is a critically
important source for Wright that holds a key to his thinking not only about
the particular plight of black people in America but also about the problems
of modern existence in general.

***

A survey of outstanding physical similarities between the fictional account
of Bigger Thomas and the actual story of Loeb and Leopold clearly establishes Wright's intentional use of this infamous case in the writing of *Native
Son.* Wright portrays the Daltons as living in Kenwood, in the 4600 block
of Drexel Boulevard, which Bessie reveals to Bigger as "that section not
far from where the Loeb folks lived" (136). Wright's Bessie has worked in
that area often as a domestic, she is quite familiar with the Loeb/Leopold
case and, as she describes it to Bigger, she unintentionally inspires him to
seek ransom from the Daltons in exactly the same amount as the ransom
demanded from the Franks family. Moreover, the actual killings of Bobby
Franks and Mary Dalton are strikingly similar in a number of significant
ways. Both young people were innocent victims of chance, both were in the
wrong place at the wrong time, and both were suffocated to death. Although
Franks was initially dazed by blows to the head with a chisel, the coroner
established that his death was caused by "suffocation" (Higdon 54) when a
rag soaked in chloroform was stuffed in his mouth to keep him quiet. Bigger
likewise suffocates Mary with a pillow to silence her. The bodies of both
victims were mutilated, as Loeb and Leopold poured hydrochloric acid over
Franks's face, torso and genitals, and Bigger decapitated Mary and inciner-
ated her corpse in a furnace. (The comparisons between such mutilations
and the destruction of the body in a lynching would surely not have passed
Wright's notice.) Bobby Franks's corpse was stuffed in a rain culvert and
his clothes burned in the furnace of the Leopold mansion, a clear parallel
to Bigger's stuffing Mary's body in the Dalton's basement furnace and then
burning her body and clothing. And Bigger, Loeb, and Leopold were all
caught shortly after their crimes were committed because they so poorly dis-
posed of the remains of their victims. Bobby Franks's body was discovered

the day after his abduction when a laborer saw his foot protruding from the culvert, and Mary's charred skeleton is discovered when Bigger neglects to clean ashes from the furnace, thereby causing smoke to fill the Dalton basement and to draw attention to her bones there.

The ransom notes used in both killings are also remarkably similar in content, although quite different in style. Loeb's carefully worded, logically structured note reveals both his privileged education and his cold amorality while Bigger's barely literate note reflects the fact that his world has provided him with little or no formal schooling. But the substance of the two notes is surprisingly similar since a $10,000 ransom is demanded in both, and the parents of each victim are instructed to place the money in a box (a cigar box for Loeb and Leopold and a shoe box for Bigger) and then to drop the money at an assigned place from a moving vehicle (a train in the historical case and an automobile in Wright's fictional narrative). Both notes make it abundantly clear that the kidnapped person will be kept alive only if these written instructions are followed scrupulously.

The trials in each narrative also share a number of significant outward similarities as they receive sensationalistic newspaper coverage that stirs Chicago's violent racism. Loeb and Leopold were Jews and their trial known to many as "the Jewish trial," whereas Wright's Bigger is, of course, black. Howling mobs calling for the deaths of the defendants form a sick chorus for each trial, and the Ku Klux Klan burns a cross outside of Bigger's cell in Wright's fiction and, in actuality, places a crude skull and crossbones on a porch across the street from the Franks's home, announcing, "If the court don't hang them, we will" (Higdon 233). Max's fictional defense is almost a carbon copy of Darrow's historical defense, as both attorneys opt for a guilty plea to avoid a jury trial and to place maximum moral pressure on a single man, the judge.

Furthermore, Max and Darrow premise their legal strategies on strongly deterministic grounds, arguing that the crimes committed were produced by unhealthy social environments that emotionally distorted their clients and stunted their human development. For Darrow, the key determinants that shaped his clients' criminal actions were chance, genetics, and a privileged background that at once eroded moral character and promoted intellectual growth. For Max, the environmental factors controlling Bigger's behavior are racism, chance, and poverty. Max and Darrow argue forcibly that environmental forces overwhelmed the consciousness, free will, and moral sense of the defendants, forcing them into violent acts that they did not fully understand or control. Just as Max pleads that the "fundamental problem" Bigger faced was his emergence "from an oppressed people" (294), Darrow stressed that the natural and social factors conditioning Loeb and Leopold were "infinite forces" (Darrow 21) beyond their understanding and control. While Max argues that Bigger was victimized by a "mode of life" that was "stunted and distorted" (389), Darrow would make the same claims for his clients. And when Darrow cries out to Judge Caverly that Loeb and Leopold "did not beget themselves" (Darrow 23), Max would apply the same idea to Bigger.

Hazel Rowley has recently observed that Wright had Darrow's *Defense of Loeb and Leopold* on his writing desk as he composed *Native Son* (153). The truth of this statement can be understood when one compares the actual and fictional discourses used respectively by Darrow and Max in court. When Darrow began the preliminary hearing by substituting a guilty plea for his early plea of not guilty, he told Judge Caverly: "Your honor, after long and honest deliberation I have determined to make a motion in this court to withdraw our plea of not guilty and enter a plea of guilty" (Higdon 163). Max uses comparable diction and syntax during Bigger's hearing: "After long reflection and thorough discussion, we have made a motion in court . . . to withdraw our plea of not guilty and enter a plea of guilty" (370). Darrow advised the judge that the defense would offer "evidence of the mental condition of the defendants" in order "to show the degree of responsibility that they had" as a way of mitigating their offense, emphasizing the "youth" (Higdon 165) of his clients. Max uses very similar words to express the same idea to the fictional judge: "I shall endeavor to show the mental and emotional attitude of the boy and the degree of responsibility he had in the crime," and he, too, stresses his intention to "offer evidence to the youth of this boy" (371). In their summations both lawyers express nearly identical ideas and similar words and phrases. Darrow reminds Judge Caverly that he has put "a serious burden on your shoulders" (Darrow 9) by obviating a jury trial and thus putting the entire moral weight of the decision on a single man rather than on 12 jurors. Max likewise tells the judge in *Native Son*, "I am not insensitive to the deep burden of responsibility on your shoulders" (383), clearly hoping to deepen the judge's awareness of the moral complexities of capital punishment. Darrow's assistant, Benjamin Bachrach, used language in his plea before the judge that the death penalty not be imposed; Wright uses a close parallel for Max's plea that Bigger's life be spared. While Bachrach says, "Your honor . . . let these boys live" (Higdon 242), Max cries out, "Your honor, give this boy life" (405).

When arguing their respective clients' motives, Darrow and Max employ similar concepts, words, and phrases. Darrow tells Judge Caverly, "This is a senseless, useless, purposeless, motiveless act of two boys. . . . There was absolutely no purpose in it at all, no reason in it at all, no motive in it at all" (Darrow 14), thereby arguing that his clients acted as mentally diseased young men mechanically driven by misshapen social impulses. Max makes a comparable point to Judge Hanley: "What was the motive. . . . The truth is, your honor, there is no motive as you and I understand motives within the scope of our laws" (399). Like Darrow, the fictional attorney views the violent actions of his client as arising from environmentally induced reflexes that have nothing to do with conscious motivation.

The rhetoric employed by the State's Attorneys in both instances also reveals important similarities. Robert Crowe at one point characterizes Loeb and Leopold as "fiendish" (Crowe 136) while Wright's Buckley refers to Bigger as a "miserable fiend" (407). Both men also attack the respective defendants by alluding to unproven sexual perversions. On many occasions during the historical trial Crowe labeled Loeb and Leopold as "perverts" (Crowe 92) just as Buckley describes Bigger as a "maddened ape," a "treacherous beast" who not only has raped Mary but then burned her body to cover up "offenses worse than rape" (412). Although, like Crowe, the fictional prosecutor has no solid evidence of sexual violation of the respective victims, he accuses Bigger of "obnoxious sexual perversions" (410). And just as Crowe inflamed the actual court by describing the murder of Bobby Franks as "the greatest, the most important, and atrocious killing that ever happened in the State of Illinois or the United States" (Crowe 174), Buckley characterizes Bigger's killing of Mary Dalton and Bessie Mears as "two of the most horrible murders in the history of American civilization" (374).

Other material similarities between the two trials abound. Buckley and Crowe each call on an inordinate number of witnesses, clear overkill considering that they were not presenting to a jury and that the defendants had already confessed and pled guilty to murder. And they sensationalized the hearing and trial by organizing grand tours of the crime scenes that had been lavishly reported in newspapers and magazines. Wright depicts Bigger as like Loeb in fainting when confronted with damaging evidence. But the most important similarity between the actual and the fictional trials is the vision shared by defense attorneys who saw the personal disasters of their respective clients as a reflection of the larger cultural calamities experienced by modern society. Each viewed his trial as a pivot on a line in history dividing barbarism from civilization. Darrow reminded Judge Caverly that he must choose between a brutal societal past that executes people instead of rehabilitating them and a more humane future in which the "disease" (Darrow 74) of crime would be rationally diagnosed and cured. For Wright, Max likewise argues that we are poised between "the night of fear" and the "light of reason" (383). If the pathological environment that spawns Bigger's violence is not understood and transformed, it will deteriorate further, resulting in the collapse of civilization, turning US history into a "wheel of blood" (392). Toward the end of his summation Darrow uses a very similar metaphor to describe the violent, anarchic world spawned by World War I as a collapsed civilization "drenched in blood" (Darrow 77).

***

These outward, rhetorical likenesses between the narrative of Bigger's crime and the Loeb/Leopold story establish a clear pattern that indicates Wright's conscious use of these legal materials to develop themes important in *Native Son*. Much more significant, however, are the comparisons between Bigger, Loeb, and Leopold as individuals and distinctively modern figures. For just as Loeb and Leopold had committed what most people at the time believed was a horrible new kind of crime that reflected the anarchy and amorality of modern life, Bigger is presented by Wright as a new kind of literary figure whose story illustrates in a bold and lucid way the central problems of American history and modern culture.

Although their social and economic backgrounds appear to be so radically different as to preclude meaningful comparisons, there are many striking similarities between Wright's character and Darrow's clients. To begin with, they are approximately the same age: when convicted, Loeb and Leopold were 19 years old, and Bigger is judged in court to be 20. All three had lonely childhoods, suffering from what Paula Fass describes in her characterization of Leopold as "fragile loneliness" (933). Bigger's loss of his father in a southern race riot traumatizes him at an early age, and Leopold's loss of his mother at age 17 had what Hal Higdon described as a "profound effect" (66) on him since she was the only person in his family to whom he was emotionally close. Loeb was outwardly very sociable but inwardly a loner who established very few genuinely close ties with people. Likewise, at one point in Book 3, Bigger reveals to Max, "I don't reckon I was ever in love with nobody" (352). Except for their own twisted relationship with one another and Leopold's relationship with his mother, Darrow's clients could say roughly the same thing. This lack of intimacy with family and friends made all three figures coldly detached from other people.

This detachment, of course, is dramatically revealed in their motives for and reactions to their killings. Loeb and Leopold, who greatly admired (and conveniently misunderstood) the philosophy of Friedrich Nietzsche and saw themselves as *ubermenschen* above the law, explained their murder of Bobby Franks as a carefully planned exercise, a "thrill killing" that gave them a sense of excitement and power. At the trial Loeb revealed that during the murder he had experienced a "great excitement" that was "pleasant" (Higdon 154). In precisely the same way, Bigger enjoys a perverse "elation" (107) from his killing of Mary Dalton and a "queer sense of power" (239) when he murders Bessie. Bigger deludedly thinks that his violence will provide him with a "new life" (105), as Loeb also thought his crimes had given him a triumphant "new life" (Higdon 127), and liberated him from conventional morality.

Wright apparently borrowed from the psychological profiles of Loeb and Leopold drawn in court by Darrow's expert witnesses to construct Bigger's mental condition. All three are split personalities who compensate for an unsatisfying outward life by indulging in wild fantasies associated with excitement, power, and rebellion. Wright stresses in *Native Son* that "There were two Biggers" (252)—a passive outer self and a turbulent inner self. For this reason, there are two basic "rhythms" of his life, "indifference and violence" *(Native Son* 29). Dr. William Healy, one of Darrow's expert witnesses or "alienists," suggested this same division in Loeb's character, classifying him as a "pathological split personality" (Higdon 217), a strange combination of brutal killer and mama's boy who at one point explained that he blamed his partner for the murder because "mompsie" (Leopold 57) would be disappointed if he were revealed as the killer. Leopold made a similar assessment of his friend's personality many years later in the autobiography he wrote in prison, stating that Loeb was "an infinitely complex mixture" who had "fundamental contradictions in his character" (Leopold 26). He observed that Loeb at times demonstrated a sunny, affable persona but had "that other side to him" (Leopold 26) that enabled him coldly to plan and execute the murder of an innocent 14-year-old boy without evincing any remorse. Leopold himself was also a curious "mixture," a noted young authority on birds that he treated with considerable tenderness and understanding, but also a remorseless killer who could snicker in court about his crimes. Like Bigger, he repressed his "tender emotions" because they made him aware of his own human inadequacies, his inability to translate these feelings into successful human relationships.

All three figures luxuriated in elaborate fantasy lives that gave them delusions of power and directed their macabre split personalities. Bigger richly enjoys this part of himself whom nobody else, particularly whites, perceive, the icy killer who can deprive the rich white world of its most cherished symbol, the beautiful white girl on the pedestal, the boss's daughter of the Alger myth. As Ross Pudaloff has observed, Bigger enacts the role of the tough gangster who kills without mercy after he has absorbed this figure from popular films and detective fiction (4). Loeb's fantasy life was likewise fed by his nearly compulsive reading of crime magazine city gangsters and dime novel western desperadoes. Like him, Bigger compensates for an outwardly disappointing life by imagining himself as a tough guy performing the perfect crime. Loeb felt much more comfortable in prison than Leopold did because such a life enabled him to prolong his fantasies of himself as a Chicago gangster, a romantic alter-ego to his previous life as a pampered rich boy, whom Darrow described once in court as a "hothouse plant" (Darrow 38).

Leopold's fantasy life was more elaborate than Loeb's or Bigger's, but it performed an identical psychological function. Avowedly ashamed of his poor health and slight physical build and stunted by the conventional life laid out for him by his parents and his social standing, he cultivated for many years a "king-slave fantasy" (Higdon 210), in which he envisioned himself sometimes as a powerful, Spartacus-like slave who would save his master by performing extraordinary feats of physical prowess. At other times, he assumed the role of king, a titanic figure situated majestically above the law.

To nourish such active fantasy lives all three figures deeply enjoyed reading newspaper accounts of their crimes. Bigger becomes greatly excited by the news reports of Mary Dalton's death because, for the first time in his life, it puts an end to his anonymity and gives him a sense of himself as an important person who can compel the attention of thousands of people. He purchases a copy of the *Chicago Tribune* so that he can read about "his story" (222), exulting in the fact that his life has acquired public importance. He takes particular pleasure in seeing "his picture" (223) in the paper, realizing that large numbers of people will finally notice him. Later in Book 3, while escaping the police, he risks capture by actually stealing a newspaper from a drugstore. Although the news account reveals he is hopelessly trapped and will soon be arrested, he takes a curious pleasure in reading about himself as he is caught in the public eye. Loeb and Leopold also enjoyed the limelight given to them in the newspapers, and escalated their crimes in part so that they could attain more press attention. In fact, Loeb actually followed reporters for days after the crime, giving them tips and false leads, getting intense psychological pleasure not only from seeing his exploits reported in the paper but from actually participating in the construction of news reports. Even after he was caught and sentenced, Loeb derived enormous satisfaction from being interviewed by reporters and providing them with reliable copy, He once jokingly claimed that he had considered committing suicide in prison but decided not to because he would be unable to read news accounts of it the next day (Higdon 290).

By thus connecting Bigger with two other men from vastly different social and economic circumstances, Wright makes an important point about capitalism in America, namely that it corrupted and alienated *all* levels of society, regardless of race and class. As a Marxist and a Communist, Wright asserted that materialism and selfishness had infected modern society from top to bottom, producing a deep alienation and moral vacuum that threatened modern civilization with anarchy and violence. Just as Mary Dalton and Bigger Thomas are finally shown as more alike than different as two "crazy" young people who cannot relate to the empty world that they have inherited and try to find meaning in rebellious acts of breaking taboos of many kinds, so too are Loeb, Leopold, and Bigger tragically alike as victims of similarly dehumanizing environments.[5] Darrow stresses that fabulous affluence has deadened Loeb and Leopold just as Wright reveals that terrible poverty has victimized Bigger. Midway through his summation Darrow claimed that "it is just as often a great misfortune to be the child of the rich as it is to be the child of the poor" (Darrow 47), arguing that his clients' "hothouse" (Darrow 48) lives prevented them from developing as normal human beings.

Leopold's description in *Life Plus 99 Years* of Loeb's motives for carrying out a murderous "perfect crime" bears a remarkable resemblance to Wright's explanation of Bigger's criminal behavior in *Native Son*. Although he hesitates to give a definitive explanation of Loeb's complex motivations, he does point out that "Dick's basic motive, I think, must be sought in his basic personality—in what he was, in how he was conditioned. Primarily, I think it was a kind of revolt—an over-reaction against the strictness of the governess who had charge of him until he was fifteen. A basic feeling of inferiority, maybe; a desire to show that he could do things and bring them to a successful end on his own" (50). Wright, likewise, stresses that Bigger explodes into violence because he sees it as a mode of action enabling him to overcome the impotence imposed upon him by conventional society. Killing Mary Dalton and successfully extorting money from her wealthy parents provides him with deep psychological satisfactions because, like Loeb, he experiences criminal action as a mode of "revolt" against a "basic feeling of inferiority."

Loeb, Leopold, and Bigger, therefore, become for Wright troubling reflections of a modern world that has dissolved but not replaced traditional ethics. As Wright stresses in "How 'Bigger' Was Born," "Bigger Thomas was not black all the time; he was white too" (441). In a "world whose metaphysical meanings had vanished" (446) because of war, depression, revolutions, and other traumatic events of modern history, political figures such as Hitler and Mussolini could enact on a large public scale the crimes that Bigger, Loeb, and Leopold commit on a personal level. Terrifying violence and anarchy, for Wright, knew no racial or national limits but infected modern society on all levels.

Significantly, when Wright describes peculiarly modern problems in "How 'Bigger' Was Born," he employs language that vividly recalls the rhetoric used to describe the killings of Bobby Franks, Mary Dalton, and Bessie Mears:

> It was a *highly geared world* whose nature was *conflict* and *action*, a world whose limited area and vision imperiously urged men to satisfy their organisms, a world that existed on a *plane of animal sensation alone.*
>
> It was a world where millions of men *behaved like drunkards*, taking a stiff drink of hard life to lift them for a *thrilling moment*, to give them *a quivering sense of wild exultation and fulfillment that soon faded and let them down.* Eagerly they took another drink, wanting to avoid *the dull, flat look of things*, then still another, this time stronger, and then *they felt their lives had meaning.* Speaking

figuratively, they were soon chronic alcoholics, men who lived by *violence*, through *extreme action* and *sensation*, through drowning in sensation (446, emphasis mine).

Such a world of "conflict and action" reduces men to "drunkards" who live on "animal sensation alone," avoiding "the dull flat look of things"; it produces not only individuals such as Bigger Thomas, Richard Loeb, and Nathan Leopold but also the cataclysmic disruptions of "Nazi Germany and old Russia" (446). When people and whole nations try to find "meaning" through "violence" and other forms of "extreme action and sensation," they might temporarily experience "a quivering sense of wild exultation" in "a thrilling moment," but ultimately this excitement fades, and nations and individuals collapse into anarchy and death. Like his favorite writer Fyodor Dostoevski, Wright understood that while a permissive society might be attractive in the short run, in the long run it experienced madness, despair, and cultural collapse.[6]

***

In the second paragraph of "How 'Bigger' Was Born" Wright describes the sources of his imaginative writing as being rooted in a mixture of deeply personal and verifiable public reality: "In a fundamental sense, an imaginative novel represents the merging of two extremes; it is an intensely intimate expression on the part of consciousness couched in terms of the most objective and commonly known events. It is at once something private and public by its very nature and texture" (433). The Loeb/Leopold case, along with the Robert Nixon murder and the Scottsboro trial, were extremely significant to Wright because they weighted *Native Son* in "public," historically verifiable events that provided the novel with an authority and resonance it otherwise would not have possessed. But Wright did not use these factual materials in a mainly literal way as Meyer Levin did in *Compulsion*, a *roman à clef* mirroring historical reality and using lightly disguised actual people in its cast of characters. While Levin's documentary novel is now quite dated because it is too firmly tied to the elements of a legal case that took place 80 years ago, Wright's *Native Son* continues to live vibrantly as a work of art because it transforms "objective and commonly known events" into a durable work of art by filtering them through Wright's unique "consciousness." In the process, it expresses a special vision of African American life that continues to speak powerfully today. To use Henry Louis Gates's term, Wright "signifies" on historical materials from mainstream culture, altering them until they express a "black difference" (xxvii). Or to cite Wright's own language in "How 'Bigger' Was Born," he took materials from white culture and then "twisted them, bent them, adapted them until they became *my* ways of apprehending the locked-in life of the Black Belt areas" (443). (In a very comparable manner, an African American jazz or blues musician might use a popular white song and then bend, twist, and adapt its lyrics and notes to shape a uniquely black sound and meaning.)

Placing Bigger's narrative alongside the Loeb/Leopold story, one immediately recognizes bitter ironies that Wright generates by juxtaposition, ironies that go to the very core of Wright's vision of African American life. For while Darrow's "boys" were young white men from wealthy, powerful families, Bigger is poor and black, and this difference ultimately accounts for his death by electrocution while his white counterparts go on living. They live even though they have in actuality committed far worse crimes and demonstrate absolutely no remorse in either their hearing or trial. Bigger's "fate" is sealed in the very moment he is arrested, but Loeb and Leopold go to prison expecting at some point in the future to be paroled, an assumption that Darrow shared. (Indeed, Leopold was paroled in 1958, due to the intervention of such influential people as Adlai Stevenson and Carl Sandburg; he spent the rest of his life living comfortably in Puerto Rico.)

Wright constructs *Native Son* such that at a critical point in Bigger's trial when Max is challenged by Buckley to provide a precedent for his defense of Bigger, the defense attorney points significantly to the Loeb/Leopold case and then asks: "Shall we deny this boy, because he is poor and black, the same protections, the same chance to be heard and understood, that we have so readily granted to others?" (376) In *Native Son* the answer to this question is a depressing "yes." Bigger clearly is not given the "same chance to be understood and heard" because he is black; what Buckley describes as his "black crimes" (375) will be punished in only one way, with death. Even though Bigger is not guilty of the murder for which he is charged whereas Loeb and Leopold confessed to what Judge Caverly described as "a crime of singular atrocity" (Caverly 150), the two white defendants evade the death penalty and Bigger is sent inevitably to the electric chair.

The millionaire parents of Loeb and Leopold could afford what was called at the time the "million dollar defense" presided over by the most distinguished defense attorney in America, himself assisted by other well-established attorneys as well as a team of research assistants and a series of extremely expensive expert witnesses who included Dr. William A. White, then head of the American Psychiatric Association. (The families of Loeb and Leopold were also willing to pay Sigmund Freud to serve as an expert witness, but he declined because of failing health [Higdon 139].)

Conversely, Bigger must settle for a bare bones defense. His attorney, Boris Max, is a despised Communist whose main goal, at least initially, is to protect the reputation of the Communist Party. He does not possess the financial resources to hire research assistants, other lawyers, or specialists who can testify to Bigger's mental condition or capacity to act responsibly. Indeed, Max is Bigger's only witness, and some of his testimony worsens Bigger's case. When Max explains to the judge that Bigger exulted over killing his victims and that his crimes were "an act of creation" (400), for example, he unwittingly weakens Bigger's case. When Wright depicts Max as employing some of the legal strategies that Darrow used successfully, particularly his stressing the youth of his client and the environmental pressures on him, he further posits that these strategies fail to evoke the judge's understanding or his sympathy for the black defendant. While Judge Caverly is reduced to tears by Darrow's eloquent summation, Judge Hanley in *Native Son* is absolutely unmoved by Max's pleas for mercy. Although Loeb and Leopold misbehaved grotesquely through the trial, showing no remorse but instead snickering, rolling their eyes and even chuckling when their victim's abused body was described, they became what Higdon has labeled "celebrities" (241) to many people and were actually viewed by young flappers as romantic figures. Bigger, who remains "numb" (331) and remorseful for the majority of his trial, draws sympathy only from Max, Jan, and his family members, all the while berated by mobs howling for his death.

The final statements made by the respective judges in each trial also demonstrate Bigger's discrimination by the law. Judge Caverly, who suffered what could be termed a nervous breakdown a few weeks after the trial, offered a tortured and detailed explanation of his decision not to impose the death penalty, citing the age of "boys of eighteen and nineteen years" (Caverly 151) as the mitigating circumstance, while agonizing over "the broad question of human responsibility" (Caverly 150). Again, approximately the same age as Loeb and Leopold, Bigger receives no such understanding, mercy, or moral agonizing. The judge in *Native Son* hands out his verdict in the coldest possible way as his final remarks formulaically elicit Bigger's final statements before he declares that "Number 666-983" will receive the death penalty "in a manner prescribed by the laws of this state" (417). The laws eased for the privileged white criminals who long continued to see themselves as above the law, are harshly applied to Bigger with full lethal force. In the final analysis, Max is exactly (W)right when he claims that Bigger's very "existence" is considered a *"crime against the state"* (400).

Caverly's argument for the mitigating fact of Loeb and Leopold's youth brings up another brutal irony. A central part of Darrow's defense was the age of his clients, to whom he referred in court as "boys" while frequently using their juvenile nicknames, Dickie and Babe, respectively. (In contrast, the prosecution referred as often to "Mr. Loeb" and "Mr. Leopold," and treated them as adults.) Defense attorney Walter Bachrach at one point in the trial implored the judge to "Let these boys live!" (Higdon 242). Years later, when Nathan Leopold sought parole, he relied on the same logic that Darrow and

Bachrach used at his trial, claiming that the murder of Bobby Franks was the "act of a child" (Higdon 312), and therefore should not be punished with the full weight of the law. He assured his parole board that he had fully repented of his crime and that, as a mature man, he was incapable of further acts of violence. Although he agreed with Darrow that he and Loeb were "diseased children" (Darrow 16) when they committed their crimes, he emphasized that he had grown morally in jail and was no danger to society.

Bigger is also referred to throughout his trial as a "boy" by Max, Mr. Dalton, and Buckley but with devastatingly different results: his youthful status earns him no special legal status. Quite to the contrary, the word *boy* worsens matters for him, evoking the age-old stereotype of the irresponsible, unpredictably violent black male who can *never* grow up and therefore can never be rehabilitated in prison so that he can become, as Leopold later claimed about himself, a reformed man and an exemplary citizen.

In his autobiography *Life Plus 99 Years,* Leopold argued, convincingly to some, that prison transformed him into a morally responsible, civic-minded adult who could and would make valuable contributions to society if paroled. In statements made later, when he lived comfortably in Puerto Rico, he often used himself as a living example of the evils of capital punishment because he was able to undergo a transformation of character as an adult and could therefore lead a useful life of service to others. In prison he had organized a school for inmates and risked his life serving as a volunteer in a medical experiment designed to develop a cure for malaria. In Puerto Rico he continued such a life of service, working in hospitals, doing research on birds, and teaching math. He claimed that "Helping others has become my chief hobby. It's how I get my kicks" (Higdon 334). In addition, he married and assumed a "normal" life, which had arguably been impossible for him as a young person. Leopold ultimately saw the reforming of criminal behavior as a function of "emotional maturing, of growing up" (198), reinforcing Darrow's belief that he and Loeb would merit parole when they reached their forties and had therefore outgrown their criminal compulsions.

But Bigger, who shows genuine remorse for his crimes throughout his trial and demonstrates convincing signs of true growth and moral rehabilitation in Book 3, does not receive the second chance offered to Leopold.[7] Just at the point where he has turned to a "new mode of life" (275) as a more mature human being who contrasts sharply with the delusional "new life" (105) earlier offered him through violence, the state decides to execute him. Bigger's remarkable conversion in jail is legally aborted by the state in a cold-blooded execution that bears a stunning resemblance to the equally cold-blooded, calculated murder of Bobby Franks. This concurrence is the supreme irony of Wright's novel.

At the end of *Native Son,* therefore, Wright certainly shares Bigger's "wry, bitter smile" (430). As the ironic juxtaposition of Bigger's narrative with the story of Loeb and Leopold narrative has surely demonstrated, Bigger is a "native son" in the sense that he, like the killers of Bobby Franks, is a product of a diseased American social environment, but unlike them, he is not fully a "native son" because he enjoys no second chances and no protections of law and privilege that Wright perceived to be the birthright of wealthy white people. To use John Dos Passos's words, the America presented in *Native Son* is really "two nations" (Dos Passos 469), a white world and a black world. As Bigger says to Gus early in Book 1, "They don't let us do nothing" (19) because "We black and they white" (20).

NOTES

1. Many critics and biographers have pointed out Wright's keen interest in detective fiction and crime stories. Pudaloff, for example, stressed that Wright's reading of men's magazines such as *Argosy All-Story Magazine* and Flynn's *Detective Weekly* provided him with plots, themes, and characters that he would use for ironic purposes in novels such as *Lawd Today!* and *Native Son.* Kinnamon noted that one of the first genres Wright was drawn to as a boy growing up in Jackson was detective fiction that appeared in magazines such as *Flynn's Detective Weekly* and *Argosy All-Story Magazine.* Fabre pointed out that Wright's reading in Memphis included not only "high literature" written by Mencken, Dreiser, and Zola but also "detective stories, dime novels, and popular fiction" (66). Rowley's recent biography quotes Wright's boyhood friend, Joe Brown, as remembering that Wright "loved western stories . . . and detective stories" (30). Wright's interest in Poe, the father of detective fiction, is also well documented. See, for example, Sisney's "The Power and Horror of Whiteness: Wright and Ellison Respond to Poe; *CLA Journal* 29 (September 1985): 82–90 and Fabre's "Black and White Cat: Wright's Gothic and the Influence of Poe" in *The World of Richard Wright.* Jackson: University of Mississippi Press, 1985, 27–33.

2. Wright's interest in Brewer was so keen that he visited him several times in prison and worked hard to get him paroled in 1942. Three months after his parole, Brewer stabbed another woman to death when she refused his offer of marriage, thereby duplicating his crime of many years earlier. Wright was intrigued by Brewer's compulsion to kill women and used him as a real life model of Erskine Fowler, the protagonist of *Savage Holiday* who also stabs a woman fatally when she refuses his offer of marriage. See Fabre, *The Unfinished Quest of Richard Wright,* and also Rowley.

3. Kinnamon's introduction to *New Essays on Native Son* traces the roots of *Native Son's* composition back to 1935 when Wright worked with troubled black youth at the South Side Boys Club in Chicago. At this time, he "sketched preliminary notes" (4) for the novel, which he then had to put on the back burner as he tried to find a publisher for *Cesspool* (later titled *Lawd Today!*) and worked on the stories included in *Uncle Tom's Children. Lawd Today!* makes an interesting reference to the Loeb/Leopold case when Jake Jackson and his friends include

"them thrill guys, Loeb and Leopold" (136) among the Chicago criminals who have impressed them.

4. Hricko's excellent unpublished doctoral dissertation briefly mentions the Loeb/Leopold case as having influenced Wright while writing *Native Son*. She points out that Wright borrowed books on the Loeb/Leopold case using Margaret Walker's library card, and also argues that Max was modeled on Clarence Darrow. She also reveals similarities between Bigger's ransom note and the one constructed by Loeb and Leopold. Rowley mentions that Wright closely followed the case in the Jackson, Mississippi, newspapers in 1924, and had a copy of Darrow's *Pleas in Defense of Loeb and Leopold* on his desk as he wrote *Native Son* (153). Kinnamon's introduction to *New Essays on Native Son* mentions Wright's careful research on both the Loeb/Leopold and Robert Nixon cases as he "was nearing the midpoint of the first draft" (5) of *Native Son*. Moreover, Kinnamon notes a letter to Walker in which Wright describes a list of research tasks that he wanted to complete at Chicago. These tasks include getting books on the trial from the Chicago Public Library as well as determining the locations of the homes of Loeb, Leopold and Bobby Franks. But aside from these four brief discussions, I can find nothing written on this important subject. Certainly no adequate analysis exists of Wright's complex uses in *Native Son* of the Loeb/Leopold murder of Bobby Franks.

5. See my *Native Son* (63–66), where I argue that Bigger and Mary, despite their obvious differences, share a common humanity that is stunted by the social roles they are forced to play and the conventional values imposed on them by a capitalist society. Wright stresses this parallel by drawing a number of important parallels between the two characters. Both, for example are described as "crazy" and "wild," problem children who upset their parents. Their acts of rebellion are attempts to work out their own definitions of themselves; they call into question the conformity, sexism, racism, and materialism of their respective environments. Wright suggests that their sexual attraction to each other is not only an attempt to attack established taboos but also a sign of their shared humanity. In a healthy society, Wright stresses, these two young people could become friends or lovers. But in a capitalist, racist society, they are locked in mortal combat that results in the death of each.

6. Meyer Levin, whom Wright knew in Chicago (Rowley 115), makes a similar connection in *Compulsion* between the personal narrative of Loeb and Leopold and widespread post-world-war cultural and political decline in Western civilization. Sid Silver, the narrator of that novel who is a lightly disguised version of Levin himself, equates the sick behavior of the boy criminals with the "tocsins" (444) of Hitler's regime and "the gathering sickness of Europe" (480) in the twentieth century. For Levin, the so-called "crime of the century" demonstrated in microcosm a century of crime characterized by anarchy and violence.

7. For a detailed discussion of Bigger's human development in Book 3, see my "The Function of Violence in Richard Wright's Native Son." While Bigger shows very few signs of remorse after killing Mary Dalton in Book 1, his conscience is activated in Book 2 as he is tormented by dream images of Mary's bloody head. Like Dostoevsky's Raskolnikov and unlike Loeb and Leopold he possesses a repressed moral nature that is at the core of the "soft" side of his divided personality. In Book 3 Bigger matures and develops meaningful relationships with Max and Jan as well as his mother, sister, and brother. This meaningful "new mode of life" (275) in Book 3 sharply contrasts with the false "new life" (105) he thinks he experiences as a result

of killing Mary. Ironically, the state kills Bigger precisely at the point where he has begun to reform.

Works Cited

Butler, Robert. "The Function of Violence in Richard Wright's *Native Son*." *Black American Literature Forum* 20 (Spring–Summer 1986): 9–25.

———. *Native Son: The Emergence of a New Black Hero*. Boston: Twayne Press, 1991.

Caverly, John R. "The Decision and Pronouncement of Sentence by Judge Caverly in the Franks Case, September 10, 1924. *Loeb-Leopold Case*, pp. 150–155.

Crowe, Robert E. "Robert E. Crowe's Demand for the Death Penalty." *Loeb-Leopold Case*, pp. 88–148.

Darrow, Clarence. "Clarence Darrow's Plea for Mercy." *Loeb-Leopold Case*, pp. 1–87.

Dos Passos, John. *The Big Money*. New York: New American Library, 1969.

Fabre, Michel. *The Unfinished Quest of Richard Wright*. New York: Morrow, 1973.

———. *The World of Richard Wright*. Jackson: University of Mississippi Press, 1985.

Fass, Paula S. "Making and Remaking an Event: The Leopold and Loeb Case in American Culture." *Journal of American History* 80.3 (1993): 919–951.

Gates, Henry Louis, Jr. *Figures in Black: Words, Signs and the Racial Self*. New York: Oxford University Press, 1987.

Higdon, Hal. *The Crime of the Century: The Leopold and Loeb Case*. New York: Putnam, 1999.

Hricko, Mary. "The Genesis of the Chicago Renaissance: The Writings of Theodore Dreiser, Langston Hughes, Richard Wright, and James T. Farrell." (Diss., Kent State University, 2004).

Kinnamon, Keneth. *The Emergence of Richard Wright*. Urbana: University of Illinois Press, 1972.

———. Wright, Ellison, "Baldwin: Exorcising the Demon," *Phylon* 37.2 (1976): 3–10.

———. *New Essays on Native Son*. New York: Cambridge University Press, 1990.

Leopold, Nathan. *Life Plus 99 Years*. Garden City, NY: Doubleday, 1958.

Levin, Meyer. *Compulsion*. New York: Random House, 1956.

The Loeb-Leopold Case: The Crime of the Century. Chicago: Wilson, 1925.

Pudaloff, Ross. "Celebrity as Identity: Richard Wright, *Native Son* and Mass Culture." *Studies in American Fiction II* (Spring 1983): 3–18.

Rowley, Hazel. *Richard Wright: The Life and Times*. New York: Holt, 2001.

Sisney, Mary. "The Power and Horror of Whiteness: Wright and Ellison Respond to Poe." *CLA Journal* 29 (1985): 82–90.

Walker, Margaret. *Richard Wright: Daemonic Genius*. New York: Amistad Press, 1988.

Wright, Richard. *Native Son: The Restored Text*. New York: Perennial Classics, 1998.

———. "How 'Bigger' Was Born." *Native Son: The Restored Text* by Richard Wright. New York: Perennial Classics, 1998, pp. 433–462.

Chronology

1908   Richard Wright born to Ella and Nathan Wright on a farm
            outside Natchez, Mississippi.

1914   Nathan Wright deserts the family.

1916–1925   Attends, with interruptions, public and Seventh-Day
            Adventist schools.

1924   Publishes "The Voodoo of Hell's Half-Acre" in the black
            newspaper *Southern Register.*

1925   Graduates as valedictorian from Smith-Robinson Public
            School; moves to Memphis.

1927–1936   Works as a postal clerk in Chicago, where he becomes an
            active writer for leftist publications. He joins the John Reed
            Club and the Communist Party USA.

1937   Becomes Harlem editor of *Daily Worker.*

1938   *Uncle Tom's Children,* a collection of short stories,
            published.

1939   Receives Guggenheim Fellowship. Marries Dhimah Rose
            Meadman.

1940   Publishes *Native Son.* Wright and Dhima are divorced.

1941	Marries Ellen Poplar. Works with Paul Green toward a stage version of *Native Son*. *Twelve Million Black Voices* published.
1942	Julia Wright born.
1945	Publishes *Black Boy*. Meets James Baldwin.
1946	Visits France.
1947	Moves to France, his home for the rest of his life.
1949	Rachel Wright born.
1949–1950	Stays in Argentina, filming *Native Son*. Wright himself appears as Bigger.
1953	*The Outsiders* published. Visits the Gold Coast (now Ghana).
1954	*Black Power* and *Savage Holiday* published. Visits Spain.
1955	Attends the Bandung Conference in Indonesia.
1956	*The Color Curtain: A Report on the Bandung Conference* and *Pagan Spain* published.
1957	*White Man, Listen!* published.
1958	*The Long Dream*, to be the first of a trilogy, published.
1959	Dies suddenly of heart failure during a hospital stay for an unrelated complaint. At the time of his death Wright was selecting the best of some thousands of his haiku for publication.

Contributors

HAROLD BLOOM is Sterling Professor of the Humanities at Yale University. He is the author of 30 books, including *Shelley's Mythmaking* (1959), *The Visionary Company* (1961), *Blake's Apocalypse* (1963), *Yeats* (1970), *A Map of Misreading* (1975), *Kabbalah and Criticism* (1975), *Agon: Toward a Theory of Revisionism* (1982), *The American Religion* (1992), *The Western Canon* (1994), and *Omens of Millennium: The Gnosis of Angels, Dreams, and Resurrection* (1996). *The Anxiety of Influence* (1973) sets forth Professor Bloom's provocative theory of the literary relationships between the great writers and their predecessors. His most recent books include *Shakespeare: The Invention of the Human* (1998), a 1998 National Book Award finalist, *How to Read and Why* (2000), *Genius: A Mosaic of One Hundred Exemplary Creative Minds* (2002), *Hamlet: Poem Unlimited* (2003), *Where Shall Wisdom Be Found?* (2004), and *Jesus and Yahweh: The Names Divine* (2005). In 1999, Professor Bloom received the prestigious American Academy of Arts and Letters Gold Medal for Criticism. He has also received the International Prize of Catalonia, the Alfonso Reyes Prize of Mexico, and the Hans Christian Andersen Bicentennial Prize of Denmark.

JACK B. MOORE was professor of English at the University of South Florida. His books include *W. E. B. Du Bois* (1981) and *Skinheads Shaved for Battle* (1993).

JEFF KAREM is associate professor of English at Cleveland State University. He wrote *The Romance of Authenticity: The Cultural Politics of Regional and Ethnic Literatures* (2004).

TARA T. GREEN is assistant professor of African American literature at Northern Arizona University. She edited *From the Plantation to the Prison: African-American Confinement Literature* (2008).

BRANNON COSTELLO is assistant professor at Louisiana State University. He wrote *Plantation Airs: Racial Paternalism and the Transformations of Class in Southern Fiction, 1945–1971* (2007).

CHERYL HIGASHIDA is assistant professor of English at the University of Colorado. She has written on African American and Asian American literature.

PETAR RAMADANOVIC is associate professor of English at the University of New Hampshire. He wrote *Forgetting Futures: On Memory, Trauma, and Identity* (2001) and edited with Linda Belau *Topologies of Trauma: Essays on the Limit of Knowledge and Memory* (2002).

QIANA J. WHITTED is assistant professor of English at the University of South Carolina. She has written on Alice Walker and Countee Cullen, in addition to Richard Wright.

CEDRIC GAEL BRYANT is the Lee Family Professor in English and American Literature at Colby College. In 1996, the Carnegie Center for the Advancement of Teaching named him Professor of the Year for the state of Maine

JEFFREY ATTEBERRY received his Ph.D. from University of California, Irvine in 2003. His dissertation was "A Gracious Freedom: The New World of Surrealist Liberation."

ROBERT BUTLER is a professor of English at Canisius College. His books include *Native Son: The Emergence of a New Black Hero* (1991) and *Contemporary African American Fiction: The Open Journey* (1998). He edited *The Critical Response to Ralph Ellison* (2000).

Bibliography

Aaron, Daniel. "Richard Wright and the Communist Party." *New Letters* 38, no. 2 (1971): 170–181.

Agosta, Lucien L. "Millennial Embroidery: The Artistry of Conclusion in Richard Wright's 'Fire and Cloud.'" *Studies in Short Fiction* 18 (1981): 121–129.

Alexander, Margaret W. "Richard Wright." *New Letters* 38, no. 2 (1971): 182–202.

Algeo, Ann M. *The Courtroom as Forum: Homicide Trials by Dreiser, Wright, Capote, and Mailer.* New York: Peter Lang, 1996.

Avery, Evelyn Gross. *Rebels and Victims: The Fiction of Richard Wright and Bernard Malamud.* Port Washington, N.Y.: Kennikat, 1979.

Baker, Houston A. *Blues, Ideology, and Afro-American Literature: A Vernacular Theory.* Chicago: University of Chicago Press, 1984.

———. *The Journey Back: Issues in Black Literature and Criticism.* Chicago: University of Chicago Press, 1980.

———. *Long Black Song: Essays in Black American Literature and Culture.* Charlottesville: University Press of Virginia, 1972.

———. *Reading Black: Essays in the Criticism of African, Caribbean, and Black American Literature.* Ithaca: Africana Studies and Research Center, Cornell University, 1976.

———. *Singers at Daybreak: Studies in Black American Literature.* Washington, D.C.: Howard University Press, 1974.

Bakish, David. *Richard Wright.* New York: Frederick Ungar, 1973.

———. "Underground in an Ambiguous Dreamworld." *Studies in Black Literature* 2, no. 3 (1971): 18–23.

Bell, Michael Davitt. *Culture, Genre, and Literary Vocation: Selected Essays on American Literature.* Chicago, Ill.: University of Chicago Press, 2001.

Bolton, H. Philip. "The Role of Paranoia in Richard Wright's *Native Son.*" *Kansas Quarterly* 7, no. 3 (1975): 11–124.

Bone, Robert A. *Richard Wright.* Minneapolis: University of Minnesota Press, 1969.

Brignano, Russell C. *Richard Wright: An Introduction to the Man and His Works.* Pittsburgh: University of Pittsburgh Press, 1970.

———. "Richard Wright: A Bibliography of Secondary Sources." *Studies in Black Literature* 2, no. 2 (1971): 19–25.

Bryant, Earle V. "Sexual Initiation and Survival in Richard Wright's *The Long Dream.*" *Southern Quarterly* 21, no. 3 (1983): 57–66.

Bryant, Jerry H. "Wright, Ellison, Baldwin: Exorcising the Demon." *Phylon* 37 (1976): 174–188.

Butler, Robert James. "Wright's *Native Son* and Two Novels by Zola: A Comparative Study." *Black American Literature Forum* 18, no. 3 (1984): 100–105.

Campbell, Finley C. "Prophet of the Storm: Richard Wright and the Radical Tradition." *Phylon* 38 (1977): 9–23.

Cobb, Nina Kressner. "Richard Wright: Exile and Existentialism." *Phylon* 40 (1979): 362–374.

College Language Association. *Richard Wright Special Number. College Language Association Journal* 12, no. 4 (1969).

Cooke, Michael G. *Afro-American Literature in the Twentieth Century: The Achievement of Intimacy.* New Haven: Yale University Press, 1984.

———. *Modern Black Novelists: A Collection of Critical Essays.* Englewood Cliffs, N.J.: Prentice-Hall, 1971.

Cripps, Thomas. "Native Son." *New Letters* 38, no. 2 (1971): 49–63.

Davis, Charles T. "From Experience to Eloquence: Richard Wright's *Black Boy* as Art." In *Chant of Saints: A Gathering of Afro-American Literature, Art, and Scholarship,* 425–439. Urbana: University of Illinois Press, 1979.

———. *Richard Wright: A Primary Bibliography.* Boston: G. K. Hall, 1982.

Demarest, David P., Jr. "Richard Wright: The Meaning of Violence." *Black American Literature Forum* 8 (1974): 236–239.

Dickstein, Morris. "Wright, Baldwin, Cleaver." *New Letters* 38, no. 2 (1971): 117–124.

Dixon, Melvin. "Richard Wright: Native Father and Long Dream." *Black World* 23, no. 5 (1974): 91–95.

Fabre, Michel. "Fantasies and Style in Richard Wright's Fiction." *New Letters* 46, no. 3 (1980): 55–81.

———. *The World of Richard Wright.* Jackson: University of Mississippi Press, 1985.

———. and Edward Margolies. "Richard Wright (1908–1960): A Bibliography." *Banner Beitrage* 24 (1965): 131–133, 137.

Felgar, Robert. *Richard Wright.* Boston: Twayne, 1980.

Feuser, Willfried F. "The Men Who Lived Underground: Richard Wright and Ralph Ellison." In *A Celebration of Black and African Writing,* edited by Bruce King and Kolowole Ogungbesan, 87–101. Oxford: Oxford University Press, 1975.

Fishburn, Katherine. *Richard Wright's Hero: The Faces of a Rebel-Victim.* Metuchen, N.J.: Scarecrow Press, 1977.

Gaffney, Kathleen. "Bigger Thomas in Richard Wright's *Native Son.*" *Roots* 1, no. 1 (1970): 81–95.

Gayle, Addison. *Richard Wright: Ordeal of a Native Son.* Garden City, N.Y.: Anchor, Doubleday, 1980.

Green, Gerald. "Back to Bigger." In *Proletarian Writers of the Thirties,* edited by David Madden. Carbondale: Southern Illinois University Press, 1968.

Gross, Barry. "Art to Act: The Example of Richard Wright." *Obsidian* 2, no. 2 (1976): 5–19.

Gross, Seymour. "*Native Son* and 'The Murders in the Rue Morgue': An Addendum." *Poe Studies* 8 (1975): 23.

Gysin, Fritz. *The Grotesque in American Fiction: Jean Toomer, Richard Wright, and Ralph Ellison.* Bern: Francke, 1975.

Hakutani, Yoshinobu. "*Native Son* and *An American Tragedy:* Two Different Interpretations of Crime and Guilt." *Centennial Review* 23 (1978): 208–226.

———. ed. *Critical Essays on Richard Wright.* Boston: G. K. Hall, 1982.

Hoeveler, Diane Long. "Oedipus Agonistes: Mothers and Sons in Richard Wright's Fiction." *Black American Literature Forum* 12 (1978): 65–68.

Jordan, June. "On Richard Wright and Zora Neale Hurston: Notes toward a Balancing of Love and Hatred." *Black World* 23, no. 10 (1974): 4–8.

Joyce, Joyce Ann. *Richard Wright's Art of Tragedy.* Iowa City: University of Iowa Press, 1986.

Kent, George E. *A Dark and Sudden Beauty.* Philadelphia: Afro-American Studies Program, University of Pennsylvania, 1977.

Kinnamon, Keneth. *The Emergence of Richard Wright: A Study in Literature and Society.* Urbana: University of Illinois Press, 1972.

———. "*Lawd Today:* Richard Wright's Apprentice Novel." *Studies in Black Literature* 2, no. 2 (1971): 16–18.

———. "The Pastoral Impulse in Richard Wright." *Midcontinent American Studies Journal* 10, no. 1 (1969): 41–47.

———. "Richard Wright: Proletarian Poet." *Concerning Poetry* 2, no. 1 (1969): 39–50.

Kostelanetz, Richard. "The Politics of Unresolved Quests in the Novels of Richard Wright." *Xavier University Studies* 8 (1969): 31–64.

Lenz, Gunther H. "Southern Exposure: The Urban Experience and the Re-Construction of Black Folk Culture and Community in the Works of Richard Wright and Zora Neale Hurston." *New York Folk Quarterly* 7, nos. 1–2 (1981): 2–39.

Margolies, Edward. *The Art of Richard Wright.* Carbondale: Southern Illinois University Press, 1969.

———. "The Letters of Richard Wright." In *The Black Writer in Africa and the Americas,* edited by Lloyd W. Brown, 101–118. Los Angeles: University of Southern California Studies in Comparative Literature 6, Hennessey & Ingalls, 1973.

McCall, Dan. *The Example of Richard Wright.* New York: Harcourt, Brace, & World, 1969.

McCluskey, John, Jr. "Two Steppin': Richard Wright's Encounter With Blues-Jazz." *American Literature* 55 (1983): 332–344.

Miller, Eugene E. "Richard Wright and Gertrude Stein." *Black American Literature Forum* 16 (1982): 107–112.

———. "Voodoo Parallels in *Native Son.*" *College Language Association Journal* 16 (1972): 81–95.

Moore, Jack B. "The View from the Broom Closet of the Regency Hyatt: Richard Wright as a Southern Writer." In *Literature at the Barricades: The American Writer in the 1930s,* edited by Ralph F. Bogardus and Fred Hobson, 126–143. Tuscaloosa: University of Alabama Press, 1982.

Nagel, James. "Images of 'Vision' in *Native Son.*" *University Review* 35 (1969): 109–115.

Negro Digest. "Richard Wright: His Life and Works." 18, no. 2 (1968).

Primeau, Ronald. "Imagination as Moral Bulwark and Creative Energy in Richard Wright's *Black Boy* and LeRoi Jones's *Home.*" *Studies in Black Literature* 3, no. 2 (1972): 12–18.

Ray, David, and Robert M. Farnsworth, eds. *Richard Wright: Impressions and Perspectives.* Ann Arbor: University of Michigan Press, 1973.

Reilly, John M. "Richard Wright's Experiment in Naturalism." *Studies in Black Literature* 2, no. 3 (1971): 14–17.

———. "Self-Portraits by Richard Wright." *Colorado Quarterly* 20 (1971): 31–45.

Relyea, Sarah. *Outsider Citizens: The Remaking of Postwar Identity in Wright, Beauvoir, and Baldwin.* New York: Routledge, 2006.

Roache, Joel. "What Had Made Him and What He Meant: The Politics of Wholeness in 'How "Bigger" was Born.'" *Sub-Stance* 15 (1976): 133–145.

Rubin, Steven J. "The Early Short Fiction of Richard Wright Reconsidered." *Studies in Short Fiction* 15 (1978): 405–410.

Savory, Jerold J. "Bigger Thomas and the Book of Job: The Epigraph to *Native Son*." *Black American Literature Forum* 9 (1975): 55–56.

Singh, Raman K. "Marxism in Richard Wright's Fiction." *Indian Journal of American Studies* 4, no. 112 (1974): 21–35.

———. "Some Basic Ideas and Ideals in Richard Wright's Fiction." *College Language Association Journal* 13 (1969): 78–84.

Skerrett, Joseph T. "Richard Wright, Writing and Identity." *Callaloo 2* (1979): 84–94.

Stephens, Martha. "Richard Wright's Fiction: A Reassessment." *Georgia Review* 25 (1971): 450–470.

Stepto, Robert B., and Michael S. Harper, eds. *Chant of Saints: A Gathering of Afro-American Literature, Art, and Scholarship.* Urbana: University of Illinois Press, 1979.

Studies in Black Literature. Special Richard Wright Issue. 1, no. 3 (1970).

Walker, Ian. "Black Nightmare: The Fiction of Richard Wright." In *Black Fiction: New Studies in the Afro-American Novel since 1945*, edited by Robert A. Lee, 11–28. New York: Barnes & Noble, 1980.

Webb, Constance. *Richard Wright: A Biography.* New York: G. P. Putnam, 1968.

Williams, John A. *The Most Native of Sons: A Biography of Richard Wright.* Garden City, N.Y.: Doubleday, 1970.

Williams, Sherley Anne. "Papa Dick and Sister-Woman: Reflections on Women in the Fiction of Richard Wright." In *American Novelists Revisited: Essays in Feminist Criticism*, edited by Fritz Fleischmann. Boston: Hall, 1982.

Acknowledgments

Moore, Jack B. "A Personal Appreciation of Richard Wright's Universality," *Mississippi Quarterly: The Journal of Southern Cultures*, Volume 50, Number 2 (Spring 1997): pp. 362–374. Copyright © Mississippi Quarterly. Reprinted by permission of the publisher.

Karem, Jeff. "'I Could Never Really Leave the South': Regionalism and the Transformation of Richard Wright's *American Hunger*," *American Literary History*, Volume 13, Number 4 (Winter 2001): pp. 694–715. Copyright © 2001 Oxford University Press. Reprinted by permission of Oxford University Press.

Green, Tara T. "The Virgin Mary, Eve, and Mary Magdelene in Richard Wright's Novels," *CLA Journal: A Quarterly Publication of the College Language Association*, Volume 46, Number 2 (December 2002): pp. 168–193. Copyright © 2002 College Language Association. Reprinted by permission of the publisher.

Costello, Brannon. "Richard Wright's *Lawd Today!* and the Political Uses of Modernism," *African American Review*, Volume 37, Number 1 (Spring 2003): pp. 39–52. Copyright © 2003 Brannon Costello. Reprinted by permission of the author.

Higashida, Cheryl. "Aunt Sue's Children: Re-viewing the Gender(ed) Politics of Richard Wright's Radicalism," *American Literature*, Volume

75, Number 2 (June 2003): pp. 395–425. Copyright © 2003 The Duke University Press. All rights reserved. Used by permission of the publisher.

Ramadanovic, Petar. "*Native Son*'s Tragedy: Traversing the Death Drive with Bigger Thomas," *Arizona Quarterly*, Volume 59, Number 2 (Summer 2003): pp. 81–105. Copyright © 2003 Arizona Board of Regents. Reprinted by permission of the publisher and the author.

Whitted, Qiana J. "'Using My Grandmother's Life as a Model': Richard Wright and the Gendered Politics of Religious Representation," *The Southern Literary Journal*, Volume 36, Number 2 (2004): pp. 13–30. Copyright © 2004 *Southern Literary Journal* and the University of North Carolina, Chapel Hill. Reprinted by permission of the publisher.

Bryant, Cedric Gael. "'The Soul Has Bandaged Moments': Reading the African American Gothic in Wright's 'Big Boy Leaves Home,' Morrison's *Beloved*, and Gomez's *Gilda*," *African American Review*, Volume 39, Number 4 (2005): pp. 541–553. Copyright © 2005 Cedric Gael Bryant. Reprinted by permission of the author.

Atteberry, Jeffrey. "Entering the Politics of the Outside: Richard Wright's Critique of Marxism and Existentialism," *MFS: Modern Fiction Studies*, Volume 51, Number 4 (2005 Winter): pp. 873–895. Copyright © Perdue Research Foundation. Reprinted by permission of The Johns Hopkins University Press.

Butler, Robert. "The Loeb and Leopold Case: A Neglected Source for Richard Wright's *Native Son*," *African American Review*, Volume 39, Number 4 (2005): pp. 555–567. Copyright © 2005 Robert Butler. Reprinted by permission of the author.

Index